the BERKSHIRE FARM TABLE COOKBOOK

the BERKSHIRES FARM TABLE COOKBOOK

*125 Homegrown Recipes from
the Hills of New England*

E L I S A   S P U N G E N   B I L D N E R
and R O B E R T   B I L D N E R

with Chef Brian Alberg

The Countryman Press
A division of W. W. Norton & Company
Independent Publishers Since 1923

This book is dedicated to Norma Weinberg Spungen, mother and mother-in-law of blessed memory, matriarch of our family, scholar, and consummate cook and entertainer.

One of her favorite places to share her love of family and friends—together with her beloved husband, Kenneth, father and father-in-law of blessed memory— was at her dining room tables in the Berkshires and in Chicago.

CONTENTS

INTRODUCTION

We raised our family in New Jersey, but the Berkshire Hills of western Massachusetts, where we've had a house for 35 years, is our "spiritual" home. The Berkshires, which refers to Berkshire County, Massachusetts, and adjacent areas in New York state, Vermont, and Connecticut, is a scenic and recreational paradise of hills, lakes, and rivers, locales where our family has hiked, fished, swum, kayaked, and canoed in the summer and downhill and cross-country skied, and snowshoed in the winter. During the summers, besides attending Tanglewood, summer home of the Boston Symphony Orchestra, like other Berkshirites we're also at Jacob's Pillow Dance Festival, Barrington Stage Company, Shakespeare & Company, Berkshire Theatre Group, the Norman Rockwell Museum, Edith Wharton's home The Mount, Hancock Shaker Village Museum, Williamstown Theatre Festival, the Clark Art Institute, the Berkshire Museum, MASS MoCA, and more. We have spent every summer, most vacations, holidays, birthdays, and even celebrated the weddings and engagement of three of our four children in the area.

We are not alone in our love for the Berkshires. Famed cellist and part-time resident Yo-Yo Ma summed it up in *Berkshire Magazine*: The Berkshires "is my psychological home. It is a place that has everything. The people are great, the people are inventive, the people care about nature, the people work hard. Traditions abound. There is a lot of talent that is built into the population. And the land, my goodness, it's magical."

You might say our interest in Berkshire farming began generations ago: Rob is the third generation of his family in the food business. We are foodies in our DNA, foodies as part of our professional backgrounds. Lawyers by train-

ing, we have founded and run food distribution and manufacturing businesses with the goal of helping farmers bring their products to market, and Elisa is a professionally trained chef and has written about food in an earlier career as a journalist. We love to cook and entertain, especially on Friday nights, when Sabbath guests and whichever of our four grown kids and their significant others happen to be in the area congregate around our dining room table.

Our youngest child, Rafi, now 26, is our family's first gardener who helped Rob plant vegetables each summer behind our Berkshires home. While still in high school, Rafi transformed our backyard into October Mountain Farm, an intensively cultivated half-acre spread of lettuces, tomatoes, and herbs as well as more exotic veggies, which he sold on a farmstand in front of our house and at farmers' markets in Otis, Great Barrington, and West Stockbridge, MA. We visited Rafi at these markets, marveling at his Red Russian kale, French radishes, All-Star Gourmet Lettuce Mix, rhubarb, flat-leaf parsley, and basil, but also cognizant of the long hours and grueling work it took to get those products to his customers—and the meager monetary return, especially considering that he didn't have to rent or buy land. At the markets, we met local farmers and were moved by stories of how they came to farm in this region, their challenges, and above all, their commitment to and passion for their livelihood. We were astounded by the taste of their offerings—of course we knew they were fresh, but each bite of a fruit or a vegetable attested to an unmatched just-picked piquancy.

We were not entirely surprised, however. With more than two decades of experience in produce and perishable distribution, we knew that even the best supermarket produce culled from the world over could end up sitting on refrigerated shelving in a New Jersey warehouse for an average of three days. Often, it arrived at the distribution center following a three-day trip by truck from California. A head of West Coast organic red leaf easily could have taken a week to get to the consumer, a week in which its flavor, nutritional content, and appearance would inevitably degrade. How different it was from the same variety Rafi grew on his small farm, a difference we could taste the moment we bit into a leaf: To be precise, it had a taste, whereas the lettuce trekked from afar rarely did. Will Conklin is president of the Berkshire County Farm Bureau and, along with his wife Amelia, owns Sky View Farm in Sheffield, MA. He adds that studies show that one's experience with food is directly related to the context in which one consumes it: "When people eat our meat products or products from another local vegetable farm that they've bought at the farm or from the farmer at a market, that whole experience, that whole context, is part of the meal, and actually makes a difference in how it tastes, and how those people feel about that meal."

There is, of course, another significant difference between the produce we saw in the farmers' markets from farms, such as Indian Line, The Berry Patch, or Rafi's October Mountain, and those sold by our former companies: Locally grown produce is more sustainable. Imagine hundreds of tractor trailers a week consuming massive quantities of diesel as they roll thousands of miles cross-country, refrigeration units humming, bringing produce from California's fields to a New Jersey distribution center. Yet another fleet of refrigerated tractor trailers then fans out from each loading dock, off to retailers in New York City and up and down the East Coast from Boston to Washington. In contrast, local food, like that sold in Berkshires farmers' markets, travels an average of 50 miles from farm to table. (Anecdotally, the produce we see on Berkshire farmers' displays often seems to come from no more than a few miles from its source.) Local produce is sustainable in yet another respect: We'd say almost all the

small farmers we interviewed voluntarily told us they avoid what they consider unsafe chemicals, even if their farms are not certified organic, because besides the danger to themselves, their families, and workers, they didn't want to be responsible for harming the soil and the environment in which they and their neighbors live.

Berkshire farming is radically changing. Although it primarily began with dairy production, in the last 50 years, according to the *Boston Globe*, New England lost 10,000 dairy farmers. Conklin told us that in the 1960s there were over 20 dairies in his town of Sheffield, but today only four remain, and he says he would not be surprised if another went out of business within the next five years. Barns and pastures still mark this rural landscape, but while farmers are generally aging, many of today's newer farmers are younger, farming small and sustainable acreage, with one member of the family often holding an off-premises job. Some are lucky to have the use of land that has been in their family, while others face the challenge of buying or renting property to break into the field. We were inspired by the idealism and commitment to their mission of those we met, denominating this eclectic group as "conscious farmers." They are motivated to farm for environmental, social, political, health, lifestyle, and even spiritual reasons, often sacrificing a comfortable living for their values.

Impressed by the farmers we met through our son and at the farmers' markets, we were inspired to relate their stories and that of Berkshire farming, through words, photographs, and recipes inspired by the fruits and vegetables they grow and the animals they raise. To understand that story, we began a journey that lasted over four years, wandering down dirt roads to meet many of them in corners of the region that most residents and visitors don't see, and hanging out with farm-to-table chefs and restaurant owners—those using local and sustainably produced foods in their businesses—to learn about Berkshires agriculture. The farmers and chefs profiled here represent only a sampling of all those we could have interviewed. In fact, this book took longer to complete than we initially planned because we kept hearing about yet one more farmer and chef we should speak to. Kudos to all those who are our subjects as well as those who are not.

These farmers and chefs, along with Barbara Zheutlin, former executive director of Berkshire Grown, whose mission is to keep local farmers farming, educated us about the high cost of farm property, especially for those who want to buy land; the financial enticement to sell farms for nonagricultural development; the difficulties of attracting younger farmers to a career that is predominantly populated by older folks and of hiring farm labor; the absence of a nearby commercial USDA slaughterhouse for those raising meat and poultry; the adverse impact of climate change on crop growing; and the expense of operating a small family farm. Added to this list is the lack of a regional infrastructure to assist in the processing, storage, and distribution of foods. But there's been a recent contribution to alleviating this problem. Former lawyer and one-time wannabe farmer Nick Martinelli started Marty's Local, a local produce and food hub that has partnerships with about 70 farms in the Berkshires, Hudson, and Pioneer Valleys.

Farmers need to overcome one more hurdle: market saturation. Too many try to sell the same products (such as ubiquitous tomatoes and kale) to a limited number of customers. As Martinelli explains when asked why there are limits to his ability to take on potential farm partners, "eight farmers are growing cucumbers, and does it make sense for us to add them to the catalog?" There's a big demand for asparagus, he notes, yet he only has two farms he can turn to for that vegetable. When he looks at the farms he perceives as the most successful of his partners, it's the ones who produce a broader variety of crops, but to be fair, they are often larger with 20 to 30 acres. The 1-acre or mom-and-pop farm, he says, may not be a match for a distributor.

Farmers have the added challenge—but one all of us can help them with—of educating consumers to understand what it takes to grow fruits and vegetables and raise livestock and why prices for these local products may be higher. This obstacle is evidenced, according to Will Conklin, by the fact that the amount of local produce consumed in the Berkshires is still only about 3 percent of the total. The Conklins also note that because of the predominance of a food supply in this country based on agribusiness and mass production, consumers expect cheap food, a point other farmers lament as well. Dairy farmers have an added burden: the government sets the minimum wholesale price for milk, which has declined in recent years, making it extraordinarily difficult for them to pull in enough to meet their costs yet alone make a profit.

These are daunting challenges, but despite them, Berkshire farmers grow fruit and vegetables that are palpably different from what's predominantly found in conventional supermarkets, and are seemingly universally committed to raising humanely treated chickens, turkeys, cows, pigs, and lambs. They are critical of agribusiness practices such as relying on massive amounts of chemical fertilizers and pesticides that harm the environment, exploiting farmworkers who toil in substandard conditions for inadequate wages, and raising animals in inhumane factory farms. They are choosing to farm in the most sustainable way, whether they are a produce or meat farmer.

The farmers we met gave us other reasons they still farm. The pride they take in delivering a product valued by their community. The joy of raising kids on a farm, which instills in them independence and an unbeatable work ethic. The ability to eat off their land. Their satisfaction in protecting the environment by using sustainable, organic and/or biodynamic farming methods.

Meeting Chef Brian Alberg was the final step of our journey to try to tell the farmers' stories. Alberg, vice president of culinary development of the Main Street Hospitality Group, and the former executive chef of their property The Red Lion Inn in Stockbridge, MA, is celebrated in western Massachusetts and beyond for championing Berkshire farmers. We bonded as fellow food entrepreneurs and supporters of the local food movement and were delighted when he signed on to help develop recipes inspired by the produce and products of the farmers we met.

Maybe you, like us, are persuaded that buying directly from local farmers who painstakingly care for the soil and treat their animals in the most humane way is more beneficial for our health, environment, and community than buying an "organic" vegetable trucked across the country for over a week in an energy-guzzling 18-wheeler. But how do you buy direct?

In the Berkshires, you can buy from farmers at any of the 19 farmers' markets regularly held over the summer. (Check out berkshiregrown.org for a comprehensive list.) There also are winter markets in Pittsfield, North Adams, and elsewhere. Almost every metropolitan area has markets: New York City has 50 in the five boroughs, Boston 25, and Miami 12, and you can search online to find those where you live. Support retail outlets and restaurants that buy directly from farmers or buy local: An increasing number of supermarkets and stores carry locally grown produce and other products, but if yours doesn't, ask them to. Ask restaurants the sources of their fruit, vegetables, and meat. Another option: join a local farmer's CSA (Community Supported Agriculture) and buy a share of the produce or products produced by that farm, ensuring the farmer a consistent stream of income and

you, the freshest, most flavorful, seasonal items. Another way to buy direct is to pick your own fruit (or vegetables). Many farms we visited—Ioka Valley Farm for pumpkins, Riiska Brook Orchard for blueberries and apples, Mountain Pasture Farm for blueberries, for example—offer pick-your-own as a way to bring consumers to the farm and reduce the costs of harvesting. Finally, you can support local farming by becoming a member of a nonprofit, such as Berkshire Grown, which produces farmers' markets, workshops for farmers, and promotes local agriculture throughout the year, or the Pioneer Valley, MA–based CISA (Community Involved in Sustaining Agriculture, buy-localfood.org/buy-local). Whichever way you choose, buying as directly as possible from farmers and eating locally helps all of us by generating a more flavorful and potentially more nutritious food supply, a more viable community—money spent on food produced locally stays in the area—a healthier environment, and, on a macro level, a more sustainable planet.

Elisa and Rob
June 2019

A NOTE ON THE RECIPES

Some recipes in this book are inspired by the products grown or raised by the farmers we met during our research. Others are prompted by something a farmer may have said to us in conversation. Farmers, we learned, are often too busy to cook, let alone develop and write recipes. (Some, though, do offer recipes to accompany what they sell via their social media accounts or in material for their CSA members.) Finally, we're most appreciative to the creative farm-to-table chefs we interviewed whose recipes were adapted for this book.

BREAKFAST

Sweet Corn Pancakes

HOWDEN FARM

MAKES 14 PANCAKES; SERVES 4 TO 5

These pancakes are great for breakfast with traditional maple syrup and butter, but also make a tasty lunch topped with black beans, salsa, and melted cheese. Pair with smoked salmon, sour cream, and a sprinkling of fresh dill, and you have an enticing dinner party appetizer. If there's corn in your freezer from last year's harvest, this recipe is a perfect way to use it up!

1 cup white or yellow cornmeal

2 tablespoons sugar, honey, or pure maple syrup

1 teaspoon salt

1½ cups buttermilk

½ cup all-purpose flour

1½ teaspoons baking powder

½ teaspoon baking soda

2 tablespoons unsalted butter, melted,
   plus more for griddle

1 large egg, beaten

¾ cup corn kernels (from about 1 ear of corn)

1. Mix together the cornmeal, sugar, salt, and buttermilk in a large bowl and let stand for 20 to 30 minutes. Mix together the flour, baking powder, and baking soda in a medium bowl and set aside.

2. Add the melted butter, egg, and corn kernels to the cornmeal mixture and stir until well combined. Add the dry ingredients to the batter and stir to combine.

3. Heat a griddle or skillet over medium heat and melt a small pat of butter in the center. Using a ¼-cup measure and a rubber spatula, scoop the batter onto the hot griddle, working in batches if necessary. Cook the pancakes for 3 minutes per side, or until beginning to turn golden. When the pancakes are first cooking, cover the pan to help them stay moist and cook faster. Transfer the pancakes to a platter in a warm oven until ready to serve.

MOON IN THE POND FARM

We walked into the following scene at Moon In The Pond Farm, in Sheffield, MA: farmer Dominic Palumbo instructing an apprentice on how to dock a lamb's tail (to prevent infection) while simultaneously apprising new interns in an adjacent rhubarb patch on how to cut the perennial ("put your thumbs way down the stem, rock side to side gently"). Thirty stalks of rhubarb were shortly on their way to a local restaurant while the always-in-motion Palumbo proceeded to weed and talk to us at the same time.

Palumbo hasn't stopped loving the idea of growing, of farming, since he was a seven-year-old cultivating corn seeds in his basement. From childhood gardening, he went on to start a landscaping business, eventually studying for two years at the New York Botanical Garden's School of Professional Hor-

ticulture. In 1991, he began farming the beginnings of Moon In The Pond, accessed off a dirt road in the southern Berkshire hills near the Appalachian Trail ("thru-hikers" trekking between Maine and Georgia can check out a day or three of farm life, and eat well at the same time). Today, he owns 35 of 100 or more acres that he farms or manages.

The farm's emphasis is on producing meat from heritage breeds, nearly 10,000 pounds annually, but Moon In The Pond also harvests heirloom vegetables and offers eggs, honey, and fruit, selling directly to families through a CSA, at the farm, at farmers' markets, and to a few restaurants. Palumbo is fiercely committed to organic and sustainable food production, but what makes his farm even more unusual is its emphasis on education—the farm itself is part of

a nonprofit, Farm Education, Inc. Moon In The Pond offers public tours and workshops, as well as apprentice and internship programs to teach sustainable agriculture to future farmers. For Palumbo, each time he sells at a farmers' market is also a chance to help people connect to what nourishes them, through conversation, through the taste of a just-picked cucumber. It's an opportunity for Palumbo to help others understand the value of buying good, clean food—including meat, which doesn't come from what he calls "a system that is morally, environmentally, and health-wise bankrupt."

Palumbo's road to farming, like that of pretty much every Berkshire farmer we spoke to, hasn't been an easy one. In 2016, he faced foreclosure, eventually raising money he needed from small and large donations—and with the help of a fortuitous tweet from Michael Pollan. He felt reassured the community valued his operation.

Not only does a landscape of farms enhance a community's beauty, but consumers get fresher food from a purveyor they know. And, Palumbo argues, small farms like his will be the savior of this country's food system, enabling us to be resilient in the face of climate change. "If most of our food comes from the Central Valley of California to Massachusetts,

you're going to be in trouble when that becomes either impossible to grow there or impossible to get it from there to here." But to keep small farms vibrant, consumers need to continue to value what they produce, just like the financial support Palumbo received from the community. "There was a very fast and publicized rise in attention to farm-to-table," says Palumbo. "And I see that fading. My concern is to try not to let that be a trend."

Palumbo himself loves to cook what he grows and raises. In fact, that includes three meals a day for his staff. He advises home cooks to be adventurous, to try unfamiliar ingredients and uncommon parts of animals, including using the bones that might otherwise be thrown away. For Palumbo, no category of food is good or bad. "Red and meat and bad should not be inextricably linked," he says. "Red meat—naturally raised—is great for you in balance. Carrots and vegetables are horrible for you if they are raised using bad chemicals and deficient soil."

Farm Hash with Poached Eggs

MOON IN THE POND FARM

SERVES 4

Start your day with this breakfast or brunch center-piece, or serve for supper as comfort food. The rec-ipe uses fresh meat for the hash, but can also serve as a vehicle for dressing up leftovers from a roast the night before.

1 tablespoon extra virgin olive oil

½ large red onion, ½-inch diced

2 cups ½-inch-diced fresh beef, lamb, or pork,
    or a combination, preferably from the loin,
    or 2 cups leftover roasted meat

Salt and freshly ground black pepper

½ cup peeled and ½-inch-diced carrot

1 medium Yukon Gold potato,
    peeled and ½-inch diced

1½ cups chicken or beef stock

1 tablespoon chopped fresh rosemary

1 cup packed, stemmed, and chopped hearty
    greens, such as kale or escarole

2 tablespoons fresh lemon juice or distilled
    white vinegar

8 large eggs

1. Heat the olive oil in a large, heavy-bottomed pan, such as a cast-iron skillet, over medium heat until shimmering but not smoking. Add the red onion and sauté, stirring frequently, for 5 to 8 minutes, until the onion is soft and translucent. If using cooked meat, add it to the pan with the onion, and season with salt and pepper if necessary, depending on how well seasoned the meat is already.

2. If using fresh meat, scrape the onion out of the pan and set aside. Season the meat with salt and pepper in a medium bowl, add to the pan, and brown on all sides. Return the onion to the pan.

3. Add the carrot and potato. Stir to combine and add the stock and rosemary. Bring to a simmer, cover, and cook for 10 to 15 minutes, until the meat is tender and the potatoes are soft.

4. Remove the cover and reduce the liquid in the pan, stirring occasionally, scraping up bits from the bottom, until the liquid is nearly gone. Add the greens to the pan and toss to combine. Continue to cook, stirring occasionally, for another 5 minutes, or until the greens have started to wilt and soften and the hash has just started to stick to the bottom of the pan. Adjust the seasoning with salt and pepper. The hash should be dark and soft, with some crispy edges. Turn off the heat, and cover while cooking the eggs.

5. Combine 4 cups of water and the lemon juice in a large, lidded sauté pan and bring to a boil. (If neces-sary, using a smaller pan, the eggs can be poached in batches.) While the water is heating, break each egg into a separate small dish. Once the water boils, turn off the heat and gently slide each egg, one at a time, into the hot water. Place the lid on the pan, allowing the eggs to poach undisturbed for 3 to 5 minutes, until the whites are firm. The yolk should still be runny inside.

6. Plate the hash. Using a slotted spoon, transfer each egg to the serving plates, placing two eggs on each serving of the hash. The yolks, once broken into the hash, will act as a sauce that incorporates all flavors of the dish.

"Red-Eye" Sausage Gravy for Eggs or Biscuits

EAST MOUNTAIN FARM

SERVES 4

Traditional sausage gravy gets a nice "red-eye" kick from the coffee in this recipe, while tomato juice boosts the flavor in this hearty merger of two beloved southern gravies. Kim Wells, owner of East Mountain Farm, took a fancy to red-eye gravy during a three-year stint working on beef farms in Kentucky in between his years at Williams College. Enjoy this version spooned over fried or poached eggs, warm fresh buttermilk biscuits, a slice of fried ham, or even steak (maybe not for breakfast . . .)!

2 slices bacon, diced

½ cup loose or ground breakfast sausage (about 5 ounces)

½ cup diced onion

1 tablespoon unsalted butter

2 tablespoons all-purpose flour

½ cup tomato juice

½ cup brewed coffee

½ cup chicken stock

½ cup half-and-half

1 tablespoon chopped fresh sage or 1 teaspoon dried

½ teaspoon kosher salt

¼ teaspoon freshly ground black pepper, or more to taste

1. Cook the bacon and crumbled sausage in a large skillet over medium heat until fully browned. Leaving the bacon and sausage meat in the pan, remove any excess fat from the pan, except for enough to cook the onion. Add the onion and sauté until golden brown, 7 to 9 minutes.

2. Add the butter, and when melted, sprinkle the flour over the meat. Cook for 8 to 10 minutes, stirring frequently to prevent the flour from burning.

3. Add the tomato juice, coffee, stock, half-and-half, sage, salt, and pepper and stir to scrape up any browned bits stuck on the bottom of the pan and to combine fully. Lower the heat to low and simmer, stirring occasionally to prevent sticking, for 15 to 20 minutes, until the gravy has thickened and is ready to serve.

EAST MOUNTAIN FARM

In 1982, Kim Wells, then a 27-year-old Williams College grad, and his wife, Linda Bundtzen, former professor of English, now emerita, at the college, purchased
East Mountain Farm, a bankrupt dairy operation in
Williamstown, MA. Wells started raising livestock,
selling his first meat five years later. A self-described
"supercarnivore," he farms 125 acres, with 12 acres of
pasture supporting 12 to 14 beef cattle and about 1,200
chickens a year. Forested acreage up the hill is home
to his pigs, 60 to 80 at a time. Wells sells his beef, poultry, and pork primarily from his farm store, housed in
a large red barn on the property, and to restaurants,
retail outlets, and at farmers' markets.

Sounds straightforward, but it's a complicated
operation, and for meat farmers like Wells, that means
caring for his animals year-round, including getting
water to his pigs in winter when the outside pipes
have frozen. One of the main challenges he has faced
is finding slaughterhouses and transporting animals
there. Wells relies on getting his beef and pork processed at Eagle Bridge Custom Meat & Smokehouse,
a USDA facility in New York state about 45 minutes
from his farm. That's not so bad, he says, but Eagle
Bridge only came on the scene in 2005. Because of the
severe shortage of local poultry processors, five times
a summer, he travels three hours to Rhode Island to
the nearest USDA facility. Days later, Wells returns
there to pick up the processed poultry and haul it
back. (Poultry must be slaughtered and processed in a
USDA-inspected operation, unless a state has its own
inspection program, which Massachusetts does not. It
can also be slaughtered and processed in a specially
licensed, on-farm facility, which only allows direct
sales from the farm.)

After slaughtering, there's the issue of keeping on
top of what Wells's customers want, which means, for
example, that he always has to have enough steaks on
hand, even though more than 40 percent of the cow
ends up as ground beef. But solving problems is what

farming's about—and why Wells says his liberal arts
education at Williams was useful. "You just never
know," he says, "because with animals, with weather,
things happen constantly." (He's by far not the lone
farmer among Williams grads. Several farmers profiled in this book graduated from the college.)

Wells is emphatic about keeping his animals
happy, with cows and chickens living in the pasture,
eating grass, devouring bugs, while the pigs are root-
ing out whatever they'd like from the forest floor. That
is, when they're not coming up to Wells for a little
affection. "They have a great life, absolutely," he says,
speaking of his pigs. "They've got mud, shade from
the woods." And his cows and chickens seem to be
pretty happy as well. Every day, Wells rotates his cows
so they can feast on new grass.

In 2016, Wells told the *Bennington Banner* that part
of the appeal of farm-to-table meat for chefs and others was the chance to work with better ingredients. "It
puts [the chefs] in touch with a quality of product that
they can't really get from the big distributors. Most
chefs are just so happy to get real meat."

DEERFIELD FARM

Deerfield Farm owner Axel Aldred never planned on growing shiitake mushrooms.

He grew up in Pittsfield, MA, then on Cape Cod, moving almost 25 years ago back to the Berkshires to property his family owned since the 1940s in Sandisfield, MA. When Aldred arrived, it was home to his late uncle's defunct Christmas tree plantation, which he saw as a "perfect diamond in the rough" for starting his own project. As we stood in what is now Deerfield Farm, Aldred gestured to a forest of healthy trees surrounding us, explaining he opted not to replant the existing monoculture, but instead create a tree farm for firewood and lumber with naturally regenerating species like oak and poplar.

Aldred was also interested in growing food, and started to plant trees and bushes—apple and pear, and blueberries—underneath and in between the existing foliage. This was the start of his permaculture operation, which he describes as a tapestry of different plants and land use woven together.

Enter the shiitakes.

Aldred was looking for something to fill up his day after spending each morning pulling together a cord

of firewood for customers. Cultivating mushrooms became part of this permaculture, added to the logging and fruit growing. He is both a passionate pupil—and teacher—embarking on a mini-tutorial for us on how to grow shiitakes.

In the spring, Aldred cuts red oak—best for growing mushrooms rather than using for firewood, because of its high moisture content—into convenient lengths. The logs "haven't come to life yet," he says, "so their defenses—their ability to fight off pathogens—aren't in place." This gives him a better chance to successfully inoculate the holes he has drilled in each log with the fresh, clean spawn of shiitake varieties. He packs the holes with sawdust, seals them with cheese wax to prevent competing fungi or bacteria from entering, and keeps the logs in the shade. Then, as he describes excitedly, the spawn "run through the log and take it over. You'll see the white end of the mycelium—the roots of the fungus—growing out through the log." To jack up the humidity level, Aldred soaks the logs in tanks for 24 hours. "It's like having a little monsoon for a day," he says. He hopes to get two flushes each summer, with his second season in August, on logs that are most productive for three or four years. Along the way, Aldred contends with interlopers, with the slugs, bugs, and chipmunks that come with raising shiitakes outside, but he manages to produce about 300 pounds of mushrooms each year from upward of about 300 logs.

Aldred feels he's lucky to be able to site his operation in the Berkshires. "We're kind of blessed here," he says. "We've got a community that appreciates local and fresh and they're willing to pay for it." He sells primarily to restaurants and through farmers' markets. The best proof, though, of the quality of his product, is that he eats what he cultivates, favoring a thick and meaty variety, the "double jewel." Even in winter, he adds reconstituted dried shiitakes, or powder made from grinding them down, to dishes for added flavor.

Shiitake Mushroom Frittata with Goat Cheese

DEERFIELD FARM

SERVES 4 TO 6

Frittata is the crust-free Italian relative of the quiche. This quick and savory classic brunch offering can also serve as a lunch or light supper.

2 tablespoons extra virgin olive oil

½ cup diced onion

2 cups sliced shiitake mushrooms, or other fresh mushrooms

1 cup packed chopped arugula, spinach, or Swiss chard

8 extra-large eggs

½ cup milk

½ cup crumbled soft goat cheese

½ teaspoon salt

½ teaspoon freshly ground black pepper, plus more for garnish

1 teaspoon fresh oregano, finely chopped, or ½ teaspoon dried

⅓ cup grated Parmesan

1. Preheat the oven to 350°F.

2. Heat the olive oil in an ovenproof skillet, preferably cast iron, over medium heat until shimmering and fragrant. Sauté the onion until soft and lightly browned, 7 to 9 minutes. Add the mushrooms and cook, stirring occasionally, until their moisture has mostly released, 8 to 10 minutes. Add the greens to the pan and toss with the mushrooms until the greens are wilted, 2 to 5 minutes, depending on the greens, until nearly all the liquid is gone. Remove the skillet from the heat.

3. While the onion and mushrooms are sautéing, break the eggs into a medium bowl. Add the milk and whisk until light and fluffy. Add the crumbled goat cheese, salt, pepper, and oregano and whisk to incorporate.

4. Pour the egg mixture into the pan and gently stir to incorporate all the ingredients. Place the skillet in the oven and bake for 15 to 20 minutes, until the frittata is lightly golden and fully set.

5. Remove the frittata from the oven and turn the oven setting to BROIL. Move an oven rack to the upper part of the oven. Scatter the grated Parmesan over the top of the frittata and broil on the uppermost oven rack for 3 to 5 minutes to melt and lightly brown the cheese. Remove from the oven and allow to cool for 15 minutes. Garnish with pepper.

6. The frittata can be served directly from the skillet or a plate. To remove from the skillet, gently run a metal spatula around the edges of the frittata and underneath, separating it from the pan. Gently slide onto a serving plate.

Balsamic Stone Fruit over Yogurt

LEAHEY FARM

SERVES 6

Stone fruit, such as peaches, plums, or nectarines, are at their supersweet best in late summer, and combine perfectly with the ubiquitous mint of the season. Using Greek yogurt gives a thick and creamy texture to this breakfast or dessert. Sprinkling granola in the bottom of the bowl or on top as a garnish makes a welcome addition. Leahey Farm, in Lee, MA, sells its milk from grass-fed cows to yogurt producer Sidehill Farm in Hawley, MA.

4 peaches, plums, or nectarines

2 teaspoons aged balsamic vinegar

¼ teaspoon salt

3 tablespoons honey

16 ounces Greek (or other) yogurt

10 fresh mint leaves, cut into tiny ribbons, reserving some for garnish

Zest of 1 lemon

1. Peel the fruit, if desired, then cut in half to remove the stone in the center. Slice into eighths and place in a medium bowl. Toss with the balsamic vinegar, salt, and 1 tablespoon of the honey. Let macerate for 15 to 30 minutes.

2. Place the yogurt in a small bowl and combine with the remaining 2 tablespoons of honey, or less if desired.

3. Just before serving, toss the fruit with most of the mint ribbons and the lemon zest. To serve, place a dollop of yogurt in each bowl, top with stone fruit slices and a little of their flavorful liquid, and garnish with the remaining mint ribbons.

Hawthorne Valley Farm Camp Oatmeal

HAWTHORNE VALLEY FARM

SERVES 5

The dried fruit plumps up in the water used to prepare this dish, adapted from a Hawthorne Valley Farm camp recipe, adding a hint of sweetness.

4 cups water

2 cups rolled oats

1 teaspoon ground cinnamon, plus more for serving

Pinch of salt

½ cup chopped dried fruit, such as apricots, prunes, raisins

Topping suggestions: local yogurt, pure maple syrup or honey, chopped almonds or other nuts

Bring the water to a boil in a heavy-bottomed stockpot or a Dutch oven over medium heat, then add the oats, cinnamon, salt, and dried fruit. Stir to combine well, cover, and remove from the heat. Let sit for 5 minutes, then check for consistency. If the oatmeal is too thick, add more boiling water and stir to combine. Sprinkle with a little more cinnamon and serve with additional toppings as desired.

HAWTHORNE VALLEY FARM

This is what really bothers Martin Ping, executive director of the nonprofit Hawthorne Valley Association, which encompasses Hawthorne Valley Farm (HVF): Only 2 percent of the US population is involved in growing food and the average age of today's farmer is about 60 years old. Ping asks: Who will grow and raise our food in the future? As our rural population diminishes, how do we connect children (and adults) with the land and food that nourishes them? How can we ask our children to be the future stewards of the earth if they've never had a relationship to it?

It is these questions that HVF is working to address. The 900-acre certified organic and biodynamic farm in Ghent, NY, with its 60 free-range dairy cows, more than 40 types of produce, creamery, bakery, 14,000-square-foot facility used primarily for producing sauerkraut and kimchi, and farm store, brings kids from kindergarten through high school and beyond close to the soil, plants, and source of food. Since 1972, when a group of pioneering educators, farmers, and artisans bought the farm, more than 24,000 kids have benefited from its residential and day programs. That includes a summer camp named one of seven best farm camps for kids by *Modern Farmer* magazine. The numbers go further: More than 200 interns and 500 summer camp counselors have worked with children in these programs. And Hawthorne Valley has trained more than 120 apprentices, most remaining in farming.

The sweetness in all this for Ping is when he watches that nine-year-old from the city pull a carrot from the ground and can almost see "the circuitry rewiring" as the child realizes his interdependence with the earth. Or, for Ping, the day camper who arrives with a baloney sandwich on white bread for lunch, but ends up a few days later asking for broccoli.

HVF not only aims to increase exposure to farming, but to a new kind of farming, what Steffen Schneider, former director of farm operations, dubs Agriculture 3.0. Preceded by Agriculture 1.0, indigenous peasant farming, and Agriculture 2.0, agribusiness that produces most of our food, 3.0 is committed to protecting the health of the earth and its people. Biodynamic farming contributes by starting with organic production, and then requiring the well-being of the

soil, plants, and animals, as well as the farmers and others on the farm. The culmination of Agriculture 3.0, according to Ping: "You should be able to eat a piece of broccoli and experience that broccoli-ness, its essence just exploding in your mouth because the conditions were created for that broccoli to come to its best expression."

Of course, consumers need to learn why it's important to buy that broccoli from a local biodynamic or organic farm even though it's sometimes cheaper to get it flown in from across the country or abroad. In answer, he says it's important to understand that the lower price reflects "externalities in the system that we're not taking into account," including a subsidized industrialized agricultural system. He's hoping that HVF contributes to helping consumers recognize the value—better tasting, healthier—of food grown in a conscious way, by adequately paid farmers—his heroes in this equation—on a farm with well-treated soil and animals.

Concerned that not all who live in Columbia County have access to locally produced food, in conjunction with Long Table Harvest, the Berkshire Taconic Community Foundation, and others, HVF launched a mobile market that visits some of these neighbor-

hoods as well as a permanent store, Rolling Grocer 19, in Hudson, NY. The hallmark of these ventures: tiered pricing based on income and the honor system. Ping is rueful, though, that even for those with the income to choose local, who can buy at a price point closer to the true cost, we still haven't figured out how to get this consumer, let alone others, to gravitate to what area farmers produce. But he's hopeful that something innovative—like this new venture—can crack this problem.

Any-Kind-of-Berry Muffins

HAWTHORNE VALLEY FARM

MAKES 12 MUFFINS

Hawthorne Valley's farm camp makes these with blueberries, but other berries will work in this simple recipe adapted from one of their favorites. The cinnamon topping is optional; you can easily make your own or use store-bought cinnamon sugar.

6 tablespoons unsalted butter, melted, plus more for pan

¾ cup sugar

1 large egg

1 large egg yolk

¾ teaspoon vanilla extract

3 tablespoons milk

1½ cups all-purpose flour

1½ teaspoons baking powder

¾ teaspoon salt

2 cups fresh blueberries, raspberries, and/or blackberries

Cinnamon sugar topping (optional):

1 teaspoon ground cinnamon

4 teaspoons sugar

1. Preheat the oven to 375°F. Lightly butter a 12-well muffin tin or line with paper liners; set aside.

2. Combine the butter, sugar, egg, and egg yolk in a large bowl and beat until creamy and light yellow in color. Add the vanilla and milk and beat until fully combined.

3. Combine the flour, baking powder, and salt in a medium bowl.

4. Gently fold the dry ingredients into the wet until they barely come together, being careful not to over-mix. Gently fold in the berries so as not to crush them.

5. Prepare the cinnamon-sugar topping (if using): Combine the cinnamon and sugar in a small bowl and mix thoroughly, breaking up any cinnamon clumps.

6. Using a scoop or spoon, fill the prepared muffin wells with the batter until nearly three-quarters full. If desired, top each muffin with a sprinkling of cinnamon sugar. Not all of the cinnamon sugar will be used.

7. Bake for 30 minutes, or until a toothpick inserted into the top of a muffin comes out clean. Remove from the oven and allow to cool in the tin for 15 minutes before using a thin knife to loosen and gently remove the muffins from the tin. Allow to cool further on a wire rack.

Haven's Morning Glory Muffins

HAVEN CAFE & BAKERY

MAKES 2 DOZEN MUFFINS OR 1 DOZEN JUMBO MUFFINS

Sweet and chock-full of hearty ingredients, these high-fiber gluten-free energy powerhouses make a great grab-and-go breakfast or snack. The recipe makes extra to freeze and save for later. Shelly Williams, owner of Haven Cafe & Bakery, from whom this recipe is adapted, says these muffins are one of her most requested items, which she loves paired with a cup of hot herbal tea.

Vegetable oil for muffin tins (optional)

2 cups white rice flour or Bob's Red Mill Gluten Free 1 to 1 Baking Flour

1¼ cups sugar

1 cup rolled oats

1 cup sweetened shredded coconut

1 cup golden or other raisins

1 apple, cored, peeled, and grated, Granny Smith, if possible

2 cups shredded carrot

2 teaspoons ground cinnamon

2 teaspoons baking powder

2 teaspoons baking soda

¼ teaspoon salt

5 large eggs

1 cup rice bran oil or vegetable oil

2 teaspoons vanilla extract

1. Preheat the oven to 350°F. Set an oven rack in the center of the oven. Prepare two muffin tins (for 24 smaller muffins total), or one jumbo muffin tin (for 12 large muffins) with liner cups or parchment paper, or lightly oil the muffin wells with vegetable oil.

2. Combine the rice flour, sugar, oats, coconut, raisins, apple, carrot, cinnamon, baking powder, baking soda, and salt in a large bowl and mix together with a wooden spoon.

3. Whisk together the eggs, oil, and vanilla in a medium bowl. Using a rubber spatula to scrape down the sides, add the wet ingredients to the dry and mix together with the wooden spoon until everything is evenly moist.

4. Divide the batter evenly among the prepared muffin wells, filling each well about two-thirds full. Bake for 13 minutes. Rotate the tins back to front and bake for an additional 5 to 7 minutes, until a toothpick inserted in the center of a muffin comes out clean. If making jumbo muffins, rotate the tins and cook for an additional 12 minutes, or until a toothpick inserted into a muffin comes out clean. Remove from the oven and allow to cool completely in the tin(s) on a wire rack before removing the muffins.

SALADS

Kale and Peanut Salad

HOLIDAY BROOK FARM

SERVES 2 AS A MAIN DISH OR 4 AS A SIDE OR SALAD COURSE

This recipe is loosely adapted from The Very Best Kale Salad on the Holiday Brook Farm website. Adding a protein—crumbled bacon, for example—easily turns this salad into a main course.

2 hard-boiled eggs, finely chopped

½ cup grated Parmesan

3 tablespoons extra virgin olive oil

1 tablespoon red wine vinegar

1 tablespoon Dijon mustard

Juice of ½ lemon (1 to 1½ tablespoons)

½ teaspoon kosher salt

¼ teaspoon freshly ground black pepper

8 cups gently packed, stemmed, and thinly ribboned kale (about 1 large bunch)

½ cup dry-roasted salted peanuts (or unsalted, if you prefer) or other favorite nut, chopped if desired

1. Prepare the dressing: Combine the eggs, ¼ cup of the Parmesan, olive oil, vinegar, mustard, lemon juice, salt, and pepper in a large bowl and mix together. Add the kale ribbons and massage into the dressing, making sure to coat all the thin strips.

2. Scatter the remaining ¼ cup of Parmesan and the peanuts on top and toss to combine. Check for seasoning, adding salt and pepper if necessary.

3. Serve in a large bowl for guests to serve themselves or on individual salad plates.

TED DOBSON, FORMER OWNER OF EQUINOX FARM

It's going to be hard not to associate arugula with Ted Dobson, who has been selling salad greens to restaurants since he started farming in 1983. Chef Michael Ballon, himself a pioneer of Berkshire farm-to-table, even denominated Dobson "the King of Greens." But this March, Dobson, farmer in chief of Equinox Farm, as he called himself, didn't plant greens on his 15-acre parcel in Sheffield, MA.

Instead, he's leasing the bulk of his property to a young farmer, and he's partnering with Theory Wellness in Great Barrington to grow cannabis on 2.5 acres of his land. Before Dobson switched to cultivating cannabis, he was an organic evangelist, growing the first organic market garden in western Massachusetts.

As a self-described 17-year-old high school dropout and stoner, Dobson had a vision that he should become an organic farmer. Three years later, he enrolled at the University of California, Santa Cruz, where his muse, biodynamic practitioner and English master gardener Alan Chadwick, had set up shop. Chadwick's spirit and focus on soil preparation infused Dobson's farming, first on 3 acres of his family's land in Hillsdale, NY, and then on Equinox Farm. As Dobson told the *Boston Globe* in 2016, his lettuces differ from the farmer's up the road because "it's all about the soil, the terroir."

Although Dobson later diversified, he admitted that he "truly adored wild arugula" and generally had "a fetish for greens. Whatever green sounded unusual, I would try it." And, strategically, from a business viewpoint, he says, everyone eats salad. Lettuces also grow and turn over quickly. He sold not only to Berkshire restaurants but to Manhattan establishments, such as the restaurants Daniel and Jean-Georges.

When we first spoke to Dobson in 2014, he felt that people were starting to recognize the value of what he grew, making the connection between fresher and better tasting. "I started with people throwing their trash on my yard; you know, why don't you get a real job? Organic farming was looked at 30 years ago as a kind of post-hippie hobby." The Berkshires had become a hub for farm-to-table eating, but he was concerned that not all residents had access to the food he and other small farmers produced. "I think it's time for people with lesser means to have the opportunity to eat just as well," Dobson says. His vision, counter to industrial agriculture, is that instead of subsidized farms' taking up thousands of acres growing GMO corn, "these farms could become scaled to grow everything in a fully diversified way and produce volume."

Dobson, circa 2019, although now passionate as

well about growing cannabis both for its use as "medicine" and for hemp as a petroleum substitute—is still of the same philosophy. "I would say the future of farming is that we become regionally self-sufficient, in that most, if not all, our food year-round is grown in the Northeast. And, I'll predict that'll happen within 15 years out of necessity."

Dobson admits he started out as a romantic about farming but soon learned that it was extraordinarily hard work, which has led him to exploring other facets of life. As he told us, "I have books in me. I have a lot of different subpersonalities that have been subsumed by being on the clock 24/7, answerable to 50 to 60 chefs, year-in and year-out. Market farming is intense." Still, Dobson is grateful that he's had "a very significant, but small, obviously, mission in life, which was to grow food" and relishes his new opportunity to grow cannabis and hemp. "Everything that can be made with petroleum—plastics, synthetics—can be woven out of hemp," he notes. Cannabis farming, says Dobson, can "reweave local economies."

Frisée, Arugula, and Tart Apple Salad

TED DOBSON,
FORMER OWNER OF EQUINOX FARM

SERVES 4

Dress this salad with the Maple Dijon Vinaigrette on page 39. Tart apples, such as Granny Smith or Jonathan, take longer to turn brown than a sweeter apple, such as Red Delicious, and their tartness adds a refreshing taste.

1 bunch frisée, rinsed, dried, and torn into bite-size pieces, or escarole, sliced into ribbons

1 cup well-packed baby arugula, rinsed and dried

1 Granny Smith, Jonathan, or other tart apple

¼ cup Maple Dijon Vinaigrette (page 39)

Salt and freshly ground black pepper (optional)

1. Combine the frisée and arugula in a large salad bowl and toss together lightly.

2. Just before serving, julienne the apple and scatter the pieces over the greens. Dress the salad with the vinaigrette, toss, taste for seasoning, and adjust with salt and pepper if necessary. Toss again and serve immediately.

IOKA VALLEY FARM

Missy Leab, a Lanesborough, MA, native, spent summers on her uncle's Pennsylvania farm. So, she was excited, she says, that her future husband, Rob, grew up on the dairy farm started by his grandparents in 1936. Together they would be the third generation of family to run Ioka Valley Farm. That is, until Rob told her he didn't want to milk a cow another day in his life. "We compromised," says Missy. "We farm, but don't do dairy. We use the land for the special treats it can give us."

And there's a bunch. The dairy herd was sold in 1996, but the Leabs—Missy, Rob, and his parents, Don and Judy—sell pumpkins in early fall, Christmas trees later in the season, maple syrup, and beef from cattle raised spring through fall in the pasture, supplemented with Ioka's ground corn and hay they can forage.

They've also perfected the farm as education and entertainment, which Don and Judy started. As Missy says, "the more we teach where [food] comes from, the happier we are." At the least, Rob says, consumers need to know "this is what a pig looked like to begin with and that it led a happy and healthy life before you picked it up in the store." At least, that's the way it's done at Ioka.

Summer brings out Uncle Don's Barnyard for kids, with a farm theme playground, hay tunnel, farm library, sandboxes, and goats, ducks, chickens, rabbits, sheep, pigs, alpacas, and cows. Fall is pumpkin-picking time, with such activities as riding a tractor wagon out to the patch and running through a mini-corn maze. And then there's Ioka's Calf-A, which serves pancakes, waffles, and French toast from mid-February to early spring on weekends, when sap from the trees is extracted to produce maple syrup. Ioka's maple sugar house is open during the season for visitors to learn about the process.

While each of the Leabs has a favorite aspect of the

farm, Rob's passion is maple sugaring. He doesn't care how hard the job is or how much snow is outside; for him, it's about the adrenaline rush he gets when that sap starts flowing. The family started maple sugaring in '93 with 100 taps and a tiny evaporator and grew to 18,000 taps with two modern boilers in the sugar house. Rob and Missy say their biggest competition isn't the syrup their fellow producers sell—they're a collegial group—but imitation products made with corn. The two are advocates for the real deal, even over cane sugar, using the lighter, golden, and sweeter varieties of maple syrup as well as the darker, more flavor-intense types. They use syrup in lemonade, cheesecake, barbecue sauce, on butternut squash and cooked carrots, on vanilla ice cream.

Missy, a keen student of regional farming trends, observes that fruit and vegetable farms on smaller acreage are popping up in the Berkshires. She foresees the difficulty new farms will have is settling on the ideal size. On the one hand, she says, if you get too big and have to hire labor, you have to deal with the fact that it's hard to find farmworkers and they're expensive. "I think agriculture's going to be in a unique situation where it's either going to be small enough for Mom and Dad to do it on their own, or they're going to have to be big enough to overcome the cost of hiring labor."

Like other Berkshire farmers, she and Rob are also mindful of the effects of climate change. Missy realizes that "if the growing season shifts a bit, we're going to have to change when we plant and harvest."

Or, to put it another way, the saying that corn needs to be knee high by the Fourth of July—or waist high, given improvements in technology—or that the time for backyard gardeners to start planting is Memorial Day weekend, may need revisiting. For maple syrup devotees like Missy and Rob, "the old-time farming, where you boil on the first of March and you're done by the first of April, those days are gone."

Maple Dijon Vinaigrette

IOKA VALLEY FARM

MAKES 1 CUP VINAIGRETTE

This dressing is extremely versatile, and works especially well with greens that are a little bitter or spicy, such as frisée or arugula.

2 tablespoons apple cider vinegar

2 to 3 tablespoons pure maple syrup, to taste

¼ teaspoon celery seeds

¼ teaspoon dry mustard

1 tablespoon Dijon mustard

¾ teaspoon minced shallot

½ teaspoon salt, plus more to taste

¼ teaspoon freshly ground black pepper, plus more to taste

6 tablespoons neutral oil, such as canola

6 tablespoons extra virgin olive oil

1. Place all the ingredients, except the oils, in a blender and blend at high speed. With the blender on low speed, slowly add the oils until fully incorporated.

2. Taste and adjust the seasonings, if necessary.

Watercress, Apple, and Cucumber Salad

WOLFE SPRING FARM

SERVES 4

A pretty plated salad that works especially well for company! Watercress is a small-leaved, tender green that is sold or packaged in different ways. If bunches have heavy stems, purchase enough to yield 5 to 6 ounces after trimming. It's not always easy to find, so substitute another peppery green, such as arugula, if necessary. The recipe also calls for Maldon salt, which has a larger flake, to use as a finishing salt. If unavailable, fleur de sel, Himalayan, or even kosher salt can be substituted. Plate this salad only when ready to serve, because watercress can get soggy quickly!

1 tablespoon honey

1 tablespoon apple cider vinegar

2 tablespoons extra virgin olive oil

2 tablespoons finely chopped fresh chives

2 apples, such as Braeburn, Fuji, or other sweet apples, unpeeled, cored, and diced

1 European seedless cucumber, diced

2 bunches watercress (5 to 6 ounces), long or thick stems trimmed, if necessary

1 teaspoon Maldon salt, other large-flaked sea salt, or kosher salt, or to taste

1. Whisk together the honey, vinegar, oil, and chives in a medium bowl. Add the apples and cucumber and mix well. Allow to sit for 10 minutes at room temperature to let the juices extract from the ingredients.

2. Dry the watercress leaves, if necessary, tear apart any larger pieces, and arrange into a fluffy pile in a medium bowl. This can be done an hour or two ahead of time and left to sit at room temperature.

3. Right before serving, drizzle the juices from the apple mixture onto the greens and toss well. Sprinkle evenly with the salt and toss again.

4. Using tongs or a pair of forks, spread a serving of watercress on each salad plate to cover it. Divide the apple mixture on top of the greens.

WOLFE SPRING FARM

Wolfe Spring in Sheffield, MA, is a farm in transition.

Today, owners June and Jim Wolfe are concentrating on marketing their chief crops, asparagus and berries, along with watercress, to restaurants. They've scaled back from when we first spoke in March 2015, the year their youngest graduated from high school and they faced a labor shortage, but today they still produce meat and poultry for their own use, and may add apples from their now-productive orchards. But instead of the CSAs that once were the backbone of their sales, they turned in the last few years to renting out a cottage on their property and a room in their house. ("People really liked the off-grid aspect of it," June says.) Now, June and Jim are standing by to see whether any of their kids might continue farming the land, so they're in a "wait-and-see mode."

Their daughter and son-in-law own a farm nearby and have a meat CSA, and one son is a full-time electrician who loves farming, works part-time on Wolfe Spring's projects, and is buying the cottage for his family. Another son, a carpenter who studied sustainable agriculture, still helps when he has time. Their daughter, an actress, comes home in May and June to manage the asparagus sales. ("She's very good at that. But she's not sticking around. Bright lights, big city, all that.") As June says with a laugh, "we have to rebuild the barn that's falling down. And we're wondering, like how's that going to work?"

One thing that June is not equivocal about is whether choosing to raise their kids on a farm was a good idea. "It's a lifestyle I would never trade," she says. "I really like what it does for your family." She says all four children are superconfident, "with a can-do attitude. They could drive a tractor when they were 10, drive a vehicle by the time they were 12. They could bake bread. They can run a table saw. And I feel that it is because there are so many skills that you have to learn to be a farmer and we didn't hesitate to put them on it young."

She's also not equivocal about her and Jim's decision to farm in the Berkshires, even after downsizing their operation. There's a supportive community here, she says, including fellow farmers. The Wolfes cooperate with others who raise chickens to share a poultry processing unit: "One guy builds it, a lot of people rent it, and we maintain it," she says. "We're small enough—referring to other farmers in the community—that we don't feel really competitive with each other."

With the help of the Sheffield Land Trust, the Open Space Institute, and money raised locally, and subject to an Agricultural Preservation Restriction (APR), the Wolfes picked up the 52-acre property in 2006 from a family that owned the land for generations but needed to settle an estate. (Massachusetts' APR program offers state and federal funds to purchase land development rights.) As one sister who sold the property to the Wolfes was quoted as saying, "The farm is Sheffield. It's what Sheffield has been, and what we want it to be."

Farm Bounty Salad

MIGHTY FOOD FARM

SERVES 4 TO 6

This summery chopped salad uses a bounty of vegetables and makes a great cookout side dish. Grating beets can get messy and the color will stain, so try doing it in the sink, or use golden or Chioggia beets, which bleed much less. Also, grated red beets will tint the salad pink, so be sure to add them right before serving to keep the colors vibrant.

Dressing:

1 tablespoon soy sauce

1 tablespoon rice vinegar

Juice of 1 lime

½ cup grapeseed or canola oil

½ teaspoon sesame oil

1 tablespoon chopped fresh cilantro

Salad:

½ cauliflower, broken into florets (about 4 cups)

2 medium carrots, ½-inch diced (about 1 cup)

1 zucchini, ½-inch diced (about 1 cup)

½ red onion, thinly sliced into half-moons (about ½ cup)

1 medium cucumber, ½-inch diced (about 1 cup)

1 medium tomato, ½-inch diced (about 1 cup)

¼ cup chopped fresh flat-leaf parsley

1 beet, peeled and shredded (about 1 cup)

Salt and freshly ground black pepper

1. Fill a medium saucepan with salted water and bring to a boil. Prepare an ice bath by combining water and ice in a large bowl.

2. Prepare the dressing: Place all the dressing ingredients in a blender or food processor and blend until the oil is fully suspended. Set aside.

3. Add the cauliflower to the boiling water and blanch for 3 to 5 minutes. Scoop the cauliflower out with a slotted spoon and quickly submerge it in the ice bath. Shocking the cauliflower will prevent it from overcooking. In the same boiling water, blanch the carrots for 5 minutes before scooping them out with a slotted spoon and placing them in the ice bath as well. Once the carrots and cauliflower are cool, drain in a colander and allow to sit for a little while to get rid of as much water as possible.

4. Combine the cauliflower, carrots, zucchini, red onion, cucumber, tomato, and parsley in a large bowl. Add the beet and toss the salad together. Pour on half of the dressing and toss again. Add more dressing, if needed, tossing together after each addition. Sprinkle with salt and pepper to taste and toss together one last time before serving.

Feta and Roasted Beet Salad

CRICKET CREEK FARM

SERVES 4

Lemon zest livens up the flavors in this striking fall salad. Use the Maple Dijon Vinaigrette on page 39 to dress the greens.

2 large beets (about 1 pound), trimmed and scrubbed

1 teaspoon extra virgin olive oil, plus more for brushing baguettes

¼ teaspoon salt, plus more for sprinkling

¼ teaspoon freshly ground black pepper

8 thin slices baguette

4 cups arugula (about 4 ounces)

¼ cup Maple Dijon Vinaigrette (page 39)

½ cup crumbled feta

Zest of 1 lemon

Sunflower seeds, salted and toasted, for garnish (optional)

1. Preheat the oven to 350°F. Place the beets on a sheet of aluminum foil large enough to wrap them both and drizzle with the teaspoon of olive oil. Season with the salt and pepper. Wrap the foil around the beets, then roast in the oven for 1 hour. Depending on the size of the beets, roasting times may vary, so check for doneness by slipping a sharp, thin-bladed knife into the heart of the beets. If the knife meets some resistance, the beets should roast for another 15 minutes before checking again. If they are still not done in the center, add another 15 minutes to the roasting time. When the beets are done, remove from the oven and allow to cool to room temperature before handling. Leave the oven on.

2. Lightly brush each side of the baguette slices with olive oil and sprinkle with salt, as desired. On a rimmed baking sheet, toast lightly in the oven for about 5 minutes per side.

3. When the beets have reached room temperature, wrap each beet with a paper towel and massage its skin off. A small knife may help if the skin is hard to remove. Cut the peeled beets into bite-size pieces and set aside.

4. To assemble, place the arugula in a large serving bowl and toss with the vinaigrette until fully coated. Toss in the crumbled feta, then carefully arrange the beets throughout the salad to prevent their color from running onto the feta cheese. Sprinkle the lemon zest evenly over the top. Add the sunflower seeds, if desired. Garnish each serving with two toasted baguette slices.

Tomato, Peach, and Cucumber Salad

HAWK DANCE FARM
RAWSON BROOK FARM

SERVES 4 AS A SIDE SALAD

A late-summer salad that touches the right notes by balancing sweet and savory, while contrasting luscious tomato and peach against the crunch of cucumber. Serve this salad as quickly as possible after tossing it together.

2 tablespoons extra virgin olive oil

1 garlic clove, minced

1 large, ripe beefsteak-type tomato

1 cucumber

2 small to medium ripe peaches

1 teaspoon Dijon mustard

1 teaspoon rice vinegar

1 teaspoon red wine vinegar

1 tablespoon chopped flat-leaf parsley

1 tablespoon basil leaves, cut into thin ribbons

½ teaspoon kosher salt

¼ teaspoon freshly ground black pepper

¼ cup crumbled soft goat cheese

1. Heat the olive oil in a small pan over medium-low heat until shimmering and fragrant. Add the garlic and sauté until translucent but not yet browned, less than 1 minute. Remove the pan from the heat and allow to cool.

2. Core and cut the tomato into ½-inch-thick wedges. Peel and cut the cucumber lengthwise to better scrape out the seeds, before cutting into ¼-inch-thick half-moons. Peel, pit, and slice the peaches into ¼-inch-thick wedges. Gently combine the tomatoes, peaches, and cucumbers in a large bowl.

3. When the garlic is at room temperature, add the mustard, both vinegars, parsley, basil, salt, and pepper to the pan and mix to make the dressing. Scrape the dressing over the salad and toss gently to coat.

4. Plate onto serving dishes and top each serving with 1 tablespoon of the goat cheese.

Watermelon and Feta Salad

DAVE'S MELONS

SERVES 8

A brightly colored and cheerful salad that nicely balances sweet and salty, this is a perfect accompaniment to grilled meat or fish. Be sure to make the salad immediately before serving, otherwise the salt in the cheese, nuts, and dressing will draw too much liquid out of the watermelon, diluting the flavors.

2 tablespoons freshly squeezed orange juice (from about ½ orange)

2 tablespoons freshly squeezed lemon juice (from about 1 lemon)

1 tablespoon minced shallot

2 teaspoons Dijon mustard

1 teaspoon kosher salt

½ teaspoon freshly ground black pepper

2 tablespoons extra virgin olive oil

6 cups 1-inch-diced watermelon, rind removed (about 2½ pounds watermelon with rind)

8 ounces feta, crumbled

4 cups lightly packed baby arugula

½ cup smoked or roasted almonds or other favorite nut, coarsely chopped

1. Whisk together the orange juice, lemon juice, shallot, mustard, salt, and pepper in a small bowl. Slowly add the olive oil in a thin stream, whisking constantly, to make a thick dressing.

2. Place the watermelon and feta in a large bowl and add 2 tablespoons of the dressing. Toss to coat. Add the arugula and toss to coat, slowly adding ¼ cup more dressing, or as needed. Top with the almonds for texture.

Kohlrabi Slaw

CARETAKER FARM

SERVES 4 TO 6

Unfamiliar to many, kohlrabi is an odd-looking root vegetable available in both purple and white varieties. First appearing in the summer, kohlrabi can grow to a tremendous size through the fall. Once scrubbed, small kohlrabi is tender enough to skip peeling, but the larger vegetables need to be peeled. Shredding the kohlrabi is easiest with the help of a food processor fitted with a shredding blade.

¼ cup coarsely chopped pecans

1 pound kohlrabi, peeled, if necessary, and coarsely shredded (about 2 large kohlrabi)

3 medium carrots, peeled and coarsely shredded

½ red onion, thinly sliced into half-moons

¼ cup chopped fresh cilantro

¼ cup dried currants or dried blueberries

¼ cup plain yogurt

2 tablespoons apple cider vinegar

2 tablespoons honey

1 teaspoon salt

1. Heat the pecans in a small skillet over medium heat for 3 to 5 minutes, stirring occasionally, until they are lightly browned and fragrant. Be sure to watch carefully because nuts can burn easily.

Remove from the heat and allow to cool a little before adding to the salad.

2. Loosely toss together the kohlrabi, carrots, red onion, cilantro, dried currants, and pecans in a large bowl.

3. Whisk together the yogurt, vinegar, honey, and salt in a small bowl.

4. Pour the yogurt mixture over the slaw and toss to coat to your desired degree. Any leftover dressing can be saved for the next batch or another use, such as a marinade for chicken before grilling.

5. Chill the slaw for an hour or more in the refrigerator to allow the flavors to develop.

RAWSON BROOK FARM

Susan Sellew's Monterey Chèvre—"a milky, sweet ice cream of a cheese" per the *New York Times* in 2016—has close to a cult following in the Berkshires.

But followers of the iconic chèvre—in original, thyme and olive, and chive and garlic flavors—are going to have to work a little harder to buy it. Beginning in 2019, Sellew, owner of Rawson Brook Farm in Monterey, MA, is paring down her operation. Not stopping, emphasizes Sellew, who at almost 70 still feels she has more to learn about cheese making, which she plans on doing "as long as I can stand up." But starting this year, she will be selling only from the farm, and at the farmers' market and Big Y in Great Barrington. Sellew's story and her influence on Berkshire farming is one worth telling, whether she's making 175 pounds of goat cheese per week or the 500-plus she churned out at the pinnacle of her production.

An idealistic child of the '60s and '70s, Sellew homesteaded property with her then husband in St. Lawrence County in upstate New York. She had what she called "the Old McDonald syndrome," collecting all sorts of animals. But after taking a cheese making workshop at the local agricultural extension, something clicked. Sellew realized she relished being self-employed, and frankly, just loved goats, which she already raised. "They are so appealing to me," she told the *Berkshire Edge*. "They're like a practical dog with much more personality—mischievous and kind of naughty."

She moved her nascent operation back to the Berkshires where she grew up, and settled on 120 acres in Monterey that her great-grandfather once owned. Her brother lives across the street; her interns have used the cabin her parents built in the '50s. Even in the more sophisticated Berkshires, selling goat cheese didn't start out easy. She remembers offering samples to potential buyers. "I would stand in places and say, 'I'm Susie Sellew; would you like to taste my cheese?' I'd wait 'til they swallowed completely before I said, 'I made it with goat's milk.' But we only had to do that for a little while."

She can't describe precisely why her chèvre has become the legend it is among residents, tourists, and chefs. She bristles at the suggestion that she has a following just because it's local. (No, they buy it because it's good.) Perhaps her success, she says, is due to routinizing production. "It's my obsessive-compulsive disorder used to good use. A lot of it's about cleanliness. A lot of it is that I resisted getting bigger." She theorizes that it's also because her small-batch goat's milk "doesn't get all banged up. I think it's really sensitive to harsh treatment." Sellew is pretty exacting about what her goats eat, or more precisely, her goats are pretty exacting about what

they want to eat. She feeds them a type of western alfalfa, but not before offering them a bunch of varieties. As she tells it, "I go, 'Ladies, which one of these do you like?' They'd kind of pick through it and go from here to there, but when it's really good, they're going 'mmmmmmm' as they dig into it." Sellew also prides herself on treating her herd well. "It's my responsibility for the goats to be as happy and well fed and well bred and just as lovely as can be."

Five years ago, she sold 20,000 pounds during a 40-week season. Even then, she began to downsize, shipping to fewer places (she sold about 85% local, 15% outside the area). She's always wanted to control the size of her business and never wanted to be too large. Sellew would have been happy staying with her original 25 goats rather than the 50 she found she needed to make her numbers, but this year, she's down to a mere 20, and milking them once, rather than twice, a day.

We asked her years ago whether we could sell her chèvre through our New Jersey–based food distribution business. Sellew firmly turned us down. Although she never intended to make a fortune—and hasn't—she is critical when sustainable farming isn't able to sustain the farmer. She's fortunate that, in her case, she could farm her family's land and that she can manage on $30,000 a year, although she needed help putting her daughter through college. "I don't think we're sustaining our farmers," she emphasizes.

Raw Slaw

ET CETERA FARM

SERVES 4 TO 6

This light and slightly sweet slaw can be served as a salad, used as a base for grilled fish or poultry, or even tucked into a sandwich. It's advisable to prepare double the amount of dressing—mayonnaise, soy sauce, sriracha, and orange juice—and save half to use on the salad the next day, since the vegetables quickly soak it up.

2 tablespoons mayonnaise or vegan mayonnaise

4 teaspoons soy sauce

2 teaspoons sriracha

Juice of 1 orange (about ¼ cup)

2 cups finely ribboned cabbage

2 cups finely ribboned kale

1 cup shredded carrot

1 cup shredded gold or Chioggia beet

3 scallions, finely chopped

¼ cup chopped fresh cilantro

¼ cup chopped nuts (walnuts, pecans, or any preferred nut)

1. Whisk together the mayonnaise, soy sauce, sriracha, and orange juice in a large bowl until a smooth dressing is achieved.

2. Add the cabbage, kale, carrot, beet, scallions, and cilantro. Using tongs or your fingers, mix together the slaw, pinching to soften the vegetables. Pour on the dressing to fully coat the vegetables, scatter the chopped nuts on top, and serve.

Salad with Goat Cheese– Stuffed Potatoes

RAWSON BROOK FARM

SERVES 3 TO 6

Ideal for a light lunch or as a salad course for dinner, this recipe combines the crunchy feel of salad with the warm creaminess of cheese-filled potatoes. You can discard the insides of the potatoes when you hollow them out, or save them to make hash browns for breakfast.

Potatoes:

6 lime-size red or Yukon Gold potatoes

2 teaspoons extra virgin olive oil, plus more for baking dish

½ teaspoon salt

2 tablespoons minced red onion

1 garlic clove, minced

4 ounces Rawson Brook Farm chèvre, or other soft goat cheese

1 tablespoon chopped fresh flat-leaf parsley

2 teaspoons chopped fresh thyme

Salad:

1 tablespoon sherry vinegar

1 teaspoon minced shallot or red onion

1 tablespoon Dijon mustard

3 tablespoons extra virgin olive oil

¼ teaspoon salt

6 cups coarsely chopped frisée or other lettuce

12 cherry tomatoes, cut into quarters

1. Prepare the potatoes: Preheat the oven to 350°F. Lightly oil a small baking dish that will hold the potatoes in one layer.

2. Toss the potatoes in a medium bowl with 1 teaspoon of the olive oil and ¼ teaspoon of the salt. Put the potatoes into the baking dish and roast for 25 to 30 minutes, until fork-tender. The time will depend on the size of the potatoes. Remove from the oven and allow to cool to a safe temperature for handling.

3. Meanwhile, heat the remaining teaspoon of olive oil in a sauté pan over medium heat and cook the red onion and garlic until soft and translucent, 3 to 5 minutes. Remove from the heat and transfer to a small bowl. Fold in the goat cheese, parsley, thyme, and remaining ¼ teaspoon of salt. Cover and refrigerate until the potatoes are ready.

4. If the potatoes roll about easily, take a tiny slice off the bottoms with a small, sharp knife to create a flat surface upon which to place them. With a melon baller or a small spoon, hollow out the potatoes so that the outside wall of each hollowed potato is ¼ to ½ inch thick. This should remove about half of the inner flesh from each potato.

5. Increase the oven temperature to 400°F. Set the potatoes back in their baking dish, so that they are stable on their flat bottoms and do not roll around.

6. Stuff each potato with the goat cheese mixture. Bake for 10 to 15 minutes, until the tops are just turning golden. Remove from the oven and allow to cool slightly, since the cheese will be quite hot.

7. While the potatoes bake, prepare the salad. Whisk together the vinegar, shallot, mustard, olive oil, and salt in a small bowl.

8. Toss together the lettuce, cherry tomatoes, and 3 tablespoons of the vinaigrette in a large bowl. Add more dressing, if necessary, to coat the lettuce leaves. Serve each plate with one or two stuffed potatoes nestled into the salad. Drizzle any extra dressing over the salad.

Warm Potato Salad

NORTH PLAIN FARM AND BLUE HILL FARM
LEAHEY FARM

SERVES 4 TO 6

Serve warm or cold, if you prefer, with a grilled pro-
tein; this pairs perfectly with the Grilled Grass-Fed
Top Round London Broil (page 190) or Grilled Turkey
Breast Paillard (page 176).

**3 large or 4 small red potatoes (about 2 pounds or a
little under), scrubbed and 1-inch diced**

2 tablespoons extra virgin olive oil

2 tablespoons Dijon mustard

1 tablespoon apple cider or red wine vinegar

**½ cup very thinly sliced red onion, cut into
half-moons**

2 tablespoons finely chopped fresh flat-leaf parsley

2 tablespoons finely chopped fresh basil

½ teaspoon salt

½ teaspoon freshly ground black pepper

1. Place the potatoes in a large pot, cover with
water, and bring to a boil over medium-high heat.
Cover and boil until fork-tender, 10 to 15 minutes.

2. Using a colander, strain the water from the potatoes and let drain for a few minutes.

3. While the potatoes are draining, with the pot off
the heat, combine all the remaining ingredients in
the pot to make a dressing. Drop the potatoes back
into the pot and toss with the dressing until fully
absorbed and incorporated. Serve warm or cold.

Taco Salad

INDIAN LINE FARM

SERVES 6

When the ingredients are fresh and at their peak,
this simple taco salad evinces summer. Depending
on the fat content of the ground beef, you may need
to drain off the fat after browning. If you wish, you
can substitute a vegetarian ground beef product to
create a vegetarian alternative. Just follow the package instructions for browning and taste for seasoning
before making any additions. If you choose, the filling may also be used in a taco or burrito.

Yogurt dressing:

½ cup plain full-fat yogurt

2 tablespoons pure maple syrup

1 tablespoon apple cider vinegar

1 tablespoon minced fresh chives

¼ teaspoon salt

Taco seasoning:

1½ tablespoons chili powder

1¼ teaspoons ground cumin

1 teaspoon dried oregano

¾ teaspoon smoked or regular paprika

¼ to ½ teaspoon cayenne pepper

Taco mixture:

1 tablespoon olive oil

1 red onion, ½-inch diced (about 1 cup)

1 tablespoon minced garlic

2 pounds ground beef or vegetarian substitute

1 teaspoon salt

½ teaspoon freshly ground black pepper

One 15-ounce can petite diced tomatoes

3 tablespoons chopped fresh cilantro

Juice of 1 lime (about 2 tablespoons)

To assemble:

2 heads romaine lettuce, sliced into ribbons (about 12 cups)

1½ cups diced ripe tomatoes

2 cups grated Cheddar (about 8 ounces)

36 tortilla chips

Sliced olives, sliced avocado, and additional chopped cilantro for garnish (optional)

1. Prepare the dressing: Blend all the dressing ingredients together in a small bowl. This is best made earlier in the day or even a day ahead to let the flavors incorporate. If a thinner dressing is desired, add a touch more cider vinegar. Set aside in the refrigerator until serving time.

2. Prepare the taco seasoning: Mix together all the seasoning ingredients in a small bowl. Set aside.

3. Prepare the taco mixture: Heat the oil in a large skillet over medium heat until shimmering and fragrant. Add the red onion and garlic and sauté until golden brown, 7 to 10 minutes. Add the ground beef and brown, stirring constantly, breaking apart as you stir to make the meat as fine as desired. Drain the fat, if necessary. Stir in the taco seasoning until well distributed throughout and fragrant. Add the salt and pepper and stir to combine. If using a vegetarian ground meat substitute, be aware that the cooking time for this stage may be shorter, and might require a little water to keep the mixture from sticking to the bottom of the pot.

4. After the ground beef is well cooked, add the canned tomatoes, scraping the bottom of the pot gently to incorporate any browned bits. Simmer for 20 minutes to marry all the flavors, then stir in the cilantro and lime juice. Remove from the heat and let cool.

5. To assemble, place 2 cups of the lettuce ribbons in each individual serving bowl and drizzle with 2 tablespoons of the dressing. Spoon on ¾ cup of the taco mixture and ¼ cup of the diced tomatoes. Top each bowl with ⅓ cup of the Cheddar and 6 tortilla chips. Serve garnished with sliced olives, sliced avocado, and chopped cilantro (if using).

SOUPS

DAVE'S MELONS

"Dave's melons are so exquisite, we donned him with the title of 'The Melon Whisperer,'" notes the website of cafeADAM in Great Barrington, MA, one of Dave Leavitt's customers. Leavitt, who operates Dave's Melons on leased land in Cheshire, MA, is not prone to hyperbole about himself but acknowledges, "I do like my melons." But not only like; he *knows* his melons. He's a lexicon of melon seeds and varieties from Johnny's Selected Seeds Sorbet Swirl to Burpee's Fordhook, and, frankly, an authority on all things melon. Ask Leavitt how to pick a melon off a supermarket display and he'll first demur, saying he can only explain how to pick from the field, but then, out flows a treatise on both subjects.

Melons, says Leavitt, let you know when they're ready to be picked. A melon in the field signals ripeness by changing from green to, perhaps, a yellow or beige, and Leavitt says, smelling like a banana on top. Without your touching the vine, it should just snap off. He picks his melons every day, even twice a day, delivering them to restaurants and supermarkets as well as Williams College. He cautions that melons in supermarket produce departments can be deceiving since it's not clear when they were picked, and could change from green to beige just from languishing in a bin. He still recommends looking for melons that are a bit more beige, although that depends on the original color. For example, an Israeli Galia will turn from green to pure yellow, so it should be picked at the green-yellow stage. Leavitt notes that customers are often told to squeeze the end of a melon to detect ripeness, but that's when it's likely rotten.

Leavitt grew up in Pittsfield, MA, exposed to, he says, "so-so" typical cantaloupes. But there was one melon he especially liked, "a casaba Crenshaw type of thing," that his father would occasionally buy at the local Stop & Shop. "We were only allowed small pieces, and if you like something, you want more." This was in the '80s, and the 20-something-Leavitt started experimenting with growing melons in his backyard. "I saw this Burpee Florida Gem, a green flesh melon but it

looked like a cantaloupe on the outside. I'd never seen anything like that and it fascinated me."

Since beginning to grow commercially in 1984, he's rotated through leasing seven fields, farming on an acre and a half or so, and growing about 10 varieties, including a rainbow watermelon that he's developed. Without a formal education in agriculture, he taught himself how to grow melons, reaching out to universities or calling seed companies with questions. When we visited, Leavitt was leasing a plot in Richmond, MA, and working with one assistant, then Williams College student Kamaar Taliafarro. Taliafarro had grown up in Pittsfield and was passionate about bringing knowledge of food—and samples of Leavitt's produce—to food-insecure families who may never have tasted freshly grown melons.

Leavitt says that despite the grueling work—we visited him on unshaded land in Richmond on a 90-some-degree day—and an ongoing battle against crows, he's about to start another season, farming in Cheshire, beginning to plant in May and staggering it so that he can supply melons from July through October.

He has some advice for those who've been sitting on packets of seeds for years, wistfully thinking that one day they might do a little fruit or vegetable gardening themselves. Use them, urges Leavitt, who himself stocks up on discontinued seeds. "There's stories about the pyramids where they found seeds that are thousands of years old."

Chilled Melon and Mint Soup

DAVE'S MELONS

SERVES 4

This refreshing cold soup is an elegant starter course or a healthy dessert on a summer evening. Zesting citrus, like the lime and oranges in this recipe, is a great way to add flavor. It's important, though, to zest only the colored surface of the fruit's skin, not the white pith, which can be bitter. This recipe lends itself especially well to being doubled (and to experimenting with different varieties of melons).

1 large lime

2 large oranges

½ large honeydew melon (2 to 2½ pounds), seeded, peeled, and 1-inch diced

3 tablespoons loosely packed fresh mint leaves

½ large cantaloupe melon (1½ to 2 pounds), seeded, peeled, and 1-inch diced

Mint sprigs for garnish (optional)

1. Place four soup bowls in the refrigerator to chill.

2. Zest the lime until you have ½ teaspoon of zest and set aside. Zest one orange until you have ½ teaspoon of zest and set aside. Juice the lime and oranges until there is 1 tablespoon of lime juice and ½ cup of orange juice. Mix the juices together in a measuring cup with a lip for easy pouring and set aside.

3. Working in batches if necessary, puree the honeydew cubes and mint leaves in a blender until smooth and the tiny pieces of mint are as fine as possible. Pour half of the juice mixture into the puree and blend again to mix well. Transfer to a glass jar or covered dish and chill in the refrigerator for 1 hour.

4. While the honeydew puree chills, rinse the blender with cold water. Working in batches if necessary, puree the cantaloupe cubes until smooth. Pour the remaining juice mixture into the cantaloupe puree and blend again to mix well. Transfer the cantaloupe puree to a glass jar or covered dish and chill in the refrigerator for 1 hour.

5. Remove the chilled soup bowls from the refrigerator and line them up on a work surface. Pour ¾ cup of the honeydew puree into the bottom of each bowl. Gently, to avoid splashing, pour ¾ cup of the cantaloupe puree down the side of each of the serving bowls, so that the two colors of soup are separate and each takes up half of the serving bowl. Sprinkle a pinch or two of the orange zest on the green honeydew soup side, and a pinch or two of the lime zest on the cantaloupe soup side, and serve. If desired, garnish with mint sprigs.

Chilled Sweet Corn Soup

HOWDEN FARM

SERVES 4

The flavor of the corn kernels in this soup is intensi-
fied by adding the stripped cobs to the pot as it simmers. Serve cold in chilled bowls as a cooldown on
hot summer nights. (And, yes, it's also good warm!)

1 tablespoon extra virgin olive oil

1 large sweet onion, diced small (about 1 cup)

4 garlic cloves, minced

**6 ears of corn, kernels (about 5 cups) and
   cobs separated**

4 cups vegetable or chicken stock

Salt and freshly ground black pepper

8 fresh basil leaves, sliced into ribbons

1. Heat the olive oil in a large stockpot over medium-
high heat. Add the onion and cook until light golden
brown, 7 to 9 minutes. Add the garlic and cook, stirring often, until fragrant, about 1 minute. Add the
corn kernels, cobs, and stock and bring to a boil,
then lower the heat and simmer for 30 minutes.

2. Using tongs, remove the cobs and discard.
Remove the pot from the heat and, using a ladle,
strain the liquid through a fine-mesh strainer into a
large bowl. Reserve both the solids and liquid, allowing them to cool to room temperature.

3. When the strained solids are at room temperature,
remove 1 cup of the solids and set aside. Using an
immersion or countertop blender, and working in
batches if necessary, puree the remaining solids,
adding only enough of the liquid as needed to puree
until smooth. The pureed soup should be thick
enough to coat the back of a wooden spoon. If there
is any strained liquid left, save in the freezer for
other soup recipes, since it is quite flavorful. Add the
remaining cup of solids back to the soup and stir to
combine.

4. Chill the soup in the refrigerator for at least
1 hour if you are planning to serve it cold. If you
prefer a warm soup, reheat gently to your desired
temperature. Before serving, taste for seasoning and
add salt and pepper to taste. When ready to serve,
ladle the soup into individual bowls and garnish with
basil ribbons.

Easy Gazpacho

CARETAKER FARM

SERVES 8

The traditional Spanish soup, paired with slices of crusty bread, makes a refreshingly light summer supper. Choose the amount of garlic to suit your taste, and consider adding a jalapeño or two for extra flavor. The Spanish tend to favor a completely pureed soup, so much so that people often drink it out of a glass, but feel free to keep some texture if that's your preference. Caretaker Farm produces a cornucopia of vegetables perfect for assembling into a gazpacho.

4 pounds ripe tomatoes (about 8 large tomatoes)

2 large cucumbers, peeled and diced large (about 2 cups)

2 green bell peppers, seeded and diced (about 3 cups)

½ cup diced red onion

2 to 3 garlic cloves, minced

2 jalapeño peppers, seeded, ribs removed, and diced small (optional)

2 tablespoons red wine vinegar

2 tablespoons freshly squeezed lime juice

6 tablespoons extra virgin olive oil

¼ cup fresh chopped cilantro, plus more for garnish

1 teaspoon salt, or more to taste

1 teaspoon freshly ground black pepper, or more to taste

Dollop of sour cream, chopped scallions, herbs, or extra diced vegetables for garnish (optional)

1. Prepare a large bowl of ice water and set aside. Bring a pot of water to a rapid boil. Meanwhile, score the tomatoes on the bottom with a paring knife by making a shallow X through the base into the skin. Working in batches if necessary, lower the tomatoes into the boiling water for about 30 seconds, then remove them with a slotted spoon and place in the ice water to shock and stop the cooking process.

2. After about a minute or two, the tomatoes should be cool enough to handle and the skin will peel off easily. Core the tomatoes and cut each in half horizontally, along its equator. Remove the seeds by squeezing the halves gently and sliding your fingertip or the point of a knife into the seed pockets and pushing the seeds out. Chop roughly and place in a large, nonreactive bowl (such as stainless steel, glass, ceramic, or enamel-coated metal).

3. Set aside a few pieces of cucumber and bell pepper for garnishing the soup later.

4. Add the remaining cucumber and bell peppers, red onion, garlic, jalapeño (if using), vinegar, and lime juice to the tomatoes and toss together. Using a blender or food processor, and working in batches if necessary, pulse the ingredients to your desired consistency—chunky, smooth, or somewhere in between.

5. Stir in the olive oil and cilantro, add the salt and pepper, and chill for at least an hour in the refrigerator before serving. Once the gazpacho has chilled, taste for seasoning and add salt and pepper as necessary.

6. Mince the reserved cucumber and pepper pieces for garnish. Ladle the chilled soup into bowls or glasses and sprinkle with your choice of the garnishes before serving.

Roasted Garlic Tomato Soup

INDIAN LINE FARM

SERVES 4 OR 5

A great way to celebrate in-season tomatoes!

1 garlic head, cloves separated but not peeled

2 tablespoons extra virgin olive oil

1 cup ½-inch-diced sweet onion, such as Vidalia

8 cups cored and 1-inch-diced tomato

1½ tablespoons chopped fresh thyme

6 fresh basil leaves, chopped

4 cups vegetable or chicken stock

3 tablespoons chopped fresh flat-leaf parsley

2 tablespoons unsalted butter or vegan butter alternative

1 teaspoon salt

½ teaspoon freshly ground black pepper

1. Preheat the oven to 400°F. Spread a piece of aluminum foil flat on the countertop. Assemble the garlic cloves in the center of the foil and drizzle with 1 tablespoon of the olive oil. Pull the corners of the foil together to the center and pinch the seams closed to make a pouch, so that the oil will not dribble out. To further prevent leakage, place the pouch on a baking pan, then roast in the oven for 30 to 35 minutes. Remove from the oven and set aside to cool until safe to handle the garlic cloves.

2. Heat the remaining tablespoon of olive oil in a nonreactive stockpot (such as stainless steel, glass, ceramic, or enamel-coated metal) over medium heat until shimmering and fragrant. Add the onion and sauté until soft and starting to turn golden brown, bringing out its sweetness, 8 to 10 minutes.

3. Add the tomato, thyme, and basil to the pot. Pinch the garlic cloves gently, squeezing the roasted garlic out of the papery skins and into the pot. Cook, stirring occasionally, until the liquid from the tomatoes has reduced and only a small amount remains. (Reducing the tomato juices adds body to the soup.) Add the stock and stir to incorporate. Simmer for 15 minutes.

4. Remove from the heat and let the soup rest until it stops bubbling. Using a countertop or immersion blender, process until smooth, in batches if necessary. Add the parsley, butter, salt, and pepper. Ladle into individual bowls.

INDIAN LINE FARM

Elizabeth Keen and her husband, Al Thorp, are co-owners of Indian Line Farm in South Egremont, MA. As Keen tells it, the idea of the CSA was born at the dining room table of their farmhouse—though she is quick to say that it wasn't their idea. Now each summer, 140 Indian Line CSA customers experience the farm's bounty, from celeriac to the humble tomato. It was Robyn Van En, the farm's owner before Keen and Thorp, who originated the concept of the CSA. With help from the Nature Conservancy, the Community Land Trust in the Southern Berkshires, and the E. F. Schumacher Society, Keen and Thorp were able to take over Van En's farm when she died, and it is now preserved for agricultural use.

Keen offers one of the best definitions of a CSA on Indian Line's website:

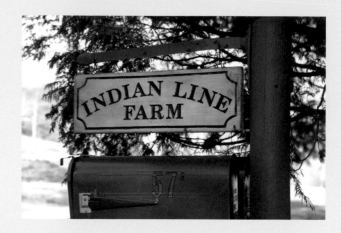

> We grow, you eat: It's a simple arrangement. The farmers at Indian Line Farm plant, cultivate, harvest, wash, and provide a bountiful selection of vegetables, fruit, flowers, and herbs. You, the CSA member, buy a share of the anticipated harvest at the beginning of the season and then pick it up from the farm in weekly increments. It's the perfect symbiotic arrangement: We have the security of an advance commitment, which helps us to plan our yields, and the funds to pay for it, you have the satisfaction of seeing where your food is grown and knowing the integrity with which it is being raised. Together we become our own food chain.

The route to CSA provider for Keen and Thorp wasn't obvious. Neither grew up farming. Keen grew up in suburban Colorado and Texas as the daughter of an Episcopal priest, Thorp in Rhode Island, bent on a career in engineering that started with a job in Olympia, Washington (he works off the farm three days a week, running his own engineering and surveying business). They met serendipitously while temping for a season at a CSA farm in Great Barrington, MA, she after working for Witness for Peace in Guatemala, he, after being newly inspired by the writings of farm and environmental activist Wendell Berry.

Keen says she immediately felt a connection with Indian Line. And that connection continues. She and Thorp have been farming the land since 1997, taking off one year in 2016 for a sabbatical during which they planted soil-building cover crops in anticipation of their return. Keen revisited Guatemala, coming back with "more energy, more creative thinking" and feeling that the time is now, as she turns 50, to take their Certified Naturally Grown farm, which follows sustainable organic practices, in new directions. The first change she made back at Indian Line was to plant

perennials, raspberries and rhubarb, on previously uncultivated land.

Keen also appreciates the farm as a place to raise the couple's two children, now young teenagers. "Their experience is going to be vastly different than that of almost anyone they encounter as adults. They have a lot of open space, a lot of freedom to be outside, and who doesn't love that as a young child?" she says. "But sometimes they don't love it, you know. Their mom is often dirty and stressed. When I go to pick them up certain places I'm sure sometimes they're like, why doesn't she wear lipstick or something?"

Keen has also organized a Berkshire farmers group in South County, modeled after New England Granges where people came to socialize. She is delighted to see new farmers coming into the region, but observes that the onus is on these and other farmers to figure out their niche. "We all can't grow kale and sell it at the Co-op and Guido's." Keen is trying to sell more in places she's already marketing to—local stores, restaurants, and at the Great Barrington farmers' market. And she's targeting her crops increasingly to what her customers want, amping up production of chard, heirloom tomatoes, parsley, dandelion greens, and escarole. She's also building a third greenhouse to extend her season and take advantage of winter farmers' markets.

But a farmer's work is never done. As Keen told the *Berkshire Eagle* in 2017, even with an additional greenhouse to extend the growing season, the farm is not yet maximizing the land's ability to produce. "There's still a lot of potential," she says.

Celery Root Soup with Granny Smith Apple

INDIAN LINE FARM

SERVES 6 TO 8

A perfect, warming fall soup, adapted from a recipe by Chef Tal Ronnen. The soup features the not-so-pretty celery root, or celeriac, whose odd appearance belies its sweet and nutty flavor. (The finished soup is quite beautiful!) Preparing the cashew cream requires the nuts to be soaked overnight, so be sure to plan ahead; it can be stored in the refrigerator for 2 to 3 days or frozen for up to 6 months.

Cashew cream:

2 cups whole raw cashews

Chive oil:

1 small bunch chives
½ cup canola oil
Pinch of salt
Freshly ground black pepper

Salt
3 tablespoons extra virgin olive oil
2 medium celery roots, peeled and 1-inch diced
2 celery stalks, diced
1 large onion, diced
2 quarts vegetable or vegetarian chicken stock, such as Better Than Bouillon brand
1 bay leaf
Freshly ground black pepper
1 tart apple, such as Granny Smith, unpeeled and finely diced

1. Prepare the cashew cream: Rinse the cashews under cold water and place in a bowl with fresh cold water to cover. Then, cover the bowl and refrigerate overnight. Drain, rinse again with cold water, and place in a blender with enough fresh cold water to just cover the cashews, about 1¼ cups. Blend on high speed for several minutes, until very smooth. If not using a professional high-speed blender, strain through a fine-mesh sieve.

2. Prepare the chive oil: Prepare a bowl of ice water and set aside. Blanch the chives in boiling water for 30 seconds, then drain and shock in the ice bath. Drain well and dry in a paper towel. Place in a blender with the canola oil, a pinch of salt and a few grinds of pepper. Blend for 2 minutes. Strain through a fine-mesh sieve. Transfer the chive oil to a plastic squeeze bottle with a small opening and set aside for garnishing the soup later. (If you don't have a plastic squeeze bottle, a spoon can also be used for drizzling the oil on the soup.)

3. Heat a large stockpot over medium heat. Sprinkle the bottom with a pinch of salt and heat for 1 minute. Add the olive oil and heat for 30 seconds, being careful not to let it smoke, so as to create a nonstick effect. Add the celery roots, celery, and onion and sauté for 6 to 10 minutes, stirring often, until soft but not browned. Add the stock and bay leaf. Bring to a boil, then lower the heat and simmer for 30 minutes. Add 1 cup of the cashew cream and simmer for 10 minutes.

4. Remove from the heat and remove the bay leaf. Using a countertop or immersion blender or food processor, and working in batches as necessary, puree the soup until a smooth texture is achieved. If using a countertop blender, put the lid on the blender, remove the center of the lid, and hold a folded towel over the opening while the machine is running, to prevent the hot liquid from spurting. Taste, and season with salt and pepper as needed. Ladle the soup into bowls and garnish with diced apple in the center of each serving, and a drizzle of chive oil around the apple.

WOVEN ROOTS FARM

We tasted our first Woven Roots carrot three years ago when Jen Salinetti, co-owner with husband Pete of the Tyringham, MA, farm, proudly pulled a bunch out of the ground and handed a single stalk to us. Imagine remembering the taste of a carrot eaten long ago? We do: sweet and unlike any supermarket carrot we've had before or after.

Jen told us that she grew up in "heavy suburbia" and didn't know where food came from, but was intrigued by a great-aunt and -uncle in Brooklyn who grew tomatoes. That was the sum of her childhood exposure to gardening, let alone farming. So, she established her own major at University of Massachusetts–Amherst in sustainable agriculture and herbal medicine. That's also where she met Pete, studying horticulture, plant, and soil science. He grew up in Lee, MA, with, as she says, "that family garden I dreamed about."

After graduation—he later transferred to the University of New Hampshire—they started growing seedlings, expanding to a farmstand selling produce from their Berkshire garden, and slowly evolved into full-time farming. As of 2019, the pair entered their ninth year as a CSA and 19th growing season—and their farming family now includes two kids: Diego, 15, and Noelia, 13. Their property is down the road from land Pete took Jen to see when they first moved back to the area. Jen remembers saying to Pete as they looked over the resplendent Tyringham Valley, "Who owns all this land? This is where I want to live someday."

While carrots are a Woven Roots signature crop, Jen and Pete are noted for their diversified output— we just bought their cherry tomatoes at Guido's Fresh Marketplace in Pittsfield, MA—and for a commitment to no till farming. That means Jen and Pete don't turn the soil but instead aerate it with a broad fork; in fact, Jen gave Pete his first as a gift when they were in their twenties. "No till" means the soil is not disturbed, allowing water and nutrients to more

easily percolate through. Jen and Pete do all their farming by hand—no tractors are used. When we met Pete, we asked whether that is part of the sales pitch for Woven Roots products. He seemed amused. "You know, we've never needed to make a pitch," he says. "I think you can just feel the difference energetically when you eat it, taste it. It's different when it's grown by hand." Their food is also different, Pete feels, because of the care they put in each square foot of soil, using ecological and regenerative practices to put carbon back into the earth.

Woven Roots is a small farm, about 10 acres total, a little less than 5 owned and 5 leased. According to

Jen, the Salinettis cultivate about 1.5 acres through their biointensive growing practices and figure out on a square-foot basis which crops are most economical. They plant only as much as needed for their 80-plus CSA customers (about 260 people per week) and for their wholesale accounts. To extend their growing season through late fall and meet their customers' needs, they plant successive crops, with 80 percent transplanted from the greenhouse and the rest grown through constant seeding.

Their kids appreciate their parents' (and their own) hard work and what they produce, and are delighted when their peers share that enthusiasm. At one point, the family became known for giving their prized carrots to their children's friends as presents. Jen recalls one birthday party where twin boys were inundated with present after present of sports equipment before opening the Salinettis' gift: carrot snack packs. "One of the boys stands up on a picnic table," says Jen, "holds up the carrots, and yells, 'YES! CARROTS!'"

Next on the Salinettis' "to do" list: building a multi-purpose barn and educational center, kicked off with a grant from the state, to help educate the next generation of farmers on soil biology. Jen is gratified "young people seek us out for information on how a farm can be viable and profitable and provide nutrient dense food to the community."

Carrot Soup with Sage and Mint

WOVEN ROOTS FARM

SERVES 8

Warm and nourishing in the chill of winter, or cold and refreshing in the heat of summer, this versatile carrot soup is welcome at the table year-round.

2 tablespoons extra virgin olive oil

1 large onion, diced (about 2 cups)

1 large celery stalk, diced (about ½ cup)

2 garlic cloves, sliced

1 tablespoon loosely packed chopped fresh sage, or 1½ teaspoons dried

5 cups diced carrots (about 2 pounds)

6 cups chicken or vegetable stock

½ teaspoon salt, or more to taste

¼ teaspoon freshly ground black pepper, or more to taste

1 tablespoon thinly sliced fresh mint for garnish

1. Heat a heavy-bottomed stockpot over medium heat.

2. Add the olive oil and heat until shimmering and fragrant. Add the onion and celery, and cook, stirring occasionally, until slightly browned, 10 to 12 minutes. Add the garlic and sage and cook, stirring occasionally, until the garlic is translucent and the sage is aromatic, about 5 minutes. Add the carrots and stock and bring to a low boil. Cook until the carrots are tender, about 25 minutes. Add the salt and pepper.

3. Remove the pot from the heat and let cool. Using a countertop or immersion blender, puree the soup, in batches if necessary, until smooth. If using a countertop blender, put the lid on the blender,

remove the center of the lid, and hold a folded towel over the opening while the machine is running, to prevent hot liquid from spurting. Return the soup to the heat and warm through, or chill in the refrigerator. Adjust the seasoning to taste with salt and pepper just before serving.

4. Ladle 2 cups of soup into each bowl and scatter the mint strips on top right before serving.

Clear Shiitake Mushroom Soup

DEERFIELD FARM

SERVES 4

This light soup can be served elegantly in a bowl, but is just as satisfying when sipped from a cup. Save the mushroom stems to make stock at another time.

2 tablespoons extra virgin olive oil

2 large garlic cloves, thinly sliced

½ cup onion, diced small (about ¼ inch)

12 ounces shiitake mushrooms, stemmed and sliced

6 cups vegetable, chicken, or beef stock

3 tablespoons chopped fresh flat-leaf parsley

1 tablespoon finely chopped fresh sage, or 1½ teaspoons dried

½ teaspoon salt, or more to taste

¼ teaspoon freshly ground black pepper, or more to taste

Croutons for serving (optional)

1. Heat the olive oil in a heavy-bottomed stockpot or a Dutch oven over medium heat until shimmering and fragrant. Sauté the garlic and onion until only slightly caramelized, 7 to 9 minutes.

2. Add the mushrooms and stir, allowing them to release their liquid and become wilted, and their edges to turn golden, 10 to 15 minutes.

3. Add the stock, parsley, sage, salt, and pepper and stir to incorporate. Bring to a simmer, cover, and adjust the heat to maintain a gentle simmer. Simmer for 30 minutes. Taste for seasoning, adding salt and pepper if needed, and serve, adding croutons if desired.

Chilled Zucchini and Roasted Tomato Soup

CHEZ NOUS

SERVES 4 TO 6

Adapted from Chefs Rachel Portnoy and Franck Tessier of Chez Nous, this soup is served chilled, garnished with a swirl of extra virgin olive oil and basil ribbons. Chilling the soup quickly in an ice bath keeps the color vibrant and helps retain the refreshing flavor.

¼ cup plus 1 tablespoon extra virgin olive oil, plus more for baking sheet and garnish

1 pound ripe heirloom tomatoes, cored and quartered

¼ teaspoon sugar

2 teaspoons salt

¾ teaspoon freshly ground black pepper

1 teaspoon herbes de Provence

1 cup diced onion

3 garlic cloves, chopped

2 cups vegetable or chicken stock

3 pounds zucchini (3 to 4 medium), diced

½ cup white wine

½ cup loosely packed ribboned fresh basil leaves, plus more for garnish

1. Preheat the oven to 450°F. Lightly oil a rimmed 13-by-18-inch baking sheet. Place four to six serving bowls in the refrigerator to chill.

2. Toss the tomato quarters gently in a medium bowl with 1 tablespoon of the olive oil, the sugar, 1 teaspoon of the salt, ¼ teaspoon of the pepper, and the herbes de Provence. When the tomatoes are coated with the seasonings and the oil, place, cut side down, on the prepared baking sheet, and roast in the oven until slightly browned, about 20 minutes. Remove from the oven and set aside.

3. While the tomatoes roast, combine the remaining ¼ cup of olive oil, onion, and garlic in a large, heavy-bottomed stockpot or Dutch oven. Cover the pot and sweat the vegetables over medium heat, stirring occasionally, for about 8 minutes, or until the onion is translucent.

4. While the onion and garlic sweat, bring the stock to a full boil in a small saucepan. When the onions are translucent, add the zucchini, stirring to combine, and then cover. Sweat the zucchini, stirring occasionally, for 10 to 15 minutes, until soft.

5. Add the roasted tomatoes and any juices from the baking sheet to the pot. Add the white wine and the boiling stock and stir to combine. Simmer for 10 minutes.

6. While the soup simmers, prepare an ice bowl to chill the soup: Using two large nesting metal bowls, or one large metal bowl that a large saucepan will fit into neatly, fill the larger bowl with ice and snuggle the smaller bowl into it so that the bottom and outer sides of the inner bowl are in direct contact with the ice. (Do not use the same pot that the soup was cooked in, since the residual heat from cooking will transfer to the soup.)

7. Add the basil leaves to the soup, stir to combine, and remove the soup from the heat. Working in batches, with a countertop blender, or in the pot with an immersion blender, puree the soup until smooth. If using a countertop blender, put the lid on the blender, remove the center of the lid, and hold a folded towel over the opening while the machine is running, to prevent hot liquid from spurting. Correct the seasoning with the remaining teaspoon salt and ½ teaspoon of pepper, or to taste.

8. Carefully pour the soup into the inner bowl of the ice bowl.

9. Gently stir the soup to help it cool in the ice bowl. Once cool, place the soup in the refrigerator until serving time, or, if cool, transfer directly from the ice bowl into the chilled soup bowls. Garnish with a drizzle of olive oil and basil ribbons.

MIGHTY FOOD FARM

Peripatetic. That's Lisa MacDougall, owner of Mighty Food Farm, in Shaftsbury, VT. Walking. Doing. All the time. The 33-year-old sole proprietor of a 154-acre diversified certified organic vegetable farm, she has to be constantly on the move, constantly working. "Did you read *Grist* magazine?" she says. "It was about the whole farmer thing being cool and sexy. I just kinda get that people have such a romantic idea about it, and it is totally awesome, but it's really hard work."

Yet MacDougall couldn't imagine doing anything else. "I can't be inside for very long so this is pretty much what I've chosen to do." She laughs. MacDougall grew up riding horses in Ipswich, MA, which is how she said she developed a tolerance—and love—for long days and hard work. After working at the Hampshire College CSA while a student at the University of Massachusetts–Amherst, she found that farming was exactly what she wanted to do, graduating with a

BS in plant, soil, and insect sciences. Her focus is still on soil, improving it at Mighty Food using compost, cover cropping, biological pest control, reduced tilling, and crop rotation.

MacDougall first farmed on 5 leased acres in 2006, then on about 25 in Pownal, VT, before moving to land she now owns in Shaftsbury, with 40 acres of tillable soil on four fields. She's also gone from a five-person CSA to more than 200 year-round free-choice CSA members, meaning customers decide what items they want. After continually getting turned down trying to buy property—MacDougall could never meet the asking price—she was offered the option to purchase land through a competitive proposal process: The Vermont Land Trust Farmland Access Program had acquired the Shaftsbury farm in 2015 from owners wanting to conserve it for agriculture. A happy MacDougall told us the ability to find affordable acreage is one of the major barriers to getting into the business. Finding commercial financing is another roadblock, since banks have difficulty assessing farm enterprises. "Agriculture can be pretty volatile in terms of cash flow," she acknowledges.

Today, MacDougall's reach extends past Vermont and into the Berkshires, selling at farmers' markets in Williamstown, Dorset, and Bennington, at Berkshire Grown Holiday Markets, and to area restaurants and co-ops, including Mezze Bistro + Bar and Wild Oats Market in Williamstown, MA.

MacDougall recognizes that her crew is essential to her success. Each member is highlighted on her website, including two draft horses. (Of the latter, she says: "We love their gentle demeanors, work ethics, and ability to get work done with their only fuel being hay and fresh water.")

"I'm definitely the human resources person," says MacDougall before telling us when we first met, that her next fun activity for her crew was "tie-dye Friday." This year, it's "show and tell" during the group's weekly check-in. She notes that while she's a "really good crew worker," she's also very organized. "You have to be willing to be organized every single day because if you're not, things fall to pieces pretty quickly." She spends the winter planning and produces "oodles of Excel spreadsheets."

For all her joie de vivre, MacDougall is astute about finance. Even in her 30s, she is starting to put money away for retirement. "You know, I don't make a lot of money, but the farm takes care of me, I have a place to live, and I really don't have many bills." She laughs yet again, returning to her more carefree self: "I'm kinda like a parasite of the farm."

MacDougall is also meticulous about what she produces. She insists that it's important to wash green leafy vegetables with a sanitizer. "Other farmers are really against it. It's like, dude…the government's cracking down and you're just gonna have to fold. I have a lot of people eating my food. I don't want anybody getting sick. I don't want to be sued. And I want people to come in and be like, 'Oh, you washed our food here? Cool; that looks good.'"

Like other farmers, MacDougall is adamant that consumers understand the real price of food, that we are paying for Big Ag through EPA cleanups, in taxes, in fuel subsidies, and through water (especially in California). She says that while the prices for some of her produce are higher, others are comparable to what one might find in a supermarket.

Beyond price, a more intangible value is infused in what MacDougall offers. "I'm not hippie-dippy or whatever," she says, but "you can tell the vibe of a place when you walk in. It translates into everything. Energy transcends whether you like it or not. That's just the way it is."

Velvety Zucchini Soup

MIGHTY FOOD FARM

SERVES 4 TO 6

Top with a few chopped scallions or a single baby arugula leaf to dress up this vibrant green soup.

2 tablespoons extra virgin olive oil

1 cup diced onion

1 cup diced scallion, white and green parts

7 to 8 garlic cloves, sliced

9 cups chopped zucchini (5 to 6 medium zucchini)

4 cups vegetable stock

½ teaspoon salt, plus more to taste

Zest of 2 lemons

2 cups lightly to moderately packed arugula

1. Heat the olive oil in a large, heavy-bottomed stockpot or Dutch oven over medium heat until shimmering and fragrant. Add the onion, scallion, and garlic. Sauté, stirring frequently, until fragrant and the onion is translucent.

2. Add the zucchini and sauté for 1 to 2 minutes. Add the vegetable stock, salt, and lemon zest and bring the soup to a boil. Lower the heat to maintain a gentle simmer and cover. Simmer until the zucchini is tender and cooked through, about 20 minutes.

3. Remove from the heat and add the arugula. Using a countertop or immersion blender, or food processor, blend the soup until completely pureed and smooth, working in batches if necessary. If using a countertop blender, put the lid on the blender, remove the center of the lid, and hold a folded towel over the opening while the machine is running, to prevent hot liquid from spurting.

4. Return the soup to the pot and continue to simmer gently for an additional 5 to 10 minutes. The soup should be on the thicker side. Season with salt to taste before serving.

ET CETERA FARM

Yong Yuk and Jeana Park came to Ghent, NY, and their farm, Et Cetera, by way of Los Angeles and before that, South Korea. Our guess is that they are the only Berkshire farmers who grow a mix of certified organic ginger, daikon, napa cabbage, turmeric, and bok choy, let alone cultivate two rice paddies. They also grow a long list of familiar staples, including mesclun, carrots, cabbage, kale, lettuce, and tomatoes. (Et Cetera also has one of the most unusual names, chosen without explanation, as Yuk tells us, by the elder of their two sons.)

Enticed by the nearby Hawthorne Valley Waldorf School for their children, Yuk and Park arrived from Los Angeles to farm a 10-acre plot of what was then mostly overgrown bushes. The property had a lot of rocks, but what attracted them was a pond that might work for growing rice. Yuk, who was in the electronic component distribution business, "always had an admiration for farming." The couple prepared for farming before leaving the West Coast by taking a master gardening course and growing in community gardens. In Ghent, they cultivate 3 acres, selling at their farmstand, to the Berkshire Food Co-op and the Hawthorne Valley Farm Store, and in Philmont and Chatham, NY.

Like other farmers we interviewed, they will tell you that farming is hard—while we were visiting, we watched Park laboriously weeding under a brutal summer sun. Although the biggest-dollar crops are lettuce and tomatoes, some of what the couple most love to grow is more challenging or doesn't bring in a lot of money, such as garlic, onions, and potatoes. They will

also never give up growing rice. And it is only the two of them doing the farming, with occasional help from their grown sons when they come home. But it is precisely this personal attention to their crops, especially during harvesting, Yuk says, that contributes to the quality of what they offer. They're also purists who won't use plastic mulch, which Yuk says he's chagrined to see on organic farms, so that means contending with weeds. A newly installed deer fence has been a big help in keeping grazers out. Off season, the couple sell firewood.

Yuk and Park eat what they grow. Park says she often makes a bok choy stir-fry with soy sauce and sesame oil, something simple and good with the short-grain brown rice from their paddies. Their children in particular liked miso soup while growing up, with lots of vegetables. Park explains that Korean miso is different from what is usually sold in grocery stores, a mix of salt and soy with no koji (a Japanese starter).

As traditionally Korean as some of their crops may be, Yuk is anything but in his eating habits. He moved to LA when he was 11; Park came later, when she was 23. He laughingly says his wife tells him he's "Mexican, Italian, American…and Korean" because he grew up eating tacos, burritos, pasta, pizza, and hamburgers. Park, on the other hand, is very conscious of the connection between food and health but finds it ironic that she's so busy, she doesn't have the time she'd like to cook. It's also ironic that she ended up farming. Her parents farmed in Korea and didn't want her to go into the business. "That's why my mother felt so sorry I'm doing this," she says with a laugh.

But Park is gratified that the many repeat customers appreciate the work it takes to bring their products to market, such as the woman who thanked her after watching her weeding carrot beds or the neighbor who brought her dahlias to beautify her stand.

Miso Soup with Daikon Radish

ET CETERA FARM

SERVES 4 TO 6

This traditional Asian soup is simple and nourishing, supplying essential minerals and vitamins. Just make sure the soup is not boiling when adding the miso, since it will destroy any health benefits. Miso paste may vary in salt content from brand to brand, so be sure to taste the soup before adding any at the end, to avoid oversalting.

2 teaspoons sesame oil

1 teaspoon vegetable oil

1 large daikon radish, peeled and ½-inch diced (about 1 cup)

1 to 2 medium carrots, peeled and ¼-inch diced (½ to 1 cup)

1 small onion, ¼-inch diced (about ½ cup)

1 tablespoon peeled grated fresh ginger

3 garlic cloves, minced

8 cups water

10 ounces extra-firm tofu, or more if desired, ½-inch diced

2 cups stemmed finely ribboned spinach, arugula, or mustard greens

1 to 1¼ cups white miso paste, to taste

Salt to taste, if necessary

1. Heat the oils together in a large, heavy-bottomed pot or saucepan over medium heat until shimmering and fragrant. Add the daikon, carrots, onion, ginger, and garlic and sauté for 5 minutes, stirring continuously to prevent burning the ginger and garlic. Increase the heat to high, add the water, and bring to a boil.

2. Once the soup has come to a boil, turn off the heat and let the boiling subside. Add the tofu and greens to the pot, and stir to combine. Add 1 cup of miso paste, whisking until fully dissolved into the soup. Taste and whisk in up to ¼ cup of additional miso, if desired. Add salt to taste, if necessary.

BIZEN GOURMET JAPANESE CUISINE & SUSHI BAR

"We're farm to tatami," quips Michael Marcus. The tatami: He's the owner of Bizen Gourmet Japanese Cuisine & Sushi Bar, in Great Barrington, MA, where his *kaiseki* (multicourse meal) rooms are furnished with woven mats and low mahogany tables. The farm: his own, an acre in Monterey where he grows organic produce for his restaurant, kabocha squash for tempura, napa cabbage, daikon, kale, and zucchini for vegetable nabe, as well as butternut squash, corn, tomatoes, and lettuce. Even in the late fall and early winter, he manages to squeeze kabocha, daikon, and carrots from his garden. Adding to this landscape are four beehives that Marcus and his girlfriend, Tasja Keetman, keep to sustain the environment, to pollinate their plants and the woods around them.

Marcus is as committed to food as he is to celebrating Japanese culture in his restaurant—more on that in a moment. He became macrobiotic in 1985, cutting out dairy, meat, and sugar, and opting for a more grain-based diet, primarily vegetarian. His principles are reflected in the Bizen menu, which also includes high-quality fish and an emphasis on organic. Marcus sources his fish as locally as possible—mostly East Coast fluke, bass, and tuna, for example—and only purchases fresh whole varieties, about 50 kinds. He also tries to cut fat and cholesterol in his dishes. "But we're not pushing it on people, and we never say we're a macrobiotic restaurant," Marcus says. "People like the food because it's high quality and real, not mass-produced."

The restaurateur says he "bends over backwards" to procure local organic produce. But he says that realistically, there's a short window to do that, from July through September. Otherwise, he says, "you're in a greenhouse and not able to get the rich variety you need to sustain the restaurant other times of the year." When Marcus can't find or grow what he needs year-round, say, organic kabocha, he'll use organic buttercup or butternut. Organic is essential for him: "If you've ever done an experiment between organic and nonorganic, it's a no-brainer. When I'm eating conventional broccoli, I'm saying I know it's broccoli, but a couple of chews later, I'm experiencing a foreign taste that I know is not really beneficial to my health." Marcus turns to an organic distributor when he can't buy local.

He is as committed to the aesthetics of eating as he is to the quality of the food, which is no surprise: Before becoming a chef and restaurateur, Marcus was a potter for over 35 years. He apprenticed in Japan for four years under master potters and kiln makers, studying Bizen ware, a wood-fired unglazed pottery. For Marcus, Japanese cuisine is a celebration of the visual, how food looks on the plate and the synergy between it and the surrounding implements, what he calls "the *morikata*, the feast of the eyes." Opening his restaurant gave Marcus the opportunity to realize a dream, using his Bizen ware for serving, showcasing food he's made on tableware he's created.

Marcus is a promoter of all things Japanese, and also of all things Berkshires. What contributes to the gestalt of his life, of being a potter and a restaurateur, is doing it in this region. He's lived here since 1982 and says the draw is the quality of life, the clear air, water, the mountains, a beautiful landscape, proximity to New York and Boston, and the fact that this is what he calls "a holistic community—people have consciousness, spirituality, a shared identity of holistic experience."

Vegetable Nabe with Kale

BIZEN GOURMET JAPANESE CUISINE
& SUSHI BAR

MAKES 4 SERVINGS

Nabe might be described as Japanese bouillabaisse. The flavorful broth, cooked here with vegetables and tofu, is traditionally prepared at the table in a hot pot called a *donabe*. This version, adapted from Bizen Gourmet Japanese Cuisine & Sushi Bar, is made in the kitchen and carried, hot, to the table for serving. The bite-size solids in the soup are removed and eaten first, and then the noodles are added to the hot broth, which is served as a second course.

Nabe:

¼ cup peeled and thinly sliced rounds of gobo (burdock root) or parsnip

½ cup peeled and julienned kabocha squash or sweet potato

¼ cup peeled and julienned carrot

¼ cup peeled and julienned daikon radish

½ cup stemmed and ribboned kale leaves

¼ cup thinly sliced onion

½ cup seeded and diced red bell pepper

¼ cup washed and thinly sliced leek, white and light green parts only, sliced into half-moons

½ cup bite-size broccoli florets

¼ cup finely shredded napa cabbage

¼ cup julienned zucchini

4 ounces firm tofu, cut into bite-size cubes

4 ounces seitan, thinly sliced into bite-size pieces

Scallions, green and white parts, thinly sliced on the diagonal, for garnish

1 pound udon or soba noodles

Dashi

5 cups water

1 large piece fresh ginger, peeled (about 2 inches)

½ cup lightly packed bonito flakes

¼ cup stemmed and thinly sliced shiitake mushrooms

Three 2-inch-wide strips dried kombu seaweed

2 tablespoons soy sauce, or more to taste, up to ¼ cup

continued . . .

1. Prepare all the nabe ingredients and lay them out prior to starting to cook. Cook the noodles according to the package instructions, drain, and set aside in a serving dish.

2. Prepare the dashi: Bring the water to a boil in a large stockpot over medium-high heat. Add the ginger. Lower the heat to maintain a simmer. Place the bonito flakes in a fine-mesh metal strainer. Position the strainer over the water so that the bonito flakes are submerged in the simmering water, but are still contained by the strainer. Allow the bonito flakes to steep for 5 minutes, then remove the strainer. Lay two layers of paper towel on a dish, hold the strainer upside down against the top layer, and tap the wet bonito flakes out of the strainer onto the paper towels. Draw the edges of the paper towel up and over the wet bonito flakes to make a package with the wet bonito flakes inside. Place the package back in the strainer, hold over the hot broth, and use your hands or the back of a large spoon to press any additional liquid out of the bonito flakes into the broth. Discard the paper towel and wet bonito flakes.

3. Add the shiitake mushroom slices and kombu to the broth. Allow the kombu to soften and flavor the broth, then, after 5 minutes, use tongs to remove and discard the kombu. Add soy sauce to taste, taking care to taste while adding so the dish does not become too salty.

4. Add the gobo, kabocha squash, carrot, and daikon to the simmering pot. Cover to avoid evaporation and cook for 5 minutes, then add the kale, onion, red pepper, and leek. Cover again and cook for 5 minutes, then add the broccoli, cabbage, and zucchini. Cover and cook for 5 minutes, then add the tofu and seitan. Use tongs to remove and discard the piece of ginger.

5. Bring the simmering hot pot of nabe to the table and place on a wooden or other heat-safe surface to protect the tabletop. Pass a slotted spoon or offer chopsticks to each person so they may serve themselves the solids from the nabe. Pass the scallions as a garnish. Once the solids have been eaten and only broth remains in the hot pot, add the noodles and allow to warm through. Serve the noodles and broth to each guest with tongs and a ladle.

Bean Soup with Smoked Ham Hock

EAST MOUNTAIN FARM

SERVES 8

This recipe features a smoked ham hock slow cooked in a delicious soup. The process is long, but the reward is a hearty, richly flavored meal. For a vegetarian version, substitute 2 cups of coarsely chopped cremini mushrooms for the smoked ham hock.

1 tablespoon extra virgin olive oil

1 cup small-diced onion

2 garlic cloves, thinly sliced

2 carrots, diced small (about 1 cup)

2 celery stalks, diced small (about 1 cup)

1 pound dried navy beans, picked over, rinsed, and drained

2 sprigs thyme

2 sprigs rosemary

1 smoked ham hock, split lengthwise by the butcher if possible

8 cups chicken or vegetable stock

Salt

1 teaspoon freshly ground black pepper

¼ cup loosely packed chopped flat-leaf parsley for garnish

1. Heat the olive oil in a large stockpot until shimmering and fragrant. Add the onion, garlic, carrots, and celery and cook until the vegetables are slightly softened. Add the beans, thyme and rosemary sprigs, ham hock (or mushrooms, if using), and stock. Bring to a boil over medium-high heat, cover, then lower the heat to maintain a simmer.

2. Allow to simmer slowly for 1½ to 2 hours, or until the meat is falling off the bone and the beans are tender and fully cooked. (If substituting mushrooms for the ham hock, keep checking until the beans are ready.) Remove the ham hock from the soup and allow to cool until easy to handle. Separate the meat from the skin, bones, and cartilage, reserving the meat but discarding the rest. There should be about 1 to 2 cups of meat, depending on the size of the ham hock. Chop the meat coarsely and set aside.

3. Remove the stems of the herbs from the soup with a pair of tongs or a fork. Scoop out 4 cups of the soup, mostly solids, and transfer to a countertop blender, food processor, or bowl, if using an immersion blender. If using a countertop blender, put the lid on the blender, remove the center of the lid, and hold a folded towel over the opening while the machine is running, to prevent hot liquid from spurting. If using mushrooms, they will become part of solids. Puree the mixture until smooth and return to the soup in the pot. Taste before adjusting the seasoning with salt and pepper, since ham hocks and stock can vary greatly in saltiness. Return the chopped meat to the pot and stir to combine evenly. Over low heat, warm the soup through and garnish with the parsley to serve.

Kale, Sausage, and White Bean Soup

CLIMBING TREE FARM

SERVES 8

This classic Italian soup recipe usually includes traditional pork sausage, but a vegetarian substitute works well, too. You can decide whether you prefer the sausage cut into slices or taken out of the casing and crumbled. Any kale could be used but lacinato, a.k.a. Tuscan kale, looks and works best. Also, if sweet corn is in season, feel free to add uncooked or cooked kernels from the cob.

1 pound dried cannellini or navy beans or three 15-ounce cans cannellini or navy beans, drained and rinsed

2 tablespoons extra virgin olive oil

2 onions, coarsely chopped (about 2 cups)

4 garlic cloves, minced

1 pound Italian pork sausage, removed from the casing, or vegan Italian-flavored sausage, removed from the casing, cut into ½-inch coins

3 celery stalks, diced (about 1 cup)

4 carrots, peeled and diced (about 2 cups)

1 bunch kale (12 to 16 ounces), preferably lacinato, stems and ribs discarded, leaves coarsely chopped

1½ tablespoons finely chopped fresh rosemary, plus more for serving

6 cups chicken or vegetable stock

2 cups fresh or frozen corn kernels, thawed (optional)

2 teaspoons kosher salt, or more to taste

½ teaspoon freshly ground black pepper, or more to taste

Grated Parmesan for serving

1. If using canned beans, skip to Step 2. Rinse the dried beans and pick over carefully for grit. Place the dried beans in a heavy-bottomed stockpot or large Dutch oven and add enough water to cover by 3 inches. Bring the beans to a boil over medium-high heat, then cover, lower the heat, and simmer for 1 hour. Drain the beans through a colander. Rinse the pot.

2. Heat the olive oil in the same pot over medium-high heat until shimmering and fragrant. Cook the onions, garlic, and sausage, stirring occasionally, for 8 to 10 minutes. Once the sausage is cooked and the onions are soft and translucent, if there seems to be too much fat, drain some from the pot. Add the celery, carrots, kale, rosemary, and beans, stir to combine, and pour the stock over the top. Stir again to distribute the ingredients evenly.

3. Return the pot to a simmer, cover, and cook for about 30 minutes, or until the beans are entirely soft, stirring occasionally, and adding the corn (if using) to the soup for the final 10 minutes of cooking. Stir in the salt and pepper, plus more rosemary, if desired. Serve with grated Parmesan sprinkled on top.

Chicken Soup,
Three Ways

SQUARE ROOTS FARM

MAKES 5 TO 6 QUARTS SOUP

Chicken soup is so simple, yet rewarding and versatile. It can be made on the stovetop, in the oven, or even in a slow cooker. Light, yet rich and flavorful, this rustic dish evokes feelings of sharing, caring, and warmth. Chicken legs and thighs are recommended because dark meat has the most flavor, but breasts can also be used. Using bone-in pieces and leaving the skin on during cooking will enhance the flavor; some prefer to keep the pieces bone-in for a chicken-in-the-pot soup, whereas others choose to take the meat off the bone and return it to the broth. This restorative soup stands alone, but can be enriched with rice or noodles.

3 pounds chicken legs and thighs, skin on

4 quarts cold water (stovetop), or 3 quarts cold water (oven or slow cooker)

1 large onion, ½-inch diced (about 1½ cups)

1 head celery, leaves removed and ½-inch diced (about 3 cups)

2 pounds carrots, peeled and ½-inch diced (6 to 7 cups)

1 large leek, cut in half lengthwise, white and light green parts sliced into ½-inch half-moons (about 3 cups)

2 tablespoons chopped fresh thyme

1 tablespoon chopped fresh rosemary

2 teaspoons salt, or more to taste

½ teaspoon freshly ground black pepper, or more to taste

¼ cup chopped fresh flat-leaf parsley

continued . . .

On the stovetop:

1. Lay the chicken pieces in a heavy-bottomed stockpot with a volume of at least 8 quarts and cover with the cold water. Cold water is important since it keeps the final broth clear; using hot water at this stage will produce a cloudy broth. Cover, bring to a boil, then lower the heat to maintain a simmer. Check periodically; if foam appears on the surface, skim it off with a spoon.

2. If you prefer chopped or shredded chicken in the soup, after the stock has simmered for 30 to 40 minutes, use tongs or a slotted spoon to remove the chicken and set on a baking sheet to cool slightly. Add the onion, celery, carrots, leek, thyme, rosemary, salt, and pepper to the broth, cover, and bring back to a simmer. When the chicken is cool enough to handle, pull the meat from the skin and bones, chop or shred it, and return it to the pot, discarding the skin and bones.

3. Let the soup continue to simmer for 45 to 60 minutes more, then taste and adjust the seasoning, adding more salt and pepper as needed. When ready to serve, stir in the chopped parsley and adjust with additional seasoning, if necessary.

In the oven:

1. Preheat the oven to 250°F and set an oven rack in the lower part of the oven.

2. Lay the chicken pieces in a Dutch oven or other oven-safe stovetop pot with a volume of at least 7 quarts and cover with the cold water. Cover and bring the pot to a simmer on the stovetop. Once the water has reached a simmer, place the covered pot in the oven. Check periodically; if foam appears on the surface, skim it off with a spoon.

3. After the stock has simmered in the oven for 4 hours, carefully remove the pot from the oven and place on a heatproof surface. If you prefer chopped or shredded chicken in soup, use tongs or a slotted spoon to remove the chicken and set on a baking sheet to cool slightly. Add the onion, celery, carrots, leek, thyme, rosemary, salt, and pepper to the pot and bring to a simmer on the stovetop while the chicken is cooling. Once the chicken is cool enough to handle, pull the meat from the skin and bones, chop or shred it, and return to the pot, discarding the skin and bones.

4. Return the pot to a simmer on the stovetop, then cover and return it to the oven. Let the soup continue to simmer in the oven for 1½ hours, then taste and adjust the seasoning, adding more salt and pepper to taste, if needed. When ready to serve, stir in the chopped parsley and adjust with additional seasoning, if necessary.

In a slow cooker:

1. Lay the chicken pieces in a slow cooker with a volume of at least 7 quarts and cover with the cold water. Set the slow cooker at LOW, and let cook for 8 to 10 hours, or even overnight. Check the pot periodically; if foam appears on the top, skim it off with a spoon.

2. If you prefer chopped or shredded chicken in soup, use tongs or a slotted spoon to remove the chicken and set on a baking sheet to cool slightly. Add the onion, celery, carrots, leek, thyme, rosemary, salt, and pepper to the slow cooker. When the chicken is cool enough to handle, pull the meat from the skin and bones, chop or shred it, and return it to the slow cooker, discarding the skin and bones.

3. Change the slow cooker setting to HIGH and continue to cook for another 2 hours, or until the vegetables are tender. Taste and adjust the seasoning, adding more salt and pepper to taste, if needed. When ready to serve, stir in the chopped parsley and adjust with additional seasoning, if necessary.

Roasted Stock

MOON IN THE POND FARM

MAKES 2 TO 4 QUARTS STOCK

Adding wine to this lovely liquid and reducing it creates a rich, dark, beautiful sauce used in professional kitchens. The stock can be thickened with flour and used as a gravy, or frozen in ice cube trays and added later to give depth to other dishes, such as Bolognese, soups, or stews.

4 pounds veal or other meat/poultry bones (ask the butcher to crosscut large bones)

1 cup coarsely chopped onion

½ cup coarsely chopped celery

½ cup coarsely chopped carrot

2 tablespoons tomato paste

4 sprigs thyme

1 sprig rosemary

6 sprigs parsley

4 quarts cold water, plus more if needed

1. Heat the oven to 450°F. Place the bones in a single layer on a roasting pan and roast in the oven for about 30 minutes. Add the onion, celery, and carrot, tossing the vegetables in the fat rendered in the bottom of the pan, and continue to roast until all is browned, 15 to 20 minutes.

2. Transfer the bones and vegetables along with any juices to a large stockpot. Add the tomato paste, thyme, rosemary, and parsley, cover with the cold water, and bring to a simmer over medium-high heat. Cover and simmer for 10 hours for red meat bones or 4 hours for poultry bones, adjusting the heat to maintain the gentle simmer. Some evaporation is expected, but if the solid ingredients are becoming crowded in the pot as the stock simmers, add small amounts of cold water as necessary through the long simmer. As the stock simmers, foam may gather around the edges, which should be skimmed off with a spoon and discarded.

3. Strain the stock through a sieve, discarding the solids and reserving the liquid. To intensify the flavor of the stock, reduce the liquid by simmering, uncovered, tasting every so often, until the flavor suits the intensity of your needs.

4. Once the stock is no longer hot, refrigerate overnight. In the morning, if desired, use a slotted spoon to skim off some or all of the fat. A little remaining fat can add flavor. Use right away in your favorite recipes or freeze for future use.

VEGETABLES

HOLIDAY BROOK FARM

Dicken Crane is as out-of-the-box a thinker when it comes to diversifying his 1,300-acre-plus farm, Holiday Brook, in Dalton, MA, as he is about his approach to cooking. Check out the headnote for "Burnt" Carrots (page 83), inspired by a Dicken original.

Among the farm's product array is screened compost ("Black Gold" or "Dicken's Dirt"), and a 50/50 soil mix of the compost and local topsoil. It's an idea that took root in the summer of '92 when his father, Fred Crane, was still alive. They would go to Otis Poultry Farm in Otis, MA, and dairy farms, and haul away chicken and cow manure. That led Dicken to add value to it as he does today with other materials he could pick up easily, such as leaves, brush from landscapers, supermarket produce scraps, and wet cardboard. Serendipitously, as Crane developed his product, the state Department of Environmental Protection decided to close all unlined landfills, eliminating a prime repository for this organic waste. Today, Crane sells about 3,000 cubic yards of compost a year to backyard gardeners, landscapers, and farmers.

Back to farming. Holiday Brook is a sustainably managed fourth-generation diversified farm on land that originated as Flintstone Farm, 3,000-plus acres amassed by Fred Crane Sr., Crane's great-grandfather

and part of the prominent New England family that owned the paper mill company Crane & Company. Crane and his two sisters and brother own the land, but Dicken owns and manages the farm business with his wife, Ruth.

At their farm store and local farmers' markets, the Cranes sell maple products, local honey, beef, lamb, pastured pork, organic vegetables, wool yarn, and Christmas trees. Besides the farm's compost, they sell firewood, hay, and straw. They also sell their meat through bulk discount and to area restaurants, such as Otto's in Pittsfield, the Dream Away Lodge in Becket, and Shire Brew House in Dalton. Add to that a 50-person produce CSA.

Holiday Brook taps 2,200 sugar maple trees that produce 850 gallons of syrup. As the *Berkshire Eagle* wrote about Crane, "there are probably a few people in Berkshire County who know as much about maple sugaring as Dicken Crane. There can't be anyone who knows more." Folks are welcome to visit Holiday Brook, says Dicken, "to enjoy our hiking trails, walk along the picturesque farm roads, and visit our barn full of friendly farm animals." The farm hosts events, including a bike race, Mother's Day brunch, and weekend pancake breakfasts during maple sugaring

season, with Ruth cooking along with other family. And, finally, the farm is a wedding venue and rents its onsite farmhouse to vacationers.

The free-thinking Crane insists the public know that although the farm is not organic certified, it follows most Northeast Organic Farming Association (NOFA) and USDA Organic standards. Crane is explicit about where he differs with those rules. His compost "is the biggie," particularly the "mixed waste" added to it. "Mixed waste means that in addition to funky squash, orange peels, coffee grounds, and plate scraping, we compost the waxed cardboard boxes in which the produce is shipped, as well as paper napkins and compostable 'plastic' plates," a no-no under organic rules, but a minuscule ingredient in the tested compost, Crane says. He argues that organic certification would be a net loss for the environment, since it would "mean rerouting more of this compostable food waste to the incinerator or hauling it farther to a different composter—both go against our goals of good environmental stewardship."

We can't end without one more story about one of Dicken and Ruth's pets, Scar the pig. In 2014, a sow, that's a mama pig, stepped on one of her piglets, creating a life-threatening tear on the animal's right side about half the length of its body. Ruth, with 16 years of veterinary technician experience, was determined to save the piglet, performing surgery on him in the farm store, which was turned into a makeshift operating room. Two days later, the pig was up and walking, engaging visitors. Scar has outgrown his original cat crate and is now 600 pounds, and he has gotten grumpier as he's gotten older ("like people," says Crane), leaving their 100-pound mini-pig, Sadie, to become the farm greeter.

We also can't end without a final observation from Dicken about Berkshire farming, specifically about the lengths farmers are going to extend the growing season. "You can see farms that used to have a greenhouse and high tunnel now have a greenhouse and three high tunnels," Crane says. (And yes, he plans to add another greenhouse, powered by alternative energy.)

"Burnt" Carrots

HOLIDAY BROOK FARM

SERVES 4 OR 5 AS A SIDE

Try using multicolored carrots to add even more pizzazz to this carrot dish inspired by Dicken Crane, owner of Holiday Brook Farm. A little freshly grated orange zest in the spice mixture, if desired, can add to the sweetness of the carrots. Crane's original recipe steamed the carrots with a little water instead of roasting them, but it was also notable for his accompanying color commentary. While the carrots are steaming, he says, "walk away and find something to do. Not too far away. Smell them when they're burning in the bottom of the pan." (Our alternative is less likely to set off a smoke detector.)

2 pounds whole carrots, peeled and trimmed

4 tablespoons (½ stick) unsalted butter, melted

1 teaspoon ground coriander

1 teaspoon kosher salt

1. Preheat the oven to 425°F. Set an oven rack in the center of the oven and line a rimmed half sheet pan with foil to facilitate cleanup.

2. Quarter the carrots lengthwise into long sticks, no thicker than your index finger. If some of the carrots are especially thick, cut into eighths instead. Lay the carrot sticks on the prepared pan. Drizzle with the melted butter and, using tongs, toss gently to coat. Spread on the baking sheet in a single layer.

3. Combine the coriander and salt in a small dish until evenly mixed. Using your fingers, take pinches of the mixture, and from at least 10 inches above the carrots, sprinkle evenly over the sticks. Sprinkling from this height will allow for more even distribution.

4. Roast in the oven for 35 to 45 minutes. The surfaces of the carrots will become darkened and caramelized and the centers will be tender. Remove from the oven and let the carrot sticks rest on the pan for 5 to 10 minutes.

5. Using tongs, shift the carrots around on the pan to mix in the remaining melted butter before serving.

Brussels Sprouts with Smoked-Almond Butter

INDIAN LINE FARM

SERVES 4 TO 6

To keep the Brussels sprouts in this recipe bright and green, an ice water bath after boiling will help retain both texture and color. The chopped smoked almonds are a stand-in for more traditional cooked bacon bits, and put a new, vegetarian-friendly face on an old favorite.

1 pound Brussels sprouts

2 tablespoons unsalted butter or olive oil

4 ounces smoked almonds (e.g., Blue Diamond Smokehouse Almonds), coarsely chopped

¼ teaspoon salt, or to taste

¼ teaspoon freshly ground black pepper, or to taste

1. Bring a large pot of salted water to a rapid boil over high heat. Prepare a large bowl of ice water.

2. While the water is coming to a boil, wash the Brussels sprouts in a colander in the sink. Trim the stems and remove any yellowed leaves. For even cooking, it is important to have the sprouts roughly the same size, so cut any larger ones in half or even into quarters. Try to cut so that each piece retains some of the center stem, to keep them from falling apart in the water.

3. Drop the Brussels sprouts in the boiling water and cover. Boil for 2 to 4 minutes, or just until the largest are fork-tender. Using a slotted spoon, remove the sprouts and shock them in the ice water bath. Allow the sprouts to cool, remove after 2 minutes, and pat dry on paper towels.

4. Melt the butter or warm the olive oil in a large sauté pan over medium heat and add the chopped almonds. As the butter begins to brown, add the sprouts and heat through, about 4 minutes. Add salt and pepper to taste, then serve.

WILDSTONE FARM

John and Joy Primmer, owners of Wildstone Farm of Pownal, VT, are all things garlic.

To be honest, we never knew there were so many garlic varieties. We knew about elephant garlic, which the Primmers sell. But we learned from them that it isn't even a true garlic, that it has a milder and sweeter flavor and is more closely related to a leek. Joy's favorite variety depends on what she's cooking, since some are better eaten raw or cooked, but she mentions Carpathian, a Rocambole variety, when we first spoke. ("Large, uniform bulbs. Nice overall tang, hot, spicy, strong and garlicky.") John gravitates to Georgian Crystal, a Porcelain variety. ("Beautiful fat cloves. Very mild and flavorful raw. Long storing.")

We think of garlic as common, ubiquitous, but

turns out, it's not easy to grow. Its season is long—John and Joy plant it in late October and don't harvest their main crop until mid-July, and then still need to leave it in the greenhouse to dry. They grade their garlic by size and quality, something you wouldn't know is possible from picking up a head or two in a grocery store, and constantly check the product from harvest through classification.

Aside from grading, they also tout the taste of their garlic, which Joy says is a result of the terroir—their fertile silt loam soil, but also their microclimate. At 1,400 feet above sea level, Wildstone is slightly cooler than the surrounding valley towns of Pownal, Bennington, and Williamstown. The Swiss Chard Gratin (page 86), which uses garlic cloves, is inspired by this signature crop, as well as the chard the Primmers grow in winter in high tunnels. Joy's garlic chicken—"tons of garlic inside, outside, all over it"—inspired the recipe on page 170.

Beyond garlic, the list of what the Primmers grow is quite long. They operate a fully diversified organic vegetable farm, offering eggs, herbs, and sunflowers. Just their root and storage crops—they have a root cellar—include onions, shallots, leeks, cabbage, carrots, beets, potatoes, four different squash, rutabaga, celeriac, broccoli, and parsnips.

The couple are fiercely committed to organic—in 1989, Wildstone became the first in Bennington County to become certified—but their principles extend beyond organic. To operate their farm as sustainably as possible, they use water drawn from a spring below their house, solar power for some of their needs, and a small walk-behind tractor and hand tools to work the land.

Supporting local food is right up there in importance. Of course, the Primmers eat off their farm. "I don't think we've bought a vegetable since we've been here," says Joy, laughing, but they are adamant about buying what they do purchase from local purveyors. They want others to have the same opportunity, and through Hoosac Harvest in North Adams, MA,

are able to offer some subsidized shares of their 50-member CSA to northern Berkshire residents. The Primmers sell at the Bennington farmers' market and Berkshire Grown Holiday Markets, and also ship. They prefer going directly to people over wholesale because they like feedback and one-on-one. "It allows us to be on a first-name basis with just about all our customers," John says.

The Primmers appreciate the collegiality of other farmers and write in their occasional newsletter that "the tri-state region that we live in is very much one large community." Yet, organic farming around the area is getting more competitive, John notes. For example, even such supermarkets as Walmart and Aldi offer organics, which are not necessarily local. He admits that he and Joy are not the best marketers—"we're kinda shy people"—so, we asked him how he confronts an increasingly tough selling environment. "This may sound weird," he says, "but the love that we put into our work, and the care for our land comes out somehow in the produce."

Swiss Chard Gratin

WILDSTONE FARM

SERVES 4

Kale seems to have received the glut of attention, but don't overlook another hearty and healthy green, leafy vegetable: Swiss chard! This gratin defines wintery comfort food: warm, flavorful, homey, easy to make, and flexible enough to work as a vegetarian or vegan dish. If preparing a vegan version, adjust the amount of vegan Parmesan to taste, since the flavor of these products can vary.

3 tablespoons unsalted butter or extra virgin olive oil, plus more for baking dish

1 tablespoon extra virgin olive oil

4 garlic cloves, minced

4 ounces hearty bread, diced small (about 2 cups)

1 tablespoon chopped fresh flat-leaf parsley

½ teaspoon salt

2 to 2½ pounds Swiss chard, stemmed and leaves cut into ½-inch ribbons

¼ teaspoon freshly ground black pepper

¼ cup heavy cream, chicken stock, or vegetable stock

½ cup grated Parmesan or vegan Parmesan, to taste

1. Preheat the oven to 400°F, and butter an 8-by-8-inch baking dish.

2. Heat 1 tablespoon of the butter in a large sauté pan over medium heat. Add one-quarter of the garlic and sauté until translucent, about 1 minute. Add the bread and parsley and sauté, stirring frequently, until lightly toasted. Season with ¼ teaspoon of the salt and toss once more. Transfer the bread mixture to a bowl and set aside.

3. Return the pan to the heat. Melt the remaining butter, add the remaining three cloves' worth of garlic, and sauté until translucent, about 1 minute. Add the chard, remaining ¼ teaspoon of salt, and the pepper and sauté until the chard is wilted, about 3 minutes. Add the cream and stir to incorporate fully.

4. Remove the pan from the heat and place half of the chard mixture in the prepared baking dish, using a spoon or spatula to spread evenly across the bottom, then sprinkle half the Parmesan evenly over the top. Layer the remaining chard mixture over the cheese and sprinkle the remaining Parmesan over all. Top with the bread mixture, spreading to cover fully. Bake for 20 minutes, remove from the oven, and let rest for 10 minutes before serving.

Butternut Squash Gratin

MIGHTY FOOD FARM

SERVES 4 TO 6

Butternut squash is the chief ingredient in this cool-weather gratin, suffused with winter spices of nutmeg and sage. The recipe will also work with precut squash from the store if you'd like a shortcut. For a lighter version, use vegetable stock instead of cream.

2 pounds butternut squash, peeled, halved, and seeded

1 tablespoon extra virgin olive oil

¾ teaspoon kosher salt

¼ teaspoon plus ⅛ teaspoon freshly ground black pepper

1 tablespoon unsalted butter, plus more for baking dish

¼ cup dried plain bread crumbs

¼ cup grated Parmesan

2 teaspoons chopped fresh thyme

2 teaspoons chopped fresh sage

⅛ teaspoon ground nutmeg

1¼ to 1½ cups heavy cream, or 1 cup vegetable stock

1. Preheat the oven to 375°F. Place the squash halves, cut side down, on a foil-lined half sheet pan. Drizzle the olive oil over the squash and sprinkle with ½ teaspoon of the salt and ¼ teaspoon of the pepper. Add ½ cup of water to the pan and roast in the oven for 25 to 35 minutes, until easily pierced with a knife. If using cut squash pieces, toss in a bowl with olive oil, ½ teaspoon of the salt, and ¼ teaspoon of the pepper and spread in a single layer on the prepared sheet pan. Cut pieces may require less time to cook.

2. While the squash is cooking, melt the butter in a small skillet and add the bread crumbs. Cook, stirring, for 3 to 5 minutes, until all are moistened with butter. Remove from the heat and let cool, then stir in the Parmesan, thyme, and sage.

3. Lower the oven temperature to 350°F. Butter an 8-by-10-inch rectangular baking dish.

4. Cut the butternut squash into half-moon-shaped slices, ¼ to ½ inch thick, and lay them in the prepared baking dish, overlapping as necessary to fill it entirely. If using cut squash pieces, arrange tightly in the pan, overlapping where possible. Some larger pieces may need to be cut in half. Sprinkle the nutmeg and the remaining ¼ teaspoon of salt and ⅛ teaspoon of pepper evenly over the squash.

5. Pour enough cream over the squash for the tops of the pieces to just poke out above the surface of the liquid.

6. Sprinkle the bread crumb mixture as evenly as possible over the top. Cover the dish with aluminum foil and bake for 30 minutes. Remove the foil and bake for an additional 10 to 15 minutes, until the top is lightly browned. Remove from the oven and allow to cool for 10 minutes before serving.

HAWK DANCE FARM

As Damon Clift and Diane Creed stood with their Realtor checking out the 3 acres of land that would become Hawk Dance Farm, two red-tailed hawks circled above, locked talons and spiraled to the ground before shooting back up, about to mate. Immediately, Clift and Creed knew something significant was about to happen in their lives. "Hawks have always been our spirit animal, our guide," Clift says.

Ten-plus years later, the husband-and-wife team are still sustainably farming that property, without chemicals, pesticides, or herbicides. They farm by hand on barely tilled soil, nourished by rich compost and cover crops. They grow diversified heirloom vegetables, herbs, and flowers, and as their website says, "by doing so, we are conserving the heritage of our forefathers."

Hillsdale, NY, where their farm is located, is about 120 miles from Queens, NY, where Clift and Creed's story begins. Clift painted houses and Creed, a former veterinarian technician, owned a pet-sitting and dog-walking business. They were urban gardeners, and swayed by the writings of back-to-the-lander Scott Nearing and organic advocate Eliot Coleman, sold their New York City home in 2007. Clift immediately began working on farms to learn the business.

Clift and Creed knew from their research that it would take three to five years to make a profit, and in 2015, when we first met the couple, they told us the year before they finally made $3,000. They acknowledge they had a romantic vision of farming, which they quickly learned was incorrect: "It's really hard," says Clift. "We weren't ready to use up our savings for this endeavor and have nothing to fall back on, no emergency fund, or anything like that." Yet, they're happy they followed their dream. "Even if we're not getting rich by it," says Creed, "at least we can say

we've done what we believed in and we're continuing to do so."

It didn't help that when they started, a tomato blight hit the Berkshires, or that climate change has made growing increasingly unpredictable. When he has been able to, Clift paints houses during the winter. The couple also have a side enterprise creating candles from 100 percent local beeswax, which they sell year-round at farmers' markets and craft fairs. Despite their own financial challenges, they have a policy that Creed says is paramount. If they have produce they are not going to use, they donate it to the local food pantry. If a CSA member doesn't show up, which occurs on occasion, that share also goes to a food pantry. "There's only so much we can eat ourselves and our tortoise can eat," says Creed. (Yes, besides a dog and two cats, they have a tortoise.)

The two are adamant about continuing to live their

ideals, as Clift says, "being in tune with the earth." They use only organic heirloom, non-GMO seeds. "We believe in supporting that kind of food because I don't want to be a genetic experiment and I don't want my customers to be either," says Creed. "I want to be able to present the freshest, healthiest food that we can grow. And everything we do grow, is done with such care and love, we want people to feel that when they eat it. We want them to feel when they bite into one of our tomatoes, the joy that we feel when we eat it, how delicious it is, and how hard it was to grow them to that state."

Clearly, the couple have a following. One woman, one of their farmers' market customers, wanting to know when she could restock her Hawk Dance cherry tomatoes, wrote on the farm's Facebook page, "Let me know if you have more before Saturday. Lucy and I ate all ours in like an hour."

To get to where they are today, they've had to experiment. For example, they started out doing everything vegan—which is how they eat—but found they couldn't generate enough plant-based compost, so they imported some with animal matter. "If it's making our plants grow better, then that's what we have to do," says Clift. They grow as far as they can into winter, with the aid of low tunnels and a greenhouse Clift built when they first bought the property. He's also resourceful at improvising equipment, such as the discarded washing machine he converted into a commercial vegetable washer and spinner.

Clift and Creed eat from their farm and have plenty to choose from—the year we visited, they grew 90 different plants. He likes Indian food, which inspired the vegan version of Aloo Gobi (page 174), and they had just finished a dinner of beet pancakes, inspiring the Savory Beet Latkes (page 98).

Mashed Cauliflower with Chives

HAWK DANCE FARM

SERVES 4

Smooth and creamy, this side dish goes with just about anything, from roasted chicken to grilled fish.

1 large to 2 small heads cauliflower (about 2½ pounds)
1 tablespoon extra virgin olive oil
¾ cup small-diced onion
1 teaspoon kosher salt
½ to 1 cup water
1 tablespoon unsalted butter
¼ cup half-and-half
1 tablespoon fresh lemon juice
¼ cup loosely packed chopped fresh chives
¼ teaspoon Maldon salt or other coarse sea salt

1. Trim the leaves from the cauliflower heads. Cut the florets and core into 1-inch pieces (about 6 cups of cut cauliflower).

2. Heat the olive oil in a large sauté pan with a lid over medium heat until shimmering and fragrant. Add the onion and sauté until translucent, about 5 minutes. Add the cauliflower, salt, and ½ cup of the water. Cover and steam until tender, 15 to 20 minutes, adding up to ½ cup more water as needed.

3. Once the cauliflower is tender, remove from the heat. Using a slotted spoon to reserve any excess liquid, transfer the vegetables to a food processor or blender, add the butter, and puree until smooth. Add the half-and-half and lemon juice and continue to puree. If the puree seems too thick, while the processor is running, slowly add liquid from the pan until the desired consistency is reached.

4. Spoon the puree into a serving dish and garnish with chives and a light sprinkling of Maldon salt.

Roasted Baby Turnips with Swiss Chard and Dijon

HAWK DANCE FARM

SERVES 8

Turnips are often overlooked because of an unwarranted reputation for being mundane. In the spring or early fall when still small, the root vegetable can be extra tender and even somewhat sweet. This recipe uses baby turnips to make a pretty side dish, paired with Swiss chard for color and fresh herbs for a flavor boost. If you find turnips with greens attached, feel free to use them and reduce the chard quantity by an equivalent amount. If your turnips are larger, be sure to trim them well and cut into smaller pieces. You may wish to double the dressing if you are not serving this immediately, reserving half of it to refresh the dish right before serving, since the chard will soak up the vinaigrette.

Neutral oil, such as canola, for baking sheet

24 baby turnips (golf ball size), scrubbed and stems trimmed to 1 inch

¼ cup extra virgin olive oil

½ teaspoon salt, plus more to taste

¼ teaspoon freshly ground black pepper, plus more to taste

Leaves from 6 thyme sprigs (about 1 tablespoon leaves)

1 tablespoon white balsamic or apple cider vinegar

2 teaspoons Dijon mustard

2 tablespoons chopped fresh flat-leaf parsley

6 cups stemmed thinly sliced Swiss chard

1. Preheat the oven to 425°F. Lightly oil a baking sheet.

2. Cut the turnips in half lengthwise, from root to stem, and place in a bowl. If you are using turnips larger than a golf ball, be sure to cut them into equal-size pieces, about 1½ by ¾ inch, for even cooking. Toss with 2 tablespoons of the olive oil and season with the salt, pepper, and thyme leaves. Transfer the turnips to the prepared baking sheet and roast in the oven until the edges are browned and the turnips are fork-tender, 20 to 30 minutes.

3. Meanwhile, whisk together the vinegar, mustard, parsley, and remaining 2 tablespoons of olive oil in a medium bowl. Season the vinaigrette with salt and pepper to taste.

4. Place the Swiss chard in a large bowl and drizzle with the vinaigrette. Once the turnips are roasted, add them to the Swiss chard and toss together. As the turnips cool slightly, the chard will wilt and absorb the vinaigrette. Transfer to a platter and serve.

Grilled Harissa Cauliflower with Corn and Avocado Relish

KRIPALU CENTER FOR YOGA & HEALTH

SERVES 4

The heat from harissa boosts the flavor of the cauliflower in this easy grilled dish, adapted from Kripalu executive chef Jeremy Rock Smith's recipe. The recipe calls for half of an avocado, but feel free to include both halves. And if you like heat, increase the harissa to your taste.

2 tablespoons rice vinegar

1 teaspoon coconut sugar or granulated sugar

2 tablespoons extra virgin olive oil

2 cups corn kernels, fresh or frozen and thawed

¼ cup seeded and small-diced red bell pepper

¼ cup small-diced red onion

¼ cup small-diced cucumber

2 tablespoons chopped fresh dill

½ avocado, peeled, pitted, and diced, or both halves, if desired

¼ cup canola oil, for grill and brushing

1 large head cauliflower, leaves trimmed

1 tablespoon dry harissa

Salt and freshly ground black pepper

1. Combine the vinegar, sugar, and olive oil in a large bowl until the sugar has dissolved. Add the corn kernels, red bell pepper, red onion, cucumber, dill, and avocado and stir gently to combine. Set aside.

2. Preheat a gas or charcoal grill to medium-high. Brush the grill rack with canola oil to prevent the cauliflower from sticking.

3. With a sharp knife, cut the cauliflower in half straight down through the stem. Cut each half into "steaks" about ¾ inch thick. Be sure to cut through the center stem so that the steaks hold together well. If there are some loose pieces that are not attached to the center stem, they can still be used by piecing them together to make up a serving. Place the cauliflower on a rimmed baking sheet.

4. Brush the cauliflower steaks and pieces evenly on both sides with canola oil. Sprinkle both sides with the harissa, and salt and pepper to taste.

5. Place the steaks and pieces on the grill and cook until lightly browned, 3 to 5 minutes. With a metal spatula or a pair of metal tongs, gently loosen the steaks from the grill rack, and flip carefully. Lower the heat to medium, or move to a slightly cooler part of the grill, and allow to cook about 10 minutes, or until lightly browned and cooked through.

6. To serve, place each cauliflower steak on a plate and top generously with the corn and avocado relish.

Cheesy Roasted Cauliflower

HOLIDAY BROOK FARM

SERVES 2 AS A MAIN COURSE OR 4 AS A SIDE DISH

Parmesan and a little red pepper elevate the mild cauliflower into a side dish to savor.

1 large or 2 small heads cauliflower (about 2½ pounds)

¼ cup extra virgin olive oil

1 tablespoon minced garlic (2 to 3 cloves)

½ teaspoon kosher salt

½ teaspoon red pepper flakes

2 tablespoons finely chopped fresh flat-leaf parsley

½ cup grated Parmesan

1. Preheat the oven to 400°F. Set an oven rack in the center of the oven and line a half sheet pan with foil to facilitate cleanup.

2. Remove the leaves from the cauliflower head and place the head securely on a cutting surface. With a large knife, slice in half. Carefully remove the center stem and set aside. Cut the florets into pieces about the size of your thumb. Cut the stem into 1-inch cubes.

3. Combine the olive oil and garlic in a large bowl. Add the cauliflower and gently toss to allow the oil and garlic to coat the cauliflower evenly.

4. Combine the salt, red pepper flakes, parsley, and Parmesan in a small bowl. Mix together well. Sprinkle half of the seasonings evenly over the cauliflower and gently mix to coat.

5. Spread the cauliflower over the baking sheet, trying to keep it as close to a single layer as possible. Using a spoon or your fingers, sprinkle the remaining seasonings from a height of 12 inches over the cauliflower. which will help distribute the seasonings more evenly.

6. Bake for 20 to 30 minutes, gently turning the cauliflower halfway through with a spatula. When the cauliflower begins to turn golden and tender, remove from the oven and serve.

Southern-Style Collard Greens

MIGHTY FOOD FARM

SERVES 8 TO 10

Traditional southern-style collards begin with bacon because of the whopping flavor it imparts. It's also tempting to add a little diced ham or tasso when serving. For those who prefer a plant-based diet, skip the bacon and sauté the onions in 2 table-spoons of butter or olive oil instead. The fat from the bacon or butter helps balance the acidity from the vinegar. Add cayenne, hot sauce, or a light sprinkling of Parmesan before serving, if desired.

8 bacon slices (about 10 ounces), diced small

1 large onion, diced small (about 1½ cups)

6 garlic cloves, sliced

4 pounds collard greens, washed, stemmed, and chopped into 1½-inch pieces

4 cups chicken or vegetable stock

½ cup apple cider vinegar

1. Cook the bacon in a large stockpot (8 to 10 quarts) over medium heat for 10 minutes, or until almost crisp. Add the onion and sauté to slightly car-amelize, 8 to 10 minutes. Add the garlic and sauté for 1 to 2 minutes. Add the collards in stages, stir-ring to help wilt and to incorporate the bacon and onion bits from the bottom of the pot. Once the greens are slightly wilted, add ½ cup of the stock. As best as possible, use the liquid to scrape up any browned bits from the bottom of the pot. Add the remaining 3½ cups of stock and the vinegar, cover, and adjust the heat to maintain a simmer for 30 to 45 minutes, until the greens are tender.

2. To serve, scoop the collards from the pot into a bowl, including the liquid from the bottom of the pot.

Celery Root Puree

INDIAN LINE FARM

SERVES 6 TO 8 AS A SIDE DISH

Celery root, a.k.a. celeriac, may look unappealing and intimidating, but simply trim off the hairy-looking fingers and peel away the dark skin, and you'll find a flavorful and aromatic center. Russet or Idaho potatoes are preferable because of their higher starch content, giving more texture and thickness to the puree, but any potato would work. This flavorful alternative to the simple mashed potato is great with meat, and can be thinned slightly with milk or stock and used as a sauce for fish or poultry.

1 pound celery root, peeled and 1-inch diced

1 pound russet or Idaho potatoes, peeled and 1-inch diced

1 teaspoon salt, plus more to taste

4 tablespoons (½ stick) unsalted butter, at room temperature

1. Place the diced celery root and potatoes in a large saucepan and cover with water by 1 inch. Sprinkle the salt on top of the surface of the water. Bring to a boil over medium-high heat and cook until tender, 20 to 25 minutes.

2. Using a colander, drain the vegetables and pat dry with a towel. Using a food processor, blender, or an immersion blender and a bowl, puree the mixture until smooth. Add the butter, mixing well, and sea-son with additional salt to taste.

Blistered Green Beans with Dijon Vinaigrette

THE RED LION INN

SERVES 4 AS A SIDE

Roasting green beans in a hot pan concentrates their flavor so they hold their own with the Dijon mustard and lemon in the vinaigrette, in this recipe adapted from Chef Brian Alberg, former executive chef of the Red Lion Inn. Be sure to allow the green beans enough time on the heat so they start to blister and get brown in spots.

Zest and juice of 1 lemon

1 tablespoon apple cider vinegar

¼ cup whole-grain Dijon mustard

¼ teaspoon salt

¼ teaspoon freshly ground black pepper

¼ cup plus 1 tablespoon extra virgin olive oil

½ medium red onion, thinly sliced into half-moons

1 pound green beans, stemmed

1. Whisk together the lemon juice, vinegar, mustard, salt, and pepper. Whisk in ¼ cup of the olive oil and lemon zest and set the vinaigrette aside.

2. Heat 1½ teaspoons of the olive oil in a large skillet over medium-high heat. Add the red onion and cook until golden, 7 to 9 minutes. Transfer to a bowl and set aside.

3. Return the pan to the heat, add the remaining 1½ teaspoons of olive oil, and spread out the beans in a single layer as much as possible. Allow the beans to cook without moving until they begin to blister and start to turn brown in spots. Stir and continue to cook to the desired tenderness, 8 to 10 minutes. Just before turning off the heat, add the onion back to the pan and stir to combine.

4. Remove the pan from the heat and pour the vinaigrette directly into the pan. Stir to combine, then let stand for 10 to 15 minutes so the beans can absorb some of the dressing. Serve warm or make ahead and serve as a cold salad.

CARETAKER FARM

It's not only sustainable food that Don Zasada and Bridget Spann, owners of Caretaker Farm, of Williamstown, MA, want to provide. It's community, including for their 270 CSA members. "Every adult member has to do two hours of work per season," explains Spann. "It's a way for them to work alongside the crew, a wonderful opportunity to be part of the experience of how their vegetables arrive at their tables." It's also a great equalizer. "It doesn't matter if you have a PhD in this or you're a doctor in that or you are on food stamps. Everyone is learning how to harvest potatoes and weed carrots. It's a neat way for people to connect over those jobs." CSA members pick up produce at the farm, but some of the crops offered are U-Pick, harvested by the members themselves.

To create even more community for CSA members, Zasada and Spann open the farm for numerous festivals and workdays, from Winter Solstice Celebrations to August Onion Harvest. They also have a volunteer program where non-CSA members can come help out. Occasional bird and wild edible walks are open to the public.

Spann is quick to credit the support they get from the community, and the community they've created, to the groundwork laid by previous owners Elizabeth and Sam Smith, who operated one of the oldest CSAs in the county. "Many of our CSA members had a longer relationship with this farm than we did," says Spann. "It's clear that it belonged as much to them as to us."

Spann and Zasada first met as volunteers organizing in rural Chile, where they encountered large-scale industrial agriculture and decided to dedicate themselves to small-scale sustainable farming when they returned to the United States. Zasada, a chemical engineer, and Spann, a social worker, eventually sought farmland in the Northeast, finding a listing for Caretaker in NOFA's *The Natural Farmer*, which they obtained with a 99-year-renewable lease and through a complicated arrangement with support from several nonprofits and the community. The land is preserved for agricultural purposes. "We never dared imagine we would be able to afford land," says Spann. "So much of the investment you make is in the soil, soil fertility, infrastructure, and to not know year by year if you're going to have to pick up and leave is terrible. If this arrangement didn't happen, we would never be able to farm here."

Caretaker Farm's 2018 summer CSA offered ample choices, too long to list, but ranging from 14 varieties of lettuce to pie pumpkins to rutabaga and even melons. The pick-your-own list is almost as long, ranging from cherry, saladette, and canning tomatoes to edamame. And opportunities to buy non-GMO free-range eggs, meats, and bakery goods.

Spann's message to home cooks is to be open to substitutions, given the plethora of choices. "I use recipes as a framework, but then expand off them,

depending on what I have available." She told us that she sometimes worked from a Moosewood Restaurant chili recipe, "but then, I had a lot of kohlrabi sitting here, so did a quick search for kohlrabi chili and sure enough, someone's putting it in their dish." See Bean Chili (page 159).

For small farmers to succeed, Spann also urges consumers to understand why it's necessary to pay what it takes to buy their food. She asks them not to compare cheap carrots from California with locally grown sustainable ones, to realize the external costs of conventional produce transported cross-country. "We're getting cheap stuff now and we'll pay later," says Spann. "I want people to connect the dots, for every person who's dealing with health issues to ask what it is in our environment that's toxic, and realize that organic farming is one answer to this puzzle."

Spann—and Zasada—think they're lucky to be able to do what they're doing, and that the Berkshires is a fantastic place to farm and raise their two kids, now 15 and 12. "This will be a farm for many generations," Zasada told the *Berkshire Eagle* in 2016. "We've been here 12 years and hopefully will be here much longer. But we're just a blip on the radar of what has happened in the history of this land. We try not to take that for granted."

Rutabaga Latkes

CARETAKER FARM

SERVES 4 TO 6

Rutabaga, the zippier relative of the turnip, is similarly overlooked as a drab winter storage crop vegetable. These simple latkes help the humble rutabaga make a star appearance over the more traditional potato pancake. Because they are dense, using a food processor to shred the vegetables is much easier than doing it by hand. These are great paired with applesauce—see the recipe on page 100.

1 large rutabaga, peeled and shredded (1½ to 2 pounds)

2 large carrots, peeled and shredded (about 6 ounces)

1 small red onion, peeled and shredded (about 3 ounces)

1 cup packed, stemmed, and ribboned spinach, Swiss chard, or kale

4 large eggs, lightly beaten

½ teaspoon salt, or more to taste

½ teaspoon ground cumin

½ teaspoon freshly ground black pepper, or more to taste

¼ cup all-purpose flour, or more as needed to hold raw latkes together

6 tablespoons neutral oil, such as canola, or more if necessary for frying

Sour cream, ricotta, pesto, or applesauce for garnish

1. Prepare a plate with layers of paper towels to drain the pancakes.

2. Place the rutabaga, carrots, red onion, and greens in a large bowl and mix well.

3. Using paper towels, squeeze out excess moisture from the vegetable mixture in the bowl. Add the beaten eggs, salt, cumin, and pepper, and toss together to fully combine. Scatter the flour over the mixture and toss together to incorporate.

4. Heat 2 tablespoons of the oil in a heavy-bottomed skillet over medium heat until shimmering. Working in batches so as not to crowd the pancakes, use a ¼-cup measure to scoop the vegetable mixture into the skillet. Flatten the mixture gently, using the back of the measuring cup or a spatula, making sure the pancakes do not touch each other. Cook until golden brown on one side, about 4 minutes, then turn and brown for about 4 minutes on the other side. Transfer the latkes to the lined plate to drain. Cook the remaining batter, adding 1 tablespoon of oil or more, if necessary, between each batch.

5. Serve warm and top with a spoonful of sour cream, ricotta, pesto, or applesauce.

Savory Beet Latkes

HAWK DANCE FARM
RAWSON BROOK FARM

SERVES 6, MAKES ABOUT 18 PANCAKES

These beet pancakes are also great for using up a variety of other root vegetables. Using a food processor will make quick work of the shredding aspect of the preparation. With a nice browned crust, the latkes are delicious served with applesauce—see recipe on page 100—or sour cream and chives, and offer a good alternative to hash browns at breakfast or brunch.

¼ cup chopped scallions, white and green parts
   (about 2 large)

1 tablespoon chopped fresh thyme

1 teaspoon kosher salt, or more to taste

2 cups peeled and shredded red beets
   (about 11 ounces, 2 to 3 medium beets)

1 cup peeled and shredded carrots
   (about 6 ounces, 2 to 3 medium carrots)

1 cup peeled and shredded celery root
   (about 8 ounces, ½ small celery root)

1 cup peeled and shredded Idaho or russet potato
   (about 12 ounces, 1 large potato)

¼ cup rye or whole wheat flour, or more as needed
   to hold the raw latkes together

1 cup crumbled Rawson Brook Farm chèvre, or other
   soft goat cheese (about 5 ounces)

1 large egg, lightly beaten

2 tablespoons neutral oil, such as canola,
   plus more as needed, for frying

Sour cream and chopped chives, or applesauce for
   garnish (optional)

1. Prepare a plate with layers of paper towels to drain the pancakes.

2. Place the scallions, thyme, salt, beets, carrots, celery root, and potatoes in a large bowl and mix well. Use a paper towel to gently squeeze out any excess moisture. Scatter the flour on top of the shredded vegetables and mix until well incorporated.

3. Combine the cheese and egg in a small bowl. Fold into the vegetable mixture until well coated.

4. Heat the oil in a heavy-bottomed skillet over medium heat until shimmering. Working in batches so as not to crowd the pancakes, use a ¼-cup measure to scoop the vegetable mixture into the skillet. Flatten the mixture gently, using the back of the measuring cup or a spatula, making sure the pancakes do not touch each other. Fry for 4 to 5 minutes on one side, until browned and crisp, and then flip to fry the other side for the same amount of time, or until browned and crisp. Transfer the latkes to the lined plate to drain. Repeat until the entire vegetable mixture has been used. If more oil is needed for frying subsequent batches, add as necessary.

5. Serve the beet latkes warm with sour cream and chives or with applesauce as a garnish.

Chunky Homemade Applesauce

RIISKA BROOK ORCHARD

MAKES 4½ CUPS;
SERVES MANY AS A LATKE TOPPING

The perfect topping for latkes!

8 large Gala apples, or any sweet variety

¼ cup apple cider or apple juice

1 teaspoon ground cinnamon

2 pinches freshly grated or ground nutmeg

1 to 2 tablespoons sugar, or to taste (optional)

1 teaspoon vanilla extract

1. Peel and core the apples. Cut into quarters, then into eighths.

2. Put the apples in a large Dutch oven or saucepan and pour in the cider. Add the cinnamon, nutmeg, sugar, and vanilla.

3. Cover and cook over medium-low heat for 10 minutes, mix, and then cook for another 10 minutes, or until the apples are soft. Remove from the heat and let cool.

4. Using an immersion blender, blend until smooth but with some chunks remaining, or to your desired texture.

MEZZE BISTRO + BAR

We'd like to introduce another term into our discussion of farm-to-table. Nose-to-tail dining: using every part of an animal in cooking, wasting as little as possible. Nancy Thomas, co-owner of Mezze Bistro + Bar and Mezze Catering in Williamstown, MA, understands this well, as does Chef Nick Moulton. Thomas once took her chefs to one of her meat purveyors, Kim Wells's East Mountain Farm, so they would understand slaughtering and develop a closer relationship with the animals. In fact, the recipe in the cookbook for Pasta Bolognese (page 146) originated because Thomas likes to buy a whole animal and use all its cuts, including ground beef.

Her embrace of farm-to-table, you could say, started as a child in Oklahoma, where her Moroccan-Greek mother, an accomplished cook, would take Thomas to source ingredients from what she referred to as "garagista backyard farms"—that's right, people farming out of their garage. "There wasn't a lot of cilantro grown or that was available in the supermarket in Oklahoma in the seventies, so we would go looking. We went to one man's garage to get peppers and tomatoes as well."

Her mom also taught her to cook. Thomas recalls learning at age five to make a vinaigrette under her tutelage, crushing garlic with a wooden mortar and pestle, adding salt, lemon, olive oil, and vinegar. "Learning balance and taste was a tool I can use forever and one I talk about in our kitchen with the chefs," Thomas says.

She started Mezze in 1996 with Mediterranean fare. Thomas quickly launched into farm-to-table, buying lettuce locally to go with the vinaigrette of her childhood. From the mid-'90s to where farm-to-table is now in the Berkshires, she says, represents a massive evolution, with more farms, food, and knowledge about what consumers and guests want to experience. Every week, Mezze gets a list of what's available from local farmers and works in concert with them. Chef Moulton's Farm Egg with Peas, Fava Beans, Garlic Scapes, and Zucchini (page 102) is a snapshot of the crops available in late spring/summer.

When Thomas arrived in the Berkshires in '92, she confronted something different from the suburban sprawl of her part of Oklahoma. "Here you could see the landscape," she recalls, "cows grazing, the apple tree orchards. I could see agriculture but I didn't know then how I was going to integrate it into my world." She soon wove it into her menu offerings, but also developed the longer vision that the Berkshires needs to tell its story through those cows and apple orchards, to become identified as a farm-to-table dining venue in the same way that the arts are considered a staple of the region's landscape.

Sharpening the area's association with farm-to-table is still a work in progress. Thomas says it's a challenge getting people to mentally connect the region to a landscape and say, "I should eat fresh pork, beef, and veal." As part of her effort to bolster this linkage, when she was on the board of Berkshire Grown, she proposed holding fall and winter holiday markets. "New England is at the heart of our Thanksgiving table," she says. "We should have farmers' markets where you can buy those things."

She's concerned that those with fewer dollars don't have the same access to local food. At Mezze, Thomas is trying to feature affordable foods with local ingredients. On Tuesdays and Wednesdays, she hosts "R & D nights," including working with lesser cuts of meat. One of her new items has Thomas reaching into her past and unburying the Okie Burger, an onion-fried hamburger created after the Depression. Shaved onions were mashed into a burger to economically plump up the sandwich.

Recently, Thomas was heartened to find a young farmer seated one night at her last table at Mezze. He was probably in his second year, a Williams College grad, and she was uplifted that he wanted to take on the hard work of farming. "I think it is fulfilling to some people, and one can understand why. It's so results oriented, especially in this divisive time we live in. It makes you feel good."

Farm Egg with Peas, Fava Beans, Garlic Scapes, and Zucchini

MEZZE BISTRO + BAR

SERVES 4

The greenest flavors and colors pair with a fresh egg in this stunning first course, adapted from a recipe by Chef Nick Moulton of Mezze Bistro + Bar. Double the vegetables for a nice luncheon dish, served with fresh bread to soak up the juices. The vegetables in this recipe are highly seasonal—it's even important that the garlic scapes are young and tender—but the alternatives (listed in parentheses) make this accessible even in the middle of winter! Feel free to cook the egg using your preferred method—soft-boiled, poached, or even fried—but don't cook too far ahead of time, to be sure you have a runny yolk, which needs to combine with the lemony, buttery broth.

4 large eggs

1 medium zucchini or yellow summer squash

1½ tablespoons extra virgin olive oil, plus more for drizzling

3 tablespoons fresh lemon juice (1 to 1½ lemons)

¾ teaspoon Maldon salt or any coarse sea salt, plus more for sprinkling

½ cup water

4 tablespoons (½ stick) unsalted butter

½ cup 1-inch-sliced young garlic scapes (or scallions, using the light and dark green parts or a combination of scallions and chives)

½ cup shelled fresh peas (or fresh snow peas or sugar snap peas, diagonally sliced into 1-inch pieces)

½ cup shelled and peeled individual fava beans, (or green beans, diagonally sliced into 1-inch pieces)

¼ cup chopped fresh tarragon

Garnish ideas: fresh pea tendrils (stripped from thicker stems), chive blossoms, nasturtium blossoms, or whole tarragon leaves

1. Bring 4 quarts of water to a boil in a medium saucepan and have a timer ready. Set the timer for 4 minutes 15 seconds. Once the water reaches a rolling boil, carefully lower the eggs into the water and begin the timer. When the timer expires, use a slotted spoon to remove the eggs and place in a pan of cold, but not icy water. (If the eggs get too cold, they are more difficult to peel.) The water should be just above room temperature after the eggs are added. Carefully peel each egg in the water and set aside the peeled, soft-boiled eggs on a plate.

2. Trim the ends from the zucchini. Cut the zucchini into long, thin ribbons with a vegetable peeler. Place the zucchini ribbons in a medium bowl and dress with the olive oil, 1½ tablespoons of the lemon juice, and ¼ teaspoon of the salt, until the ribbons are well coated. Do not allow the ribbons to sit in the dressing for too long as they will become soggy and difficult to work with. Using your fingers, curl each zucchini ribbon into a spiral or a coil so that it looks like a blossom (see photograph). Some blossoms may require more than one zucchini ribbon. Make 8 to 12 zucchini blossoms and set aside.

3. Bring the ½ cup of water and ¼ teaspoon of the salt to a boil in a medium saucepan over medium-high heat. Melt the butter into the water and reduce until most of the water has gone and the buttery broth coats the back of a spoon, 6 to 8 minutes.

4. Add the garlic scapes, peas, and fava beans, or their substitutes, to the butter broth and delicately warm them through for only 1 minute. Remove from the heat and, using a slotted spoon, gently transfer the vegetables to a bowl, reserving the broth in the saucepan. Toss the warm vegetables with the remaining 1½ tablespoons of lemon juice and remaining ¼ teaspoon of salt, and then gently mix in the tarragon.

5. Divide the vegetables equally among four serving bowls and pour the reserved buttery broth evenly over each portion, about 2 tablespoons per portion. Position two or three zucchini blossoms in each bowl. In each serving, make a little nest with the vegetables and place an egg into the indentation. Sprinkle a pinch of the salt on each egg.

6. Arrange any of the garnishes artfully on top, if desired. Finish with a light drizzle of olive oil and serve immediately.

Vegetable Ratatouille with Basil Gremolata

THE BERRY PATCH

SERVES 6

Salting the eggplant is not necessary here since the vegetable is married with the sweet flavors of the tomatoes and onions. This recipe uses a two-step method for sautéing so that the vegetables are not overcrowded in the pot. When they are jam-packed, they steam instead of sauté, resulting in a soggy, less flavorful dish. Feel free to fold in fresh spinach or any other chopped hearty greens with the herbs at the end. Scattering the gremolata on top just before serving lends a lovely crunch to the final dish.

½ cup dried plain bread crumbs

¼ cup plus 2 teaspoons extra virgin olive oil, plus more for pan

2 teaspoons fresh thyme, chopped

½ cup fresh basil, chopped, plus 1 chopped and lightly packed tablespoon for gremolata

½ teaspoon kosher salt

¾ teaspoon freshly ground black pepper, or more to taste

2 pounds fresh ripe tomatoes or one 28-ounce can diced tomatoes, with juices

1 large yellow onion, diced

4 garlic cloves, minced

1 cup seeded and diced green bell pepper

1 cup seeded and diced red bell pepper

2 cups diced zucchini

1 globe eggplant, skin on and diced (about 1 pound, yielding about 4 cups)

½ cup chopped loosely packed fresh flat-leaf parsley

1 teaspoon salt

1. Preheat the oven to 350°F. Lightly oil a rimmed half sheet pan.

2. Prepare the gremolata: Combine the bread crumbs, 2 teaspoons of the olive oil, the thyme, the packed tablespoon of basil, the kosher salt, and ¼ teaspoon of the black pepper in a medium bowl. Spread evenly on the prepared pan and bake for 5 to 10 minutes, until golden. Remove from the oven and set aside to cool.

3. Meanwhile, prepare the tomatoes: If using fresh tomatoes, fill a large stockpot with water and bring to a boil over high heat. Prepare an ice water bath by filling a large bowl with water and ice. Score the blossom end of each of the tomatoes with a tiny X and gently place in the boiling water for about 1 minute to blanch and crack the skins. Quickly remove the tomatoes from the boiling water and place in the ice bath to stop the cooking process. The skins will slip off easily when cool enough to handle. Core the tomatoes and dice into 1-inch pieces. Set aside.

4. Heat 2 tablespoons of the olive oil in a large, heavy-bottomed pot or Dutch oven over medium heat until shimmering and fragrant. Add the onion, garlic, and green and red bell pepper and sauté for 10 minutes. Transfer to a bowl and set aside.

5. Return the pot to the heat and add the remaining 2 tablespoons of olive oil. Once hot, add the zucchini and eggplant and cook until tender, stirring frequently to prevent sticking, about 10 minutes.

6. Add the pepper mixture back to the pot, and cover with the diced tomatoes, ¼ cup of the basil, and ¼ cup of the parsley. Season with the salt and the remaining ½ teaspoon of pepper, or to taste, and simmer for 20 to 30 minutes, stirring to incorporate the flavors. The vegetables should be cooked and thickened but still identifiable. Just before serving, stir in the remaining ¼ cup of basil and ¼ cup of parsley and sprinkle the gremolata over the top.

Corn and Mushroom Conserva

HOWDEN FARM

MAKES 1 QUART CONSERVA

A conserva is a food preserved by canning, often used as a condiment, side dish, or spread on bread. This relish, a creative interpretation of the traditional concept, can serve as a side for your favorite meat, fish, or poultry dish, but can also embellish a main course salad or bruschetta appetizer. You could even try it on toast with a poached egg for breakfast.

2 pounds mixed mushrooms, including shiitake, oyster, maitake (hen of the woods), or portobello

4 ears sweet corn, husked, or 3 cups frozen corn kernels, thawed

¼ cup extra virgin olive oil, plus up to 1½ cups for topping off jar

4 garlic cloves, minced

2 shallots, thinly sliced

1 sprig rosemary

4 sprigs thyme

¼ cup sherry vinegar

½ teaspoon kosher salt, or to taste

1. If using shiitakes, discard the stems before slicing thinly. If using portobellos, be sure to remove the gills with the edge of a paring knife before slicing. Otherwise, trim and thinly slice all the mushrooms.

2. If using fresh corn, bring a large stockpot of water to a boil over high heat. Prepare a large bowl of ice water. When the water reaches a boil, add the corn ears and allow to return to a boil. From the start of the boil, blanch for 4 minutes. Remove from the boiling water and cool in the ice water bath. When cool enough to handle, use a sharp knife to cut the kernels from the cobs into a large bowl and set aside.

3. Place a large, heavy-bottomed stockpot or a Dutch oven over medium heat. Add ¼ cup of the olive oil and heat until shimmering and fragrant. Add the garlic and shallots and cook for about 3 minutes, or until translucent. Add the mushrooms, rosemary, and thyme, stirring to coat with the oil. Cook for about 20 minutes, stirring occasionally, or until the mushrooms have given up most of their liquid and are gently sticking to the bottom of the pan. Deglaze the pan with the vinegar, scraping any bits from the bottom, and cook for another 5 minutes, or until most of the liquid from the vinegar is gone. Add the corn kernels and stir until heated through, about 3 minutes. Stir in the salt and remove from the heat.

4. Remove and discard the herb stems, leaving in the conserva any leaves that have fallen off. Allow to cool for about 30 minutes. Once it has reached room temperature, transfer to a clean quart-size glass container that can be sealed. Press down gently on the mixture with the back of a spoon to compact and reduce any air bubbles. Top off with the remaining olive oil so the mixture is completely covered, seal, and refrigerate. The conserva will last up to 2 weeks because it is slightly pickled and preserved in olive oil, but its flavor may become more muted by then.

HOWDEN FARM

Bruce Howden, 78, owner of Howden Farm, posted on Facebook on September 20, 2018, "Today is the last day at the farm for our delicious sweet corn. Thank you for another successful season." Customer response was immediate: "Can't be the last week! Please say it ain't so!!!" and "Going to be a long wait till next year."

At 250-acre Howden Farm in Sheffield, MA, it's not only sweet corn that's king. Howden's father, John, started growing pumpkins in the 1940s, and his son attests that he did for the pumpkin industry what Henry Ford did for cars. The senior Howden developed the eponymous "Howden Pumpkin" in the 1970s, which became the industry standard. Later, he developed the Howden Biggie, about 42 pounds, the product of one large pumpkin found in a field of Howden Pumpkins.

Howden refers to the farm as his dad's "empire," and growing up there, raised by his grandmother and widowed father, he was determined to escape. And he did, for 30 years, living in New Hampshire and Vermont, running a bed-and-breakfast and graphic arts business.

Then, he reconsidered. When his father passed away while chasing heifers at age 88 in 1997, Howden decided to keep the farm, partially because of its pumpkin legacy. He told *Berkshire Magazine*, "before my father died, I visited him to help out, and I looked at all he had built and knew that it was too good of a thing to let go." With his partner, David Prouty, now 90, a former Middlebury College professor, Howden bought out his brother's interest, and the two have been farming, depending on the year, 20 to 40 acres of pumpkins and 35 to 50 acres of corn. They've sold the development rights to the state to keep the land agricultural in perpetuity. When Howden first returned to farm, he'd send out six or seven trailer loads of product

a season. Today, he has a U-Pick field and relies more on retail and less on wholesale customers.

Howden not only came back for the family legacy but added to it, developing the Howden XXX from the original Howden Pumpkin, with sturdier stems (*peduncles* is the proper term). The farm website says "the people at DP Seeds and New England Seed Co. claim that 'it is probably the best Halloween pumpkin grown.'"

We sat in the living room with Howden and Prouty and one of their cats, named Pumpkin, of course. Copies of *Eating Well* and *Food & Wine* lay scattered on the coffee table. Howden says that he and his partner like to eat and drink, and not surprisingly, like corn. (See the recipes for Sweet Corn Pancakes, Chilled Sweet Corn Soup, and Corn and Mushroom Conserva, pages 19, 57, and 105). He also has a strong opinion on how to cook it. "We bring a pot of water to boil. Use enough water just to cover the corn (husks off!). We put corn in and bring back the boil. Cover the pot. The way you tell if it is done is to take the cover off. Waft the steam. If it smells like corn, it's done. Maybe three minutes." He gets exasperated when speaking about people who overcook corn, including one customer who boiled his for 20 minutes and then complained it was tough.

A digitally up-to-date Howden uses Facebook to promote the farm ("The Big Y corn is 80 cents per ear and ours is 60 cents per ear and ours was picked fresh this morning. Hey gang come and get it"). He's concerned that the mean age of farmers is around 60 and that even the increasing number of small organic farms in the Berkshires run by idealistic young people won't offset the backlog of this older generation. "We live in a pocket—Berkshire County—that is not reality," he acknowledges, contrasting this burst of interest to the demographic trend.

"It's a very tough business," Howden says. "It has to be a passion." Listening to him discourse enthusiastically on pumpkins—as well as corn—our guess is that for him, it is.

Corn, Feta, and Summer Savory Fritters

CAFEADAM

SERVES 8 TO 10 AS AN APPETIZER, 4 TO 6 AS A MAIN COURSE

Adapted from a recipe by Chef Adam Zieminski, owner of cafeADAM, these crispy-on-the-outside, tender-on-the-inside fritters make great appetizers for a party, as well as a perfect accompaniment to a bright and vinegary summer salad. Any extra fritters can be frozen on a sheet pan, then placed in a plastic bag and reheated in a 400°F oven directly from the freezer.

8 tablespoons (1 stick) unsalted butter

1½ to 2½ cups all-purpose flour

4 teaspoons baking powder

1 teaspoon fine Himalayan salt, or fine sea salt, plus more for finishing

¼ cup extra virgin olive oil

2 large eggs, lightly beaten

2 cups corn kernels (fresh, or frozen, thawed, and drained of extra liquid)

1 cup crumbled feta (about 4 ounces)

1 teaspoon Thai chile or jalapeño pepper, seeded and finely minced

1 tablespoon chopped fresh summer savory, or 1 teaspoon dried

1 tablespoon pure maple syrup

½ cup plain yogurt

½ cup whole milk

3 cups canola, peanut, or vegetable oil for frying

Freshly ground black pepper

1 lemon, cut into wedges

continued . . .

1. Melt the butter in a small saucepan over medium heat until the solids in the butter have started to brown, 8 to 10 minutes. Remove from the heat and allow the browned butter to cool to room temperature.

2. Combine 1½ cups of the flour, the baking powder, and the teaspoon of salt in a medium bowl.

3. Pour off the liquid butter into a large bowl, leaving the solids behind in the saucepan. Discard the solids. Add the olive oil, eggs, corn kernels, feta, chile, summer savory, maple syrup, yogurt, and milk to the liquid butter and mix together until well combined.

4. Heat the oil in a large, heavy-bottomed skillet over medium-high heat until the oil reaches 350°F on an instant-read thermometer. Line a half sheet pan with paper towels and set aside.

5. Make sure the corn mixture is well mixed, then add the flour mixture and fold together to make a thick and rough-textured batter. Use at least 1½ cups of the flour and keep adding up to 2½ cups, if the moisture in the batter will absorb it. The baking powder will make the batter expand as the wet ingredients are mixed in, so work quickly after the batter is mixed together.

6. Working in batches to avoid crowding, use a ⅛-cup measure to scoop the batter into the hot oil, making sure each mound doesn't touch the next. A spoon mounded with batter to equal 2 tablespoons will also work. Fry the fritters until they are crisp and golden brown, flipping with a slotted spoon to cook on both sides. Transfer the cooked fritters to the paper towels to drain.

7. Season the fritters with salt and black pepper to taste, spritz with lemon juice from the lemon wedges, and serve while still hot.

Rhubarb Compote

MOON IN THE POND FARM

MAKES 1 QUART COMPOTE

Rhubarb in season most famously evokes sweet strawberry-rhubarb pie—it's thought of as a fruit, but is actually a vegetable. This bright red stalk goes beautifully with poultry, pork, or lamb in this gingery, savory condiment. It also complements a cheese board for an elegant hors d'oeuvre. For a sweeter version to serve over ice cream or the Maple Cheesecake (page 215), chop 1 pound of rhubarb into ¼-inch pieces. Place in a medium saucepan with ¼ cup each of chopped walnuts and raisins, and sprinkle with ⅔ to 1 cup of sugar and 1½ to 3 teaspoons of lemon juice (adjust per your sweet tooth!). Cook over medium heat, stirring occasionally, until soft, 8 to 10 minutes.

½ cup sugar

½ cup pure maple syrup

½ cup small-diced red onion

½ cup dried cranberries

1 tablespoon minced fresh ginger

½ teaspoon ground allspice

½ teaspoon ground cinnamon

¼ teaspoon crushed red pepper flakes

2 pounds rhubarb, leaves and ends removed and discarded, ½-inch diced

1. Combine all the ingredients, except the rhubarb, in a large saucepan and bring to a simmer over medium heat. Stirring frequently to make sure the sugars don't burn, let simmer for about 10 minutes, or until the sugar is fully dissolved.

2. Add the rhubarb and continue to cook, stirring often, until tender and the sauce is slightly thickened, 10 to 15 minutes. Remove from the heat and let cool before pouring into a quart-size glass jar or other sealable container. Seal and store in the refrigerator.

Baked Eggplant with Tomatoes, Mozzarella, and Basil

HOLIDAY BROOK FARM

SERVES 8

This dish looks especially attractive if you can make the slices of eggplant, tomato, and mozzarella roughly the same diameter. This is more easily done by using the equivalent amount of small Italian eggplants, if you can find them, and plum tomatoes. To make your own flavored bread crumbs, toast some stale bread, then use a food processor to pulse into crumbs along with some finely chopped fresh flat-leaf parsley, salt, and a little extra virgin olive oil.

¼ cup extra virgin olive oil, plus more for half sheet pans and baking dish

2 to 3 large eggplants (1½ to 2 pounds total), or 5 to 6 Italian eggplants

1½ teaspoons salt, or more to taste

½ teaspoon freshly ground black pepper, or more to taste

4 to 5 ripe medium tomatoes, (about 1½ pounds total) or the equivalent of plum tomatoes (about 6 to 7)

¾ cup Italian-style bread crumbs

1 pound fresh mozzarella

15 to 20 large fresh basil leaves, ribboned

Pasta or tomato sauce (optional)

1. Preheat the oven to 400°F. Set an oven rack in the center of the oven. Lightly oil two half sheet pans with olive oil, or to facilitate cleanup, line with foil and lightly oil the surface. Lightly oil the sides and bottom of a 9-by-13-inch baking dish and set aside.

2. Leaving the peel on the eggplant, cut off and discard the ends and slice into circles ¼ to ½ inch thick, at least 24 slices total, depending on how thick you choose to cut your eggplant. Place the eggplant in a large bowl. Toss the eggplant with the ¼ cup of olive oil, salt, and pepper. Allow the eggplant to absorb the olive oil and salt fully by resting in the bowl for 5 minutes.

3. Place the eggplant slices in a single layer on the prepared half sheet pans and bake until slightly soft, 15 to 25 minutes. Check for softness and remove from the oven before the timer is up if necessary.

4. Meanwhile, slice off and discard the ends of each tomato. Starting from the blossom end, slice into ½-inch rounds, at least 16 slices. Pour the bread crumbs into a shallow dish and dip each tomato

continued . . .

slice into the crumbs, coating on both sides, so that the bread crumbs stick to the juicy, cut surfaces. Set aside.

5. Slice the mozzarella evenly into at least 16 slices.

6. Place the baking dish facing you horizontally. Starting in one corner of the dish, place one of the smallest pieces of eggplant snugly in the corner as a stabilizer, over which place a second, larger slice at an angle, half-standing up. Lay a slice of breaded tomato on top, overlapping like fish scales, and then a slice of mozzarella, slightly overlapping. On top of the mozzarella, place another circle of eggplant, and continue the layering in this same order—eggplant, tomato, mozzarella—finishing the row with a piece of eggplant or whatever you choose.

7. Arrange a second row in the same manner as the first row, and then a third, and then a fourth, until the pan is full. Feel free to be creative with the layering, depending on the size of your eggplant, tomato, and mozzarella slices. Press the layers gently into each other to allow room for more rows or more layers. Some extra slices may be left over, so feel free to find an attractive looking spot for them.

When the pan is filled, or the ingredients have been used, place in the oven and bake until the mozzarella has just softened and barely started to melt, 15 to 20 minutes.

8. Remove from the oven and place on a wire rack. Scatter the basil over the finished dish. Serve warm with tomato or pasta sauce on the side, if desired.

BERKSHIRE BOUNTY FARM

"I had a previous life." That's how Steve Cunningham, proprietor of Berkshire Bounty Farm of Southfield, MA, begins his tale of becoming a farmer on second-home land he owns with his husband, Daryl Wickstrom.

In that former life, for almost 20 years Cunningham jetted around the world working for companies investing in renewable energy in developing countries. It was while living in London with Wickstrom that he started to burn out from the travel and "the idea for the farm came."

To be more exact, that idea struck in a bucolic setting in rural Uganda, as Cunningham sat across from a woman asking for a $50,000 loan to expand her solar dried fruit business. "I'm listening and I'm thinking, God, this is beautiful. I wish I knew somebody who had land. I'm on the plane coming back and I said, 'Wait, I have land! We have this house!'"

Two years later, Cunningham quit his job and spent five weeks working for a 32-acre CSA, but it was not until he visited UK farmer Charles Dowding, author of books on no-dig and organic gardening, that he knew how he wanted to farm. "He's on 2 full acres. Does the whole thing himself—it is a Garden of Eden. I just got goosebumps."

Cummingham returned to Southfield and spent a year setting up his 1.5 acre, certified organic, no-till diversified farm, with its 110 to 120 crops, bent on creating a property like Dowding's. "There wasn't a stitch of landscaping," he says of his land, a cleared grass field on a steep hill. Cunningham is a one-man outfit, up at 5 a.m., working 'til 9 p.m. He's had to figure out how to farm while living between Southfield and Hong Kong, where his husband was posted after London. They moved back to the United States fulltime in 2016.

"I am so incredibly blessed because I found something I love and happen to be good at it," Cunning-

kets in 2016 after he developed a solid commercial business and, two years later, was able to succeed with only two accounts, Gedney Farm, an inn and special events venue, and Cantina 229 in New Marlborough, MA.

Summer 2019 is different. Cunningham says that good soil management, especially on organic farms, requires that fields lie fallow every seven years or so. He's farmed for 10 and never done that, rotating crops and adding amendments to improve the soil instead. He is letting almost all his beds rest, using cover crops. Instead of farming, he's offered to plant raised beds for his customers, planning to focus his time on infrastructure, finishing the irrigation, "all the stuff you never get to when you're running around."

He's keeping his personal garden for cooking, though. Cunningham describes himself as "a trash cook" who opens the cupboard and makes dinner. "I stumble upon something that I've knocked out of the ground while weeding or a crop that's bolted that I can't sell but is still tasty. That's part of dinner."

He doesn't eat meat, so he'll prepare a lot of stir-fries, influenced by his time in Asia. He's also a fan of roasted vegetable pizzas. "I buy the Berkshire Mountain Bakery crust and everything else is mine," he says. When we first met, he had just prepared a pizza with "49 colors, three different squashes, cherry, Brandywine tomatoes, onion, garlic."

Cunningham stops. He apologizes—unnecessarily—for talking too much. "If you haven't been able to tell, I have a passion." He has no regrets about leaving global corporate life, having "created this wonderful microcosm for the growth of food that was woods, that can stay this way. After I die, somebody can still grow here, eat from here, and I've made the earth a little more productive. That's sort of my legacy I guess."

ham says, confessing that "I've always known plants. I don't know why." Perhaps it's in his blood—his Irish grandfather was a farmer, his dad cultivated a large garden. In grad school, he and his roommate had 88 plants in their apartment.

Cunningham is emphatic that the first thing he grows is soil, but the first products he produced were standard greens and tomatoes before branching out into Asian varieties—mizuna, tat soi, bok choy, and herbs. He stopped going to farmers' mar-

Kimchi Summer Rolls

BERKSHIRE BOUNTY FARM
HOSTA HILL

SERVES 4 TO 5

Savory and succulent, these light and quick Vietnamese-inspired summer rolls are like a salad in your hand. Try either dipping sauce, or better yet, both, one thin and sweet, the other thick and a little spicy. Because these rolls are made with fresh avocado, they should be eaten immediately or placed in a dish covered tightly with plastic wrap and briefly stored in the refrigerator before serving.

Kimchi summer rolls:

2 ounces thin rice or cellophane noodles

½ cup kimchi

1 red bell pepper, seeded and cut into 2-inch-long, very thin matchsticks

½ European cucumber, seeded if necessary, cut into 2-inch-long, very thin matchsticks

1 carrot, shredded

¼ cup chopped fresh cilantro

1 ripe avocado, peeled, pitted, and sliced into ¼-inch-thick wedges

2½ to 3 cups roughly chopped Asian greens, or another sharp green, such as arugula or mustard

10 to 12 rice paper rounds

Sesame citrus dipping sauce:

½ teaspoon sesame oil

1½ teaspoons fresh lime juice

1½ teaspoons soy sauce

2 tablespoons pineapple juice

2 tablespoons fresh orange juice

Peanut dipping sauce:

¼ cup peanut butter (either smooth or chunky)

2 tablespoons water

1 tablespoon hoisin sauce

Zest and juice of ½ lime

1 tablespoon soy sauce

1¼ teaspoons sriracha

1. Prepare the summer rolls: Break the noodles into smaller pieces with your hands and place in a shallow dish. Cover with boiling water and let sit for 10 to 15 minutes. Drain when done.

2. Combine the kimchi, red pepper, cucumber, carrot, and cilantro in a bowl and mix well.

3. Set up a filling assembly line with the bowl of kimchi mixture, the sliced avocado, and the greens. On a clean work surface, place a bowl of cold water large enough to accommodate the diameter of the rice paper rounds.

4. Dip a rice paper round into the water to submerge fully, remove, and lay out flat on the work surface. Work quickly but carefully, since the water will soften the rice paper and make it increasingly fragile to handle. Place ¼ cup of very loosely packed greens in the center of the rice paper round, shaping the greens into a thick line across its equator and leaving about 2 inches bare on each side. Leaving space on each side is very important. Cover with a scant ⅛ cup of the softened noodles, arranging compactly on top of the greens. Layer on a few slices of the avocado, then a scant ¼ cup of the kimchi mixture.

5. The amounts of filling ingredients may need to be adjusted, based on what works for the size of the rice paper round, but most important, there needs to be room to fold up the rolls. To do this, fold the bottom of the round up and over the filling in the center, pressing down gently with your palm to press some of the air out of the filling. Fold in the right side, then the left side, to cover the filling and close the sides. Roll the center up toward the top of the roll to make a tight, burrito-like shape. Place the rolls, seam side down, on a plate without touching each other, or they may stick together as they dry. While the sauces are being made, let the summer rolls set and dry slightly in the air before serving.

6. Prepare the sesame citrus dipping sauce: Combine all ingredients in a small bowl. Pour into four or five dipping-size dishes and serve alongside the summer rolls.

7. Prepare the peanut dipping sauce: Combine all ingredients in a small bowl. Pour into four or five small dipping-size dishes and serve alongside the summer rolls.

Stir-Fried Bok Choy

ET CETERA FARM

SERVES 2 TO 4 AS A SIDE

Bok choy headlines this slightly sweet and savory stir-fry. As usual when cooking with this technique, the pan should be very hot, and the fresh ingredients should stay in motion so that they don't overcook. Serve over rice or noodles, or alongside a grilled protein, such as chicken or fish.

1 pound bok choy

1 tablespoon canola oil

2 garlic cloves, thinly sliced

2 teaspoons grated fresh ginger

2 teaspoons soy sauce

2 tablespoons rice vinegar

¼ cup vegetable stock

¼ teaspoon kosher salt

½ teaspoon honey

Zest of ½ orange

2 scallions, white and green parts, minced

1. Trim the bottom of the bok choy, rinse, and dry. Separate the leaves and stalks and chop both into 2-inch bite-size strips.

2. Heat the canola oil in a sauté pan over medium heat until shimmering. Add the bok choy stalks and sauté for 5 minutes, or until they start to soften. Add the garlic, ginger, and bok choy leaves and sauté for about 2 minutes or until the leaves barely wilt. Mix the stalks and leaves in the pan to incorporate the flavors.

3. Combine the soy sauce, vinegar, stock, and salt in a small bowl. Increase the heat to high and add the liquid mixture to the pan. Stirring constantly, cook until the liquid is half evaporated, about 5 minutes. Remove from the heat.

4. Toss with the honey, orange zest, and scallions and serve.

Kabocha Squash Tempura

BIZEN GOURMET JAPANESE CUISINE & SUSHI BAR

MAKES 6 SERVINGS

Kabocha is a winter squash also known as Japanese pumpkin, with a green skin so thin that it is edible when cooked. If it is not available for this recipe, adapted from a Bizen Gourmet Japanese Cuisine & Sushi Bar standard, good substitutes include peeled acorn or butternut squash, or even peeled sweet potatoes. The tempura batter mix can sometimes be found in supermarkets, or in Asian markets and online.

1 kabocha squash

1 cup dashi (make ½ of the broth from the Vegetable Nabe with Kale recipe, Steps 2 and 3, page 73), or other favorite vegetable stock

¼ cup pure maple syrup

¼ cup sake

¼ cup mirin

¼ cup soy sauce

Two 10-ounce packages dry tempura batter mix (Kikkoman brand works well; buy enough batter mix of whatever brand you choose to make 3 cups)

1½ quarts sunflower oil (what Bizen uses) or canola oil

6 tablespoons peeled and grated fresh ginger

6 tablespoons grated daikon radish

1. Wash the outside of the kabocha and cut out the stem or scoop it out with a large spoon. Cut the squash in half from top to bottom with a large, sharp knife. Scrape the seeds and stringy pulp out of the squash. The seeds can be washed and saved for roasting, or can be discarded with the pulp. Cut the blossom end out of the kabocha halves and slice the squash into thin crescents, not more than ½ to ¾ inch thick.

2. Mix together the dashi, maple syrup, sake, mirin, and soy sauce in a medium saucepan. Bring to a simmer over medium-high heat and remove from the heat. Keep the mixture covered and warm while preparing the rest of the dish.

3. Line a rimmed baking sheet with a few layers of paper towels to wick any extra oil away from the tempura before serving. Keep this baking sheet close to your work area.

4. Follow the tempura batter mix package instructions to make 3 cups of batter. Use very cold water. When stirring, use chopsticks so as not to activate any gluten with too much motion. Pour the batter into a shallow dish that is large enough to accommodate a kabocha crescent.

5. Heat the oil in a large, heavy-bottomed pot over medium heat. When the oil has reached 350°F on an instant-read thermometer, check it with a tiny drop of the batter. The batter should sizzle and start to puff right away as soon as it hits the oil. As Bizen's owner, Michael Marcus, instructs, "sprinkle a bit of batter into the oil; the resulting clumps should be short, not long."

6. Arrange the dishes of ingredients relatively close together, so that the kabocha crescents can be dipped into the batter dish and from there dropped into the hot oil. Whenever frying with hot oil, be cautious of splattering.

7. Work on only a few slices of kabocha at a time to avoid overcrowding the oil in the pot. Begin by dipping a batch of crescents into the batter, turning them over with tongs to make sure they are coated completely. Gently slip each battered crescent into the hot oil, and let fry for 3 minutes, turning once with tongs. Pull each slice out of the oil, allowing the excess to drip back into the oil in the pot, and place on a paper towel.

8. Dip the fried crescent back into the batter, and turn to cover with a second coating of batter. Gently slip back into the hot oil and allow to fry for another 3 or 4 minutes, turning once with tongs. Kabocha tempura is done when the batter has puffed and taken on a nice golden color. Using tongs, move the finished pieces to the paper towel–lined baking sheet. Repeat with the remaining pieces of squash until done.

9. To serve, place 5 or 6 pieces of kabocha tempura, a small bowl of sauce, and 1 tablespoon of grated ginger and 1 tablespoon of grated daikon radish on each plate. Diners should mix the ginger and daikon into the sauce before dipping the tempura pieces.

SANDWICHES, PIZZA, AND SAVORY PIES

CRICKET CREEK FARM

Cricket Creek Farm, in Williamstown, MA, is a small, grass-fed dairy farm producing raw milk, seven styles of artisanal farmstead cheese, grass-fed beef, and whey-fed pork. There are a lot of other moving parts to the operation, including a farm store, bakery, event space, and weekly community potluck dinner, but if we had to pick just two topics on which to drop the most ink, it's Cricket Creek's cheese and the farm's focus on how it treats its animals.

Topher Sabot, owner and manager, says that the cheese is the clear economic driver of the farm because it can be marketed farther afield and is not limited by local demand. In 2002, his father, Richard, an economist and Williams College professor, with his wife, Judith, concerned about the development of one of the largest dairy farms in Williamstown then for sale, bought the land. Faced with what to do with it, and aware of the challenges of running a midsize dairy, Richard posed the question of what value-added product could make a smaller sustainable dairy farm successful. The answer for the Sabots: cheese, which led to visiting regional cheese makers and a fact-finding and tasting trip to northern Italy. But his father's sudden death in 2005 led Topher, who had been salmon fishing in Alaska, to return to help manage Cricket Creek and eventually take over running the farm in 2009.

Speaking to Sabot about dairy farming and producing cheese, you would never know that he hadn't planned on this career. He manages 10 people, sells 28,000 pounds of cheese yearly, and while he doesn't like to pick his favorite "child," admits it's Maggie's Round, Cricket Creek's flagship offering, a semifirm raw milk variety named after the family's black Lab.

It's the nature of small-scale artisanal farmstead cheese—handmade with milk from that farm—to vary, and Maggie's Round does. Cricket Creek's former cheesemaker Suzy Konecky says the complexity of fresh milk is a major factor in how a cheese ages. If it's summer, if the cows are agitated, if they are pastured, or even if the cow was stressed because a new person is milking, all these variables affect the milk. It's an art, and the variations should be celebrated, she says, because it demonstrates the cheesemaker is working with a natural and pure product.

Sabot's last word on artisanal cheese, at least for this profile, is to suggest trying it in a grilled cheese sandwich. "You say, ugh, grilled cheese, but put good cheese on it. It's awesome. A classic." He recommends commingling different kinds in a sandwich, such as Maggie's Round and Cricket Creek's Tobasi. A recipe for Open-Faced Grilled Cheese follows.

Sabot's focus on how he treats his 75 to 80 cows manifests itself in his efforts to continuously improve their existence. The biggest recent change, he says, is in the lives of male calves. Often, they're treated like a waste product. Even if a farmer is using bulls for breeding, he might keep one, maybe two a year. Sabot says that most farms "just put them in a truck, send them to auction, and they end up in the conventional veal or beef supply. It's not a pleasant experience." He decided a few years ago that this was something Cricket Creek would not participate in and the farm works hard to market calves they don't keep. This year, they sold 23 to people as far as Rhode Island for breeding, or who will raise them for beef in a small home-style operation. "That's a wonderful thing because we know they're going to be well cared for with a high quality of life," says Sabot.

Sabot urges consumers to think critically about the source of their food. "Just because it's local, doesn't mean it's good," he says, adding that the best way to understand what you're eating is to buy directly from farmers. "Obviously, for a lot of people, that's not possible. But you can still ask. People email me from Boston: 'Oh, we saw your cheese and here's a question: How do you treat your cows?'"

Open-Faced Grilled Cheese

CRICKET CREEK FARM

SERVES 4 (OR 2 HUNGRY PEOPLE)

This simple comfort food can be made with any of your favorite artisanal or other cheeses. The appealing texture here comes from using one soft and one hard variety. If you love Camembert or Brie, match it up with Cheddar or Gouda—experiment!

One 8-inch loaf ciabatta, French baguette, or other crusty bread

1 tablespoon unsalted butter, at room temperature

4 ounces soft, ripe cheese, such as Cricket Creek Farm's Tobasi (or Taleggio, Brie, or a good Fontina), thinly sliced

2 large vine-ripened tomatoes, cored and sliced ½-inch thick

⅛ teaspoon freshly ground black pepper, or more to taste

4 ounces hard, slicing cheese such as Cricket Creek Farm's Maggie's Round (or Manchego or Pecorino Romano), thinly sliced

1. Preheat the oven to 400°F. Set an oven rack near the top of the oven. Line a half sheet pan with aluminum foil.

2. Meanwhile, slice the ciabatta loaf in half horizontally down its length so that there is a top and bottom. Then, slice the loaf in half so that there are four 4-inch pieces. Lay out the pieces of bread, crust sides down, on the prepared pan.

3. Spread the butter evenly over all the interior sides of the bread. Top each piece with 1 ounce of sliced soft cheese, then top with 1 to 2 slices of tomato and a sprinkling of pepper, and cover with 1 ounce of sliced firm cheese.

4. Bake for 10 minutes. Then, turn on the broiler, but leave the oven door open a crack and check frequently to prevent burning. The cheese should turn golden and crusty after 1 to 2 minutes under the broiler. Remove the pan from the oven and let sit on a wire rack for 5 to 10 minutes before serving since the cheese may be too hot to eat right away.

HOSTA HILL

Western Massachusetts cookbook author and self-described Berkshires ambassador Alana Chernila says the area's food identity goes beyond being a farm-to-table hub. "Berkshire food is centered around a certain resourcefulness and an ability to think outside the box," she writes in *Rural Intelligence*. It's a perfect description of the story and evolution of Maddie Elling and Abe Hunrichs's Hosta Hill, a niche, value-added business that creates fermented products out of local organic produce.

Elling graduated from Monument Mountain Regional High School in Great Barrington in 2006, and started WWOOFing—yes, it's a verb. (Worldwide Opportunities on Organic Farms offers volunteer working homestays on sustainable farms.) Hunrichs is a Californian who was introduced to food production and farmers' markets working at a Eugene, OR, bakery after college. The two met in 2010 when he came east to visit family in western Massachusetts. The couple decided to figure out what food business they could create together in the Berkshires, a community they cherished. In 2011, they started Hosta Hill.

Both Elling and Hunrichs were influenced by the writings of Sandor Katz, a self-described "fermentation revivalist." Hunrichs, a biology and outdoor education major, happened upon the process in an undergraduate microbiology class. "We made yogurt and sauerkraut, and once I learned the role of microbes in fermentation, I was hooked," he told Benjamin Wolfe of MicrobialFoods.org. On Elling's family property in West Stockbridge, the two experimented with growing perennial food crops, raising animals, as well as cooking all types of cultured food, baking bread, brewing beer, fermenting vegetables. They narrowed their search for products to tempeh, sauerkraut, and its Korean cousin, kimchi, but eventually dropped their prized artisanal tempeh. We first met the duo in their West Stockbridge kitchen, deep into perfecting tempeh, and became steadfast customers, only to be dismayed when we went to purchase it one day at Guido's

Fresh Marketplace and discovered it was no longer carried. As Hunrichs explains, they couldn't keep two product lines—fermented vegetables and unpasteurized tempeh—that were manufactured and sold differently. The sauerkraut and kimchi, with such intriguing names as Gochu Curry Kraut, Scape Kraut, Crimson Kraut, and Daikon Kimchi, were more "accessible" to consumers, says Elling.

Elling and Hunrichs also added products—hot sauces and kraut juices (Krautonics). Then, they made another strategic decision: opting to outsource the farming, but keeping their commitment to local, sustainable growing. Again, the issue was struggling to balance separate businesses: manufacturing and farming. They are currently focusing on their vegetable fermentation business, purchasing produce from local organic growers.

In 2018, Elling and Hunrichs reported sourcing over $40,000 of organic vegetables for their ferments. A local company selling fermented products can be a boon to area farmers looking to sell produce that may not otherwise make it in markets or local food stores. "It's a great way to use up vegetables that aren't necessarily pretty, or in perfect condition," says Elling. "We're able to take some bruised vegetables—our vegetables are really high quality, but they can sit in storage, and their outer leaves get wilted." She and Hunrichs are proud that they can "turn them into beautiful sauerkraut, in a jar with an awesome label, and benefit the farmers who might not be able to sell those vegetables."

That year, 2018, was big in two ways: First, the couple had a baby, and then at the same time, Hosta Hill transitioned from their 900-square-foot West Stockbridge kitchen to a 3,500-square-foot facility in Pittsfield. Elling and Hunrichs sell at farmers' markets, at stores in the Berkshires, the Pioneer Valley, Boston, and New York City. But they're delighted to still produce in the Berkshires because of the communal support for local food and small businesses.

Tempeh Reuben

HOSTA HILL
STARVING ARTIST CAFE & CREPERIE

SERVES 4

This hearty and filling deli staple is reinvented as a vegetarian offering that both meat and non-meat eaters alike will love! It's a Starving Artist favorite and features Hosta Hill sauerkraut (feel free to experiment with the variety). As an extra, the stock from cooking the tempeh can be used as a protein-rich base for a soup.

8 ounces tempeh, sliced ¼ to ⅓ inch thick

1 small onion, thickly sliced into rounds

1 celery stalk, coarsely chopped

2 garlic cloves, minced

1 cup vegetable stock

¼ cup mayonnaise

2 tablespoons ketchup

1 teaspoon hot sauce (Cholula or sriracha, if possible)

2 tablespoons sweet pickle relish

1 cup sauerkraut

2 tablespoons extra virgin olive oil

8 slices rye or pumpernickel bread

8 slices Swiss or Gruyère

1. Place the tempeh, onion, celery, garlic, and stock in a medium saucepan. Add water, if necessary, to top the tempeh, cover, and bring to a boil over high heat. Then, remove from the heat and allow to stand, covered, for 10 minutes, or until the tempeh is tender. Transfer the tempeh to a plate and let cool to room temperature. Discard the liquid and vegetables.

2. Combine the mayonnaise, ketchup, hot sauce, and relish in a medium bowl and set aside.

3. Warm the sauerkraut in a small saucepan over medium heat.

4. To assemble each sandwich, heat a small amount of the olive oil in a large skillet or griddle, reserving the remaining oil for the other sandwiches. Working in batches if necessary, lay one slice of bread in the skillet and top with one slice of cheese. Let the cheese start to melt, about 4 minutes, then lay one-quarter of the tempeh pieces on top. Top with one-quarter of the sauerkraut, arranging to cover the tempeh. Top with another slice of Swiss cheese. Spread a second slice of bread with the mayonnaise mixture and place it, dressing side down, on the stack. Using a wide spatula, carefully flip the sandwich. Allow the second side to cook for about 2 minutes, then transfer to a serving plate. Repeat to make the remaining sandwiches, keeping the extra dressing for dipping on the side.

Roasted Asparagus and Lemon Ricotta Tartines

WOLFE SPRING FARM

SERVES 8

Fresh asparagus is a welcome springtime delicacy after a long winter, showcased here in a tartine, a French open-faced sandwich. Serve accompanied by a small soup or a salad of dressed greens, or as a starter course for a larger meal. A mini-version makes an enticing hors d'oeuvre.

1½ pounds asparagus, tough stem ends trimmed

¼ cup extra virgin olive oil, plus more for drizzling

¾ teaspoon kosher salt

1½ cups ricotta

Zest and juice of 1 lemon

⅓ cup tightly packed finely ribboned fresh basil leaves

1 baguette

2 ounces Parmesan, grated finely (about 1 cup)

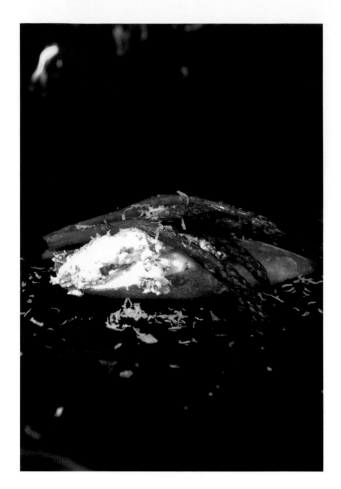

1. Preheat the oven to 400°F. On a rimmed half sheet pan, toss the asparagus with 1 tablespoon of the olive oil and ¼ teaspoon of the salt to coat. Roast in the center of the oven for 10 to 15 minutes, until tender. Thicker asparagus stalks will take longer to cook than thin ones.

2. Meanwhile, combine the ricotta, lemon zest and juice, 2 tablespoons of the olive oil, the remaining ½ teaspoon of salt, and the basil in a medium bowl. Set aside.

3. Cut the baguette lengthwise into two long halves. Cut each half into four equal pieces. Place, cut side up, on a baking sheet. Drizzle with 1 tablespoon of the olive oil and place in the oven to toast lightly for 5 minutes.

4. Remove the bread from the oven. Divide the ricotta mix equally among each of the bread slices, spreading a thick layer to cover the cut surfaces of the bread. Lay the asparagus pieces on top, cutting the stalks to fit neatly onto the top of the bread, if desired, or left to drape over the edges. Sprinkle each tartine with Parmesan and place back in the oven for 5 to 10 minutes, until the Parmesan has melted. Serve warm, drizzled with a little olive oil.

STARVING ARTIST CAFE & CREPERIE

There's often a line waiting to order at Starving Artist Cafe & Creperie, in Lee, MA, which sells sweet and savory crepes as well as sandwiches, soups, and salads. (Our favorite: the gluten free and vegan "Herbivore," a buckwheat crepe stuffed with tempeh, sautéed spinach, mushrooms, and caramelized onions, with ume scallion dressing.)

For Emmy Davis, co-owner of the popular spot with her husband, Ryan, crepes are perfect for farm-to-table eating. They're a blank slate, she says, better than a sandwich because you can put so much more in them, and anything—whatever a local farm produces—can be wrapped inside.

Davis didn't always gravitate toward making crepes. As a teenager, she visited Paris with her dad, whom she credits with the cafe's motif. "I wasn't sold on it because I don't have a sweet tooth. Like, that's what I thought of as a crepe." When she decided to open Starving Artist, she and her staff took one week to master the art of crepe making. "I made up all these recipes with a little pan at home, hoping they would work out." They obviously did. The creperie's website proclaims itself as "Local/Organic/Gluten-Free/Vegan/Vegetarian," but there's meat on the menu, too. Davis says that 90 percent of what she sells is organic, and if not, it's non-GMO or local.

She has long had a penchant for working with food, especially local and organic. After she and Ryan had their first child, Davis worked for a Pittsfield-area market that specialized in local and organic produce. She got to know area farmers, and when Clover's, a Lee health food store, came up for sale around the corner from where Starving Artist is now, she and Ryan purchased it and turned it into Berkshire Green Grocer. "I learned so much being there from the reps that came in. They just wanted to teach you about health food." Her favorite part of the operation, though, was its small cafe, so it made sense for Davis to ultimately sell the grocery and focus on her creperie. Starving Artist, by the way, is in a building owned by her father, which houses his College Internship Program that helps young adults on the autism spectrum and with learning differences transition to college or employment. The cafe itself shares space with CIP's Good Purpose Gallery, and Starving Artist patrons eat under and circulate around the artwork.

It turns out that Lee, MA, is a great location for a Berkshires-based business. Davis says the town "used to be kind of a drive-through, but we get tons of people that come from upstate New York going to Boston. This is their meeting spot, their stomping ground. There's not many places you can get off the Mass Pike and have lots of options. And we're a bit different than other restaurants around. People really do want organic, non-GMO." Starving Artist also attracts participants in the area's cultural offerings who are looking for healthy choices, such as the Jacob's Pillow dancers who drop in from Becket, MA.

The cafe's focus on local continues unabated, purchasing Hosta Hill sauerkraut, High Lawn Farm dairy, Rawson Brook chèvre. "If you want this area to succeed, it's what you have to do," says Davis. "You get a better product, too, one that's not going to be on a train or a plane for a month."

Davis is also adamant that whatever she cooks is uncomplicated. As the mother of three, she says she doesn't have four hours to fuss with a dish. "Everyone's searching for these crazy recipes to make something fun and new. But sometimes, simple is good."

Portobello and Spinach Crepes

STARVING ARTIST CAFE & CREPERIE

SERVES 4 OR 5 (MAKES 9 TO 10 CREPES)

These crepes, adapted for the home cook from Emmy Davis's Starving Artist Cafe & Creperie, can be made in advance and gently reheated. The piquant pesto recipe makes more than you need, so save it in the freezer for use in another dish.

Pesto:

4 cups gently packed fresh basil leaves

½ cup chopped walnuts (toasting optional)

¾ cup grated Parmesan

2 garlic cloves, coarsely chopped

1 teaspoon salt

¼ teaspoon red pepper flakes

½ cup extra virgin olive oil

Zest of 1 lemon

Crepes:

1 cup all-purpose flour

2 large eggs

1 cup milk

¼ cup half-and-half

2 tablespoons melted unsalted butter

¼ teaspoon salt

Extra virgin olive oil for cooking crepes

Filling:

2 tablespoons extra virgin olive oil

½ red onion, thinly sliced into half-moons

1 garlic clove, minced

1 pound portobello mushrooms, stemmed, thinly sliced and then cut in half if especially large (about 6 cups)

2 cups packed, stemmed, and coarsely chopped fresh spinach

2 tablespoons chopped fresh flat-leaf parsley

1 cup shredded mozzarella

¼ cup grated Parmesan

½ teaspoon salt, or as needed

1. Prepare the pesto: Place the basil, walnuts, Parmesan, chopped garlic, salt, and red pepper flakes in a food processor or blender and pulse to combine, then process until uniformly chopped. Add the olive oil in a slow stream through the opening of the processor lid while the food processor is running. Add the lemon zest and pulse a few times, just to incorporate. Scrape the pesto into an airtight container and store in the refrigerator.

2. Prepare the crepes: Combine all the crepe ingredients, except the olive oil, in a food processor or blender and blend until smooth. Prepare a plate lined with paper towels on the side of the stovetop. Heat an 8- or 10-inch nonstick or well-seasoned cast-iron skillet over medium heat and add only enough olive oil to barely coat the bottom of the pan. When the oil is hot, pour ¼ cup of the batter into the center of the pan. Quickly, before the batter sets, use a spatula to spread out the batter to the edges of the pan, keeping it as thin as possible. Cook the crepe gently until the top looks dry, 1 to 2 minutes. Flip, using a spatula or your fingers, by flicking the crepe over quickly as if you were turning the page of a book. Cook for 20 seconds more on the second side, and then transfer from the pan to the paper towel–lined plate. Repeat the process until there is no more batter, adding more oil only every three or four crepes.

continued . . .

3. Prepare the filling: Heat the olive oil in a skillet over medium heat until shimmering and fragrant. Sauté the red onion until soft and translucent, 5 to 7 minutes. Add the garlic and sauté for 1 minute. Add the mushrooms and sauté until cooked through and they have given up most of their moisture, 5 to 7 minutes. Add the spinach and parsley, and sauté until the spinach is wilted. Remove from the heat and fold in the cheeses, allowing to melt slightly. Taste for salt and add as needed.

4. To assemble, lay out a crepe on a clean work surface. Scoop ¼ cup of the filling onto the lower half of the circle and then fold the top down over the filling to meet the bottom. Gently fold one side over the other to make a triangular shape. Alternately, arrange ¼ cup of the filling down the middle of the circle and fold one side, then the other, up over the filling, overlapping on top. Garnish each crepe with a heaping tablespoon of pesto.

Pizza Dough

MAKES 1 POUND DOUGH

This basic pizza dough recipe can be made in under a few hours. It's worth noting that most pizzerias ferment their dough for as long as 24 hours to develop maximum flavor in the crust. If there's a local pizza parlor that you like, feel free to buy a ball of their dough, but this crust certainly can work.

¾ cup lukewarm water (about 110°F)

2¼ teaspoons (one 9-gram packet) active dry yeast

½ teaspoon sugar

1½ cups all-purpose flour, plus more as needed and for dusting

½ cup bread flour (all-purpose will work, but bread flour gives more structure to the dough)

1 teaspoon salt

3 tablespoons extra virgin olive oil, plus more for bowl

1. Pour the warm water into a small bowl. Stir in the yeast and sugar. Let stand at room temperature until the yeast has dissolved, about 5 minutes. The yeast is active when bubbles are on the surface of the mixture.

2. Combine the flours and salt in a food processor. Pulse a few times to mix the dry ingredients.

3. Add the yeast mixture and olive oil. Pulse until a dough ball comes together. If you don't have a food processor, you can mix the dough in a bowl with a wooden spoon until all the ingredients are incorporated. Add more water, if necessary, until the dough forms a cohesive ball. Transfer to a lightly floured work surface and knead until the dough is smooth to the touch but slightly sticky. Add more flour while kneading if the dough is too sticky.

4. Lightly oil a large bowl. Place the dough in the bowl and turn so that the oil also coats the dough lightly. Cover with a piece of plastic wrap or dry, clean cloth and let rise in a warm area until doubled in size, 1 to 1½ hours. If your room is cooler, the dough will rise more slowly.

5. Punch down the dough ball by pressing the center with your fist, and then reshape it into a ball by gathering the edges toward the center and tucking them into the middle of the ball. It can be helpful to put the dough on a counter and cup your hands around it while turning to form a ball. If using the dough at another time, return the ball to the bowl, cover with plastic wrap, and refrigerate until ready to use. The dough may be made up to 2 days prior to making the pizza, but should sit for 20 minutes to come to room temperature before using. If you are using the dough right away, cover the ball with plastic wrap or a floured towel, and allow to rest for 30 minutes.

GOOD DOGS FARM

Owned by Roberto Flores in Ashley Falls, MA, Good Dogs Farm isn't really a farm anymore. Save for Flores's long row of asparagus on the property, most of the acreage once devoted to the farm is his partner Maria Nation's horse riding ring and pasture. But it was a farm for a number of years before that, and Flores and Nation's thoughtful perspective on their Berkshire farming experience is worth telling.

Flores's third career was farming—after banking in Texas and running Seven Hills Inn in Lenox. When Flores sold the hotel, he decided to try farming on their property, which Nation had purchased in the '90s. He didn't start cold: Flores sought advice from neighboring farmers including Ted Dobson and Dominic Palumbo, and spent six weeks shadowing a California farmer. He had also gardened extensively. Nation, whose expansive gardens are a Berkshire legend, told *Rural Intelligence* that together they "have touched or gardened at one point every one of the 8 acres of our property."

Enticed by the loamy soil of the Housatonic River basin, Flores set up Good Dogs, farming 2.5 acres at its height, selling vegetables at farmers' markets and area restaurants. In 2014, Flores told *Rural Intelligence* that his new work was deeply satisfying, saying, "it's such a right thing to do." At the Millerton Farmers' Market late one summer, tea makers Michael and Paul Harney of Harney & Sons, in Salisbury, CT, approached the Good Dogs farmstand. They shopped at Millerton frequently and loved talking food with Flores, so they asked whether he'd like to work for them during the off-season. What started out as temporary became permanent, and Flores eventually stopped farming. We asked Nation whether she thought he might go back to a career he had embraced with such enthusiasm. She laughed. "We already lost too much money trying that one!" That's when another farmer, Joe Scully, who now works at Indian Line Farm, took over Good Dogs for the 2014 season. Nation and Flores, who had met Scully earlier at the farmers' market, generously offered him the opportunity to use their land without

charge to grow ingredients—celery, an heirloom New England dried bean—for Prairie Whale restaurant, in Great Barrington, MA.

Nation is emphatic that she didn't farm, giving sole credit to Flores. But she acknowledges that for most Berkshire small farms, someone in the family needs to work an off-farm job to support the operation. She was that person, she says, laughing, probably because she hadn't seen herself exactly that way until we spoke recently. "I was writing screenplays to sort of help support the farm." (Nation started selling scripts while living in New York, and moved to the Berkshires in '97.)

Flores and Nation were and are frequent entertainers. They cook from their garden, and when they had their farm, from that as well, often making pizzas in an outdoor oven, topping them with their produce, inspiring the Greek Salad Pizza (page 129).

Looking back at their experiment with mixed feelings, Nation says the experience changed her perception of agriculture. "It's really a sobering reality, the state of small farmers in America," she says. "They don't get subsidized by the government like agribusinesses do. You work so unbelievably hard, such horrible hours, and you know, a quarter of the things that you've raised from seeds and nurtured, that you've harvested that morning at dawn, you've washed and taken to market—you compost because nobody bought them."

But their stint at farming positively influences how Nation cooks and eats today. "Before we started farming, I would go through recipes, and it could be the middle of December and I would say, 'How about this strawberry tart? This tomato something?' I still can't bring myself to use strawberries or tomatoes in the winter, or things that are going to be flavorless, even though they're in abundance in the supermarket."

Even now, the visual image Nation has of farming is an overpoweringly pleasurable one. "I still love photos of the spring, when the fields are all freshly turned, and the rows are up, and it means hope and promise of the future, optimism and all that. It's just a beautiful graphic, so evocative."

Greek Salad Pizza

GOOD DOGS FARM

SERVES 4 TO 6

Each slice of this unique pizza offers a great flavor combination from the cool crunch of the salad topping to the hot cheese and tart olives right underneath. If you'd like, the salad can be served as a delicious side dish, but our friends on the farm enjoy it right on top!

Flour for dusting work surface (all-purpose is fine)

1 pound pizza dough (page 126), or store-bought dough, or other prepared crust (e.g., from Berkshire Mountain Bakery, Housatonic, MA)

1 tablespoon extra virgin olive oil, plus more for half sheet pan if not using pizza stone

¼ cup grated Parmesan

½ cup very thinly sliced red onion, cut into half-moons

1 cup quartered cherry tomatoes

¼ cup pitted Kalamata olives, halved

½ cup crumbled feta

¼ teaspoon salt

Freshly ground black pepper

½ cup ¼-inch-diced seedless cucumber

1 cup chopped arugula

2 tablespoons plain yogurt

1. If using a pizza stone, place it on the center rack of the oven before preheating. If not using a pizza stone, lightly oil a rimmed half sheet pan. Preheat the oven to 450°F.

2. Flour a work surface on which to stretch the pizza dough. Then, if using a pizza stone, gently shape the dough into a shape to match, and with the desired thickness. If using a half sheet pan, gently shape or roll the dough to fit. If stretching the dough is difficult, let it relax for 5 minutes and then return to working it. Make sure there is enough flour under the dough to prevent sticking.

3. Drizzle the shaped dough with the olive oil and, using your fingers or the back of a spoon, gently spread the oil around the surface of the dough. Sprinkle the Parmesan, red onion, tomatoes, olives, and half of the feta evenly over the dough. Season with ⅛ teaspoon of the salt and a sprinkling of pepper to taste.

4. If using a pizza stone, gently slide a pizza peel under the dough, trying not to disturb the toppings. A pizza peel can be improvised by using the underside of a baking sheet as a giant spatula, easing the pizza carefully onto the back of the sheet. From here, slide the pizza from the peel carefully onto the pizza stone. If the pizza was assembled on a half sheet pan instead of a stone, just put the pan into the oven.

5. Bake for 10 to 18 minutes, until the crust is slightly risen and golden in color. Remove the pizza from the oven using either the pizza peel underside of a baking sheet, or by sliding the half sheet pan from the oven. Allow the pizza to cool for a few minutes.

6. While the pizza bakes, combine the cucumber, arugula, remaining feta, and the yogurt in a bowl as a salad. After the pizza has cooled, top the pizza evenly with the salad and sprinkle with the remaining ⅛ teaspoon of salt. Cut into pieces and serve.

Roasted Zucchini and Cherry Tomato Pizza

BERKSHIRE BOUNTY FARM

SERVES 4 TO 6

This pizza makes the most of late summer garden bounty—tomatoes and zucchini. Be sure to let the pizza cool to a comfortable temperature before serving, since the cheese and tomatoes can hold a surprising amount of heat from the oven.

1 teaspoon extra virgin olive oil, plus more for half sheet pan if not using pizza stone and for drizzling

1 medium zucchini, cut into ¼-inch rounds

12 cherry tomatoes, cut in half

2 garlic cloves, chopped

½ small red onion, sliced very thin into half-moons

¼ teaspoon salt

Flour for dusting work surface (all-purpose is fine)

1 pound pizza dough (page 126), store-bought dough, or other prepared crust (e.g., from Berkshire Mountain Bakery, Housatonic, MA)

½ cup ricotta

2 tablespoons grated Parmesan

8 ounces fresh mozzarella, thinly sliced

6 fresh basil leaves, thinly sliced into ribbons

1. If using a pizza stone, place it on the center rack of the oven before preheating. If not using a pizza stone, lightly oil a rimmed half sheet pan, plus another foil-lined, rimmed half sheet pan for roasting the vegetables. Preheat the oven to 400°F.

2. Combine the sliced zucchini, cherry tomatoes, garlic, and red onion in a medium bowl. Toss together with ⅛ teaspoon salt and 1 teaspoon of the olive oil. Place the vegetable mixture on the foil-lined sheet pan and spread evenly, distributing across the pan. Roast the vegetables for 15 minutes to allow them to soften and the moisture to be drawn out. Remove from the oven and set aside to cool. Increase the oven temperature to 450°F. The pizza stone, if using, should still be in the oven.

3. Flour a work surface on which to stretch the pizza dough. Then, if using a pizza stone, gently shape the dough into a shape to match, and with the desired thickness. If using a half sheet pan, gently shape or roll the dough to fit. If stretching the dough is difficult, let it relax for 5 minutes and then return to working it. Make sure there is enough flour under the dough to prevent sticking.

4. Spread the ricotta evenly over the surface of the pizza, leaving about ½ inch of dough uncovered around the edges. Sprinkle the ricotta evenly with the Parmesan. Top with the roasted vegetable mixture, evenly distributing across the surface of the pizza. Layer the sliced mozzarella on top of the vegetables, making sure to keep the mozzarella away from the crust area around the edges so that the cheese won't melt over the sides. Season with the

remaining ⅛ teaspoon salt and drizzle with a little olive oil.

4. If using a pizza stone, gently slide a pizza peel under the dough, trying not to disturb the toppings. A pizza peel can be improvised by using the underside of a baking sheet as a giant spatula, easing the pizza carefully onto the back of the sheet. From here, slide the pizza from the peel carefully onto the pizza stone. If using a half sheet pan instead of a pizza stone, just put the pan into the oven.

5. Bake for 10 to 18 minutes, until the crust is slightly risen and golden in color. Remove the pizza from the oven using either the pizza peel or the underside of a baking sheet, or by sliding the half sheet pan from the oven. Scatter the basil ribbons evenly over the pizza. Allow the pizza to cool for 5 to 10 minutes before serving.

Savory Piecrust

MAKES A SINGLE PIECRUST

This is a simple piecrust recipe, perfect for quiches, galettes, and other savory crusted dishes.

1¼ cups all-purpose flour

1 teaspoon salt

8 tablespoons (1 stick) unsalted butter, cut into pea-size pieces, chilled

¼ cup ice water

1. Combine the flour, salt, and butter in a food processor and process until a granular mixture is achieved. With the processor running, gradually add the ice water through the opening of the processor lid until the dough balls up. This should only take a few minutes from start to finish.

2. On a floured work surface, shape the dough by hand into a thick disk and wrap in plastic wrap.

Refrigerate until firm, at least 1 hour, before using. At this point, the dough can be refrigerated for up to 2 days, or frozen for 4 to 6 weeks.

3. Follow your recipe instructions for rolling and filling.

4. If the recipe does not specify a particular way to roll out the dough, use a rolling pin to roll it into a wide circle, about 15 inches in diameter. Carefully transfer the crust circle to the pie plate. One way to do this is to roll the dough partially onto the rolling pin so that half of the crust is supported by the pin and the other half hangs down. Transfer the crust to the pie plate and unroll to allow it to gently lie in the pie plate. Press down the center gently with your fingers and up the sides. Trim any crust overhang according to the recipe instructions.

Caramelized Onion Galette with Blue Cheese and Carrots

WOVEN ROOTS FARM
HIGH LAWN FARM

SERVES 8

There's nothing like the aroma of slowly caramelizing onions to evoke a feeling of homecoming. The key to getting good color and flavor from your onions is allow them to cook slowly in their own sugars, without rushing or scorching them. Serve this rustic galette at room temperature, along with a salad on a warm day, or a hot bowl of soup on a chilly fall evening.

Galette topping:

2 tablespoons extra virgin olive oil

2 large red onions, thinly sliced into ¼-inch half-moons (about 1½ pounds, or 6 cups)

4 carrots, peeled and sliced into ¼-inch matchsticks (about 2 cups)

1 tablespoon pure maple syrup

2 tablespoons white balsamic or other favorite vinegar

1 tablespoon finely chopped fresh rosemary

¼ teaspoon salt

¼ teaspoon freshly ground black pepper

Flour for dusting (all-purpose is fine)

6 ounces High Lawn Farm blue cheese, or other local blue cheese, crumbled

1 recipe Savory Piecrust (page 131), or store-bought

Egg wash:

1 large egg, lightly beaten

1 tablespoon water

1. Preheat the oven to 375°F. Place parchment paper on a rimmed baking sheet and set aside.

2. Heat the olive oil in a 10-inch skillet over medium heat until shimmering and fragrant. Add the red onions and gently coat with the oil, using a pair of tongs. Move the onions around in the pan every few minutes and watch for scorching. The onions should soften slowly and become more translucent, getting golden brown on their edges. This should take about 15 minutes. Add the carrots, maple syrup, vinegar, rosemary, salt, and pepper. Increase the heat to high and slightly reduce the liquid while continuing to stir the mixture gently. The carrots should still be slightly firm after about 5 minutes. Remove from the heat and set aside to cool to room temperature.

3. On a floured work surface, roll out the pie dough into a wide circle, about 15 inches in diameter. Carefully transfer this circle to the prepared baking sheet. One way to do this is to roll the dough partially onto the rolling pin so that half of the crust is supported by the pin and the other half hangs down. Unroll it so that it lies flat on top of the parchment paper, gently smoothing out any wrinkles.

4. Mix the egg with the water in a small dish to make an egg wash and set aside.

5. Add the blue cheese to the onion mixture and fold in carefully. Mound the onion mixture in the middle of the galette crust. With the back of a large spoon, gently push the filling evenly out from the center of the mound to within 1½ inches of the edge of the crust, leaving that space bare. Fold the crust edges in toward the center, drawing the edges up and over the filling. Fold or crimp the crust in places so that the filling will not leak out during baking. Gently brush the crust with a thin layer of the egg wash, being careful to brush over the crust only, not the vegetable filling.

6. Bake the galette for 30 minutes, or until the edges of the crust are golden brown and the filling is bubbling slightly. Remove from the oven and allow the galette to cool to room temperature before serving in wedges.

Yellow Squash and Spinach Quiche

MIGHTY FOOD FARM

SERVES 8

This quiche can also be made without the crust as a gluten-free alternative—just be sure to lightly oil the pie plate.

1 tablespoon extra virgin olive oil, plus more for pie plate, if necessary

½ cup small-diced onion

1 cup diced yellow summer squash

1 cup packed ribboned baby spinach

1 recipe Savory Piecrust (page 131)

8 large eggs

½ cup whole milk

½ teaspoon salt

½ teaspoon freshly ground black pepper

1 tablespoon chopped fresh flat-leaf parsley, or 1 teaspoon dried

1 tablespoon chopped fresh basil, or 1 teaspoon dried

¾ cup crumbled feta

1. Preheat the oven to 350°F. Set an oven rack in the middle of the oven.

2. Heat the oil in a sauté pan over medium heat. Add the onion and allow to slightly caramelize, about 5 minutes. Add the squash and sauté for 5 minutes. Add the spinach and cook until wilted and the water has evaporated from the pan, about 3 minutes. Remove from the heat and let cool to room temperature.

3. Roll out the pie dough to fill a 9-inch pie pan. Lay the crust in the pan and trim it to the edge of the pan. If choosing to make a crustless quiche, lightly oil the pan with olive oil. Place the pan on a foil-lined rimmed baking sheet to catch any drips.

4. Whisk together the eggs, milk, salt, pepper, parsley, and basil in a large bowl. Add the vegetable mixture and stir to combine.

5. Sprinkle the feta evenly over the dough in the bottom of the pie pan. Fill with the quiche filling, smoothing the top evenly with a spatula.

6. Place the baking sheet in the oven and bake until the quiche is just set in the center and golden on top, 55 to 65 minutes. Remove from the oven and let cool at least 15 minutes before serving.

Leek Tarts with Chèvre

RAWSON BROOK FARM

SERVES 4 TO 6

These sturdy little tarts can be served warm or at room temperature, as appetizers at a summer party, or tucked into a picnic basket or school lunchbox in the fall. Small enough to be eaten out of hand, they are equally elegant on a plate at brunch. They also freeze well in zippered plastic freezer bags with most of the air pressed out.

Flour for dusting (all-purpose is fine)

1 recipe Savory Piecrust (page 131)

6 medium or 4 large leeks (about 2½ pounds)

4 tablespoons (½ stick) unsalted butter

7 ounces chèvre, or goat cheese, crumbled (about 1¾ cups)

3 large eggs, beaten

½ cup milk

1 teaspoon fresh thyme leaves, or a heaping ¼ teaspoon dried

¼ teaspoon salt

¼ teaspoon freshly ground black pepper

1. Preheat the oven to 400°F. Set a 12-well nonstick muffin tin in the center of a rimmed half sheet pan so that any overflow is contained.

2. On a lightly floured surface, roll out the piecrust to 1/16-inch thickness. Using a large biscuit cutter or the lip of a 4½-inch-diameter bowl and the tip of a sharp knife, cut circles of dough. Reroll the scraps and cut out the remains of the dough to make up 12 circles total. Press the dough circles gently into the muffin wells, smoothing out any wrinkles and flattening the dough against the bottom and sides. The bottom and sides of a shot glass work well here. Place the muffin tin in the refrigerator to chill the dough while working on the filling.

3. Discard the darkest green, thickest portions of the leeks and keep the lighter green and white parts. Slice the leeks lengthwise through the root and wash the leek halves carefully in cold water, swishing to be sure to remove any grit hiding between the layers. Slice the leeks thinly into half-moons and discard the root end.

4. Melt the butter in a large skillet over medium heat. Add the leeks and gently sauté for 20 minutes, or until soft and slightly caramelized. Remove from the heat and allow to cool slightly.

5. Mix together the crumbled chèvre, eggs, milk, thyme, salt, and pepper in a large bowl.

6. Remove the muffin tin from the refrigerator and measure 2 mounded tablespoons of leeks into each tart, evenly distributing any remaining leeks over all. Pour a scant ¼ cup of the chèvre mixture over the leeks. With the end of a butter knife, poke the egg mixture around a little in the leeks to release any air pockets. Use any remaining liquid to top off any crust cups that seem to have slightly lower levels.

7. Carefully put the half sheet pan along with the muffin tin in the oven and bake for 25 to 30 minutes, until the tarts are set in the center and browned lightly on top. Remove from the oven and allow to cool in the muffin tin for 15 minutes. Carefully remove the tarts from the muffin tin and serve warm or at room temperature.

PASTA, GRAINS, AND BEANS

Carrot Gnocchi

WOVEN ROOTS FARM

SERVES 2 AS A MAIN, 4 AS A SIDE DISH

Gnocchi are the tasty potato pillows of the pasta world. In this recipe, carrots add an earthy sweetness, complemented by a simple sage and butter sauce. Serve with a salad for a lighter dinner, or as a side with a protein.

1 large baking potato, preferably Idaho or russet (about 12 ounces)

1 tablespoon extra virgin olive oil, or more as needed for sautéing and oiling dish

½ cup minced onion

1 tablespoon grated fresh ginger

2 cups shredded carrot (about 8 ounces)

2 large egg yolks

½ teaspoon salt

1 cup all-purpose flour, plus more as needed and for dusting

2 tablespoons unsalted butter

1 tablespoon packed chopped fresh sage

½ cup grated Parmesan

1. Preheat the oven to 350°F. Pierce the potato in a few places with a fork and bake until tender, 60 to 90 minutes.

2. Meanwhile, heat the oil in a medium sauté pan over medium heat until shimmering and fragrant. Add the onion, ginger, and carrot and sauté until the onion has slightly caramelized and the carrot is cooked through and soft, 15 to 20 minutes. Remove from the heat and allow to cool slightly. Place the vegetables and egg yolks in a food processor and puree until smooth. Transfer to a bowl and set aside.

3. Split the baked potato in half and let the steam escape. When cool enough to handle, scoop out the flesh and put through a ricer or food mill, or shred on a box grater directly into the bowl of puree. Add the salt and blend with a spatula to mix well.

4. Bring a large pot of salted water to boil over high heat. Lightly oil a large platter or two dinner plates for the finished gnocchi.

5. Place the flour on a cutting board, put the potato mixture on top, and knead into a dough, adding more flour as needed.

6. Once kneaded into a firm dough, divide into six equal pieces. Dusting the work surface lightly as needed, roll each piece into a long strand about ¾ inch in diameter, similar to a thick rope. Using a sharp knife or dough scraper, cut the ropes into ¾- to 1-inch gnocchi.

7. Working in three or four batches, drop the gnocchi into the boiling water and boil for about 3 minutes, or until they float. Remove with a strainer or spider and place on the oiled dish. As the water returns to a boil, continue to add and cook the gnocchi, one batch at a time.

8. When the last batch of gnocchi goes into the boiling water, melt the butter in a large sauté pan over medium heat, then add the sage. When all the gnocchi are done, add to the sauté pan as much in one layer as possible. Allow the gnocchi to sit in the pan without stirring until one side starts to crisp, 3 to 5 minutes. Toss with the Parmesan and serve immediately.

JOHN ANDREWS FARMHOUSE RESTAURANT

Chef/owner Dan Smith of John Andrews Farmhouse Restaurant, in South Egremont, MA, could fill a scrapbook with articles about his restaurant and him. But we thought *Harvard Magazine* had the best description of his culinary philosophy: "Smith offers a locavore ethic, cooking whatever's freshest, with no showboating about it." In fact, our favorite part of interviewing Smith was his similarly low-key, but lengthier description of how he approaches creating dishes, one which truly captures the idea of farm-to-table.

Smith has been cooking farm-to-table long before it became trendy, supporting local farmers and artisan food producers in the Berkshires, Hudson Valley, and northwestern CT. He and his then wife started the restaurant in 1990 in an 18th-century renovated farmhouse surrounded by perennial gardens and forest views. Among its accolades: the *Daily Meal* named it one of the World's 25 Best Farmstead Experiences. Smith is involved locally, teaching a culinary class for at-risk teenagers at the Railroad Street Youth Project in Great Barrington, MA, and is grateful in turn for the communal support he and his restaurant have received.

A hallmark of his style is spontaneity. "The other night," he remembers, "I was trimming strawberries and some were a little too ripe to serve. I recalled, maybe 30 years ago, making strawberry vinegar. So, I just poured Champagne vinegar over the ripe strawberries and then kinda mashed them, and made a strawberry vinaigrette for an Indian Line Farm tomato salad. That tiny bit of fruit in the vinaigrette went really well with the tomato." He's particularly delighted when customers give him the go-ahead to ad lib, and mentions a wedding party—the restaurant can handle outdoor tented parties for up to 220—that came for a tasting, told him "We loved it," but then said do what you want.

The way Smith buys products from local farmers guarantees improvisation. Rather than telling a farmer what he wants him or her to grow, Smith prefers to ask, "What do you grow best?" He's also happy to work with a farmer's excess, whatever shows up at his door. "A light clicks on in my head," he says. "I have to have that visual connection and my brain gets really engaged. I use my hands a lot, too. Once it's in my hands, I'm like, 'whoa.'"

Working with farmers transports Smith back to his childhood. His dad still farms a 700-acre produce and livestock farm near Villisca, Iowa, population 1,250, where he grew up. Originally Smith studied agriculture and planned to farm, but preparing food won out, especially when he found that some of the required courses in his major were "basically supported by chemical companies." Growing up as he did, Smith understood eating fresh. He humorously recalls his farming grandfather's understanding of what that meant in relation to sweet corn. "He's like, the house was here and the garden was here, and by the time it takes to pick the sweet corn and get it

to the house and eat it, it's almost too late. It's been picked too long."

On WAMC Northeast Public Radio, Smith told a listener who said he had little cooking savvy that it's simple and quick to prepare a healthy meal. Just one example: Go to a farmstand, grab vegetables, roast them, slice local tomatoes, and add some cheese. "That's the easiest meal to make." He says that you may fail here and there (he does), but "don't be afraid to try something you don't know."

As a steadfast proponent of farm-to-table, Smith is concerned that fads in farming and food—good ones—may be temporary. "It's almost become hip for people to come and do a year farming," he says, but is concerned if that fades away, where are farmers going to find help? Ditto for the farm-to-table concept. "Just that coined phrase is huge. I mean, what happens when that trails away?" He's hopeful eating local is here for the long run, especially when people learn about its health benefits, when that means buying from farms that don't use pesticides or growth hormones. Home in Iowa years ago after his mom and sister died, he offered to help out on the farm. "I didn't even recognize the soybeans they were planting. What are these?"

Ricotta Gnocchi with Butternut Squash and Sage Brown Butter Sauce

JOHN ANDREWS FARMHOUSE RESTAURANT

SERVES 4 AS A MAIN, 6 AS A SIDE

These light, tender puffs of ricotta and Parmesan create a perfect canvas for the combination of nutty brown butter, fragrant sage, and sweet squash. Because this recipe, adapted from Chef Dan Smith of John Andrews Farmhouse Restaurant, yields a lot of gnocchi, be sure to use a very large skillet at the end so you can mix everything together gently. The gnocchi can be made ahead and refrigerated for a day, or frozen for longer. If you choose to freeze them, place the gnocchi in the freezer on a sheet pan before transferring to a plastic bag. Drop the gnocchi into boiling water straight from the freezer and cook until they float, three to four minutes.

In the spirit of Smith's philosophy that a cook should experiment, try another version of this recipe, if you'd like, by adding the butternut squash to the ricotta mixture. Reserve some pieces of squash to add color to the dish in Step 10.

2½ pounds butternut squash, peeled, seeded, and diced into ½-inch cubes (about 4 cups)

2 tablespoons extra virgin olive oil

1½ teaspoons, plus a generous pinch of kosher salt

1 pound fresh ricotta

1½ cups grated Parmesan (4 to 5 ounces), plus more for serving

1 cup all-purpose flour, plus more for kneading and dusting

3 large egg yolks

1½ teaspoons freshly ground black pepper

¼ cup minced fresh flat-leaf parsley

continued . . .

2 tablespoons minced fresh chives

12 tablespoons (1½ sticks) unsalted butter

24 fresh sage leaves

1 to 2 shallots, finely minced

1 to 2 garlic cloves, finely minced

1. Preheat the oven to 350°F. Toss the butternut squash with the olive oil and a generous pinch of the salt and spread in one layer on a foil-lined rimmed sheet pan. Roast for 30 to 40 minutes, until tender. Set aside until ready to use.

2. To drain some moisture out of the ricotta, place 2 or 3 layers of paper towels on a plate and, using a rubber spatula, spread out the ricotta as much as possible on the paper towels. Place another 2 or 3 layers of paper towels on top and press gently to absorb some of the moisture. When the paper towels are wet, change both the top and bottom paper towels so that more water can be absorbed from the cheese. (This should yield 12 to 13 ounces of ricotta when finished.)

3. Combine the ricotta, Parmesan, and flour in a large bowl and mix well with a wooden spoon or rubber spatula. Add the egg yolks, remaining 1½ teaspoons of salt, and the pepper, parsley, and chives and mix well until the mixture forms a ball.

4. Scrape the dough out of the bowl onto a well-floured surface and, with floured hands, knead for about a minute, pulling in flour as needed, maybe even as much as ¼ cup, to form a moist but not sticky dough.

5. Divide the dough into 6 to 8 pieces. Working with one piece at a time, roll out the dough into a long rope ½ to ¾ inch in diameter. Flour a cutting implement (a sharp knife or dough scraper is fine) and use to cut the rope into ½- to ¾-inch pieces. Place the gnocchi onto a parchment-lined or floured rimmed sheet pan and dust lightly with flour. If there are too many gnocchi to arrange in one layer, place parchment or waxed paper between the layers. Place in the refrigerator until ready to boil, for up to 24 hours. (At this point they can be frozen for later use, if desired.)

6. Bring a large pot of salted water to a boil.

7. Place the butter and sage leaves in a small, heavy-bottomed saucepan. Melt over medium heat, and cook, stirring constantly, until the butter is browned and the sage leaves are crisp, about 15 minutes. Watch carefully as butter can go from brown to burnt quickly. Remove from the heat and set aside in a warm place while the gnocchi cook.

8. Working in four or five batches, boil the gnocchi for 3 to 4 minutes, until they are floating close together. Remove gently with a spider or slotted spoon and drop into a large skillet. (Do not turn on the heat under the skillet yet.) Drizzle some of the brown butter sauce on the gnocchi to keep them from sticking. Cook the first several batches of gnocchi.

9. When the second-to-last batch comes out of the water, turn on the heat to medium under the skillet. Clear out a space in the skillet, add more brown butter sauce, and sauté the shallots and garlic while boiling the last batch of gnocchi. Make sure there is enough butter in the skillet to keep the gnocchi already in there from sticking.

10. Transfer the last batch of gnocchi from the boiling water to the skillet, add the remaining brown butter sauce and butternut squash, and mix gently while heating through. Serve immediately with grated Parmesan.

MICHAEL BALLON, OWNER OF THE FORMER CASTLE STREET CAFÉ, GREAT BARRINGTON, MA

Chef Michael Ballon was the proprietor of the former Castle Street Café, in Great Barrington, MA. Sadly, Ballon passed away in September 2019 at the age of 63, but during his life he was easily one of the earliest adopters of farm-to-table in the Berkshires. He described the café in his 2014 personal book of essays and recipes, *A Chef's Life: Farm-to-Table Cooking in the Berkshires*, as "farm-to-table since 1989." (He sold the restaurant in early 2017, telling the *Berkshire Eagle* that 38 years in the restaurant industry is like 60.) Even before Ballon opened Castle Street, an unexpected occurrence tipped him off to the existence of the local food movement. "I came to the Berkshires in 1982 when I was still a chef in New York City," he recalled. "I was shipping in goat cheese to New York from California, and found someone making it here."

Yet Ballon found the farm-to-table movement, of which he was a pioneer, ironic. "Up until a hundred years ago," he said, "that was the only way people ate. People talk about it as if it were a revelation. This idea of supporting local farms is not new; what's really new is the industrialization of food." While he was growing up, his family ate seasonally, like everyone else at the time. "My father's birthday was the beginning of June and we had blueberry pie each year to celebrate because that's when blueberries were around. The idea of blueberry pie in January was heretical. But things changed pretty quickly after that," Ballon said. "I don't know too many people who give up chocolate or citrus because they grow it far away."

Blueberries remained one of Ballon's favorite ingredients, and continued to define summer for him. (In the same way he said that cranberries define Thanksgiving, although Ballon thought they should be used year-round. Check out the recipe for Warm Cranberry Cobbler, page 203.)

When he took over the Castle Street space, it had been a "'70s hippie crunchy health food restaurant" in an early incarnation. "There was a chalkboard. One of the menu items was millet stew." Ballon said he'd be hard pressed to include something like that: He could put it on the menu, but few would order it. He also wasn't blind to the economics of farm-to-table. "There's a price point above which people won't pay. You may be growing something virtuous and so wonderful and of such high quality," but there is still a limit to local, mentioning a "ridiculously" expensive potato that he knew he couldn't afford to put on the menu.

In his essay "Farmers' Market Menu Planning," Ballon suggested how to approach shopping there. "Rather than arriving at a farmers' market with a list of desired purchases, it is perhaps more in keeping with the spirit of the place to be open to surprises and see what looks freshest and most appealing. Instead of deciding the evening's menu before you arrive, allow the serendipity of the garden's harvest to decide your menu."

One reason Ballon delighted in operating a restaurant in the Berkshires, he told us, is here "people think about where their food comes from. We've been serving Berkshire Mountain Bakery bread and Turner Farms maple syrup forever." There is something about this "milieu," he said, an area where people gravitate to farmers' markets, that gives diners the luxury of focusing on a food's origin.

Fettuccine with Blue Cheese

MICHAEL BALLON, OWNER OF THE FORMER
CASTLE STREET CAFÉ
HIGH LAWN FARM

SERVES 6 TO 8

Many blue cheeses tend to be dry and crumbly, but for this recipe, look for a local blue that is rich and creamy, which makes a delicious sauce for pasta. Walnuts are a traditional accompaniment to blue cheese, and they garnish this dish adapted from Chef Michael Ballon.

½ cup walnuts, coarsely chopped

1 pound dried fettuccine

1 tablespoon unsalted butter

1 teaspoon minced shallot

1 teaspoon minced fresh thyme

2 tablespoons all-purpose flour

1 cup chicken or vegetable stock

1 cup heavy cream

10 to 12 ounces creamy blue cheese, such as High Lawn Farm blue cheese, to taste

1. Watching carefully to avoid burning, toast the walnuts in a small skillet over medium heat until fragrant, about 5 minutes. Set aside.

2. Bring a large pot of salted water to a boil and cook the fettuccine according to the package instructions.

3. To make the sauce, heat the butter in a medium saucepan over medium heat and add the shallot, stirring occasionally. When the shallot is lightly browned, add the thyme and the flour and stir well.

4. Add the stock to the saucepan in a slow stream, stirring constantly to evenly incorporate the liquid into the flour. When the stock is fully incorporated, add the cream in a slow stream, stirring constantly.

Bring the sauce to a simmer and allow to thicken slowly for 5 minutes.

5. Lower the heat to a low simmer and whisk in the cheese, stirring well, allowing the cheese to melt through the sauce evenly.

6. Drain the pasta and toss with the sauce. If the sauce feels too thin to cover the pasta at first, allow it to cool a little while, tossing constantly to coat the pasta evenly. The sauce will thicken slightly as it cools. Serve on plates and garnish with the toasted walnuts.

Whole Wheat Penne with Vegetables and Herbed Ricotta

WOLFE SPRING FARM

SERVES 4 TO 6

This quick and simple, yet visually stunning dish, makes a nice dinner in the spring when asparagus is at the peak of freshness.

16 ounces whole wheat penne

1 cup ricotta

1 cup packed fresh basil leaves, plus 2 tablespoons minced

1 tablespoon grated lemon zest (from about 1 medium lemon)

½ cup grated Parmesan

2½ teaspoons salt

¼ teaspoon freshly ground black pepper

3 tablespoons extra virgin olive oil

4 teaspoons minced garlic, or to taste

2 cups bite-size broccoli florets

2 cups sliced asparagus spears (1-inch lengths)

2 cups halved cherry or grape tomatoes

½ cup vegetable or chicken stock

1 tablespoon chopped fresh flat-leaf parsley

continued . . .

1. Bring a large pot of salted water to a boil and cook the pasta according to the package instructions, then drain.

2. Combine the ricotta, the cup of basil, lemon zest, Parmesan, ½ teaspoon of the salt, and the pepper in a food processor or blender. Process until smooth and set aside.

3. Heat the olive oil in a large, heavy-bottomed stockpot or a Dutch oven over medium heat until shimmering and fragrant. Sauté the garlic for less than 1 minute, stirring constantly to prevent scorching. Add the broccoli, asparagus, and cherry toma-

toes, sautéing until they are bright in color but still crisp, 4 to 5 minutes.

4. Deglaze the pot with the stock, using a wooden spoon or spatula to gently scrape up any bits from the bottom. Add the parsley, 2 tablespoons of minced basil, remaining 2 teaspoons of salt, and the cooked pasta. Toss together in the pot over medium heat for a few minutes to allow everything to warm through.

5. Fill the bottom of four to six large dishes with the pasta mixture. Divide the herbed ricotta evenly on top of each portion.

Ditalini Pasta with Sugar Snap Peas and Pancetta (or Mushrooms)

THE RED LION INN

SERVES 2 TO 3 AS A MAIN COURSE, 4 TO 6 AS A SIDE

When the first sugar snap peas appear at farmers' markets early in the growing season, it's the perfect time to enjoy their sweet crunch in this pasta recipe, adapted from Chef Brian Alberg, former executive chef of The Red Lion Inn. As with any cream-based pasta recipe, it is best eaten as soon as it is made. Any small, tube-shaped pasta would make a good substitute if ditalini can't be found. For a vegetarian version, substitute a variety of mushrooms for the pancetta. The mushrooms' meaty, earthy flavors provide a good alternative to the pancetta, but you may want to use more olive oil as well as salt and pepper.

2 cups dried ditalini pasta (about 8 ounces)

1 tablespoon extra virgin olive oil, or 2 or more tablespoons for vegetarian version

4 ounces sliced pancetta (about 2 thick slices), diced, or 8 ounces mushrooms, preferably of more than 1 variety, diced small, for vegetarian version

½ medium red onion, thinly sliced into half-moons (about ½ cup)

1 teaspoon salt, for vegetarian version

½ teaspoon freshly ground black pepper, for vegetarian version

2 cups sugar snap peas, trimmed and cut vertically into 1-inch lengths (about 6 ounces)

¾ cup High Lawn Farm or other heavy cream

¼ cup grated Parmesan, plus more for serving, if desired

¼ cup chopped fresh chives (optional)

1. Bring a large pot of salted water to a boil and cook the pasta according to the package instructions, until al dente. Drain the pasta, reserving ½ cup of the pasta water, and return to the pot over no heat and cover, just to keep warm.

2. If using pancetta: Heat the tablespoon of olive oil in a large sauté pan over medium heat, add the pancetta, and cook until most of the fat has rendered and the pancetta is nearly crisp. Add the onion and sauté until it is translucent and caramelized, 6 to 8 minutes.

For the vegetarian version: Heat the 2 tablespoons of olive oil in a large sauté pan over medium heat and sauté the red onion with ½ teaspoon of the salt. After 2 to 3 minutes, once the onion has softened slightly, add the mushrooms with the remaining ½ teaspoon of salt and ½ teaspoon of pepper. Depending on the variety of mushrooms, a little more oil may be needed if they seem too dry. Cook until the mushrooms have given up most of their liquid, 5 to 7 minutes.

3. Toward the end of sautéing either version, add the pea pods to the pan, and stir to cook slightly, 1 to 2 minutes.

4. Add the warm ditalini, then add the cream and allow to warm through while stirring gently. Add the Parmesan and stir again. If it seems dry, add some pasta water or a bit more cream. You may not need any pasta water, and if so, it can be discarded. Stir until well incorporated and the pea pods are still slightly crunchy.

5. Garnish with the chives and additional Parmesan, if desired.

Pasta with Roasted Cherry Tomatoes, Kalamata Olives, and Capers

BERKSHIRE BOUNTY FARM

SERVES 4 TO 6

Late-summer cherry tomatoes shine in this traditional Italian recipe. Roasting the tomatoes, along with the other ingredients, enhances the flavor of this dish.

¼ cup extra virgin olive oil, plus more for
    baking sheet

50 cherry tomatoes, halved

4 garlic cloves, minced

½ cup diced red onion

¼ cup red wine vinegar

2 teaspoons freshly ground black pepper

¼ cup chopped fresh flat-leaf parsley

1 pound thin pasta, such as capellini or
    other thin spaghetti

½ cup pitted Kalamata olives, roughly chopped

¼ cup capers, rinsed and drained

¼ cup grated Parmesan

½ cup crumbled Cricket Creek Farm feta,
    or other local feta

1. Preheat the oven to 400°F. Lightly oil a foil-lined rimmed baking sheet.

2. Toss together the tomatoes, olive oil, garlic, red onion, vinegar, pepper, and parsley in a large bowl. Transfer the vegetables to the prepared baking sheet. Use a spatula to spread them out into a single layer, and arrange tomatoes cut side up. Bake for 20 minutes.

3. Bring a large pot of salted water to a boil and cook the pasta according to the package instructions so that it is done at the same time as the vegetables. Drain the pasta.

4. Toss together the roasted vegetables and cooked pasta in a large bowl. Add the olives, capers, Parmesan, and feta and toss well. Serve immediately.

Pasta Bolognese

MEZZE BISTRO + BAR

SERVES 6 TO 8

Thick and heartwarming, this traditional Bolognese sauce, adapted from a favorite of Chef Nick Moulton of Mezze Bistro + Bar, simmers for a few hours before serving, and it's so worth the wait. It also freezes well, so you can double the sauce and put half in the freezer for an easy weeknight dinner. If you have trouble finding all three ground meats separately, some stores stock a meat loaf or meatball mix that includes beef, pork, and veal, which is a good substitute, even if they are not in the exact same proportions. Choose a pasta with small crevices, such as rotini, farfalle, or penne, to catch pieces of the sauce.

2 tablespoons extra virgin olive oil, plus more for serving (optional)

½ cup minced yellow onion

¾ cup minced celery

¾ cup minced carrot

1 teaspoon kosher salt, plus a large pinch and more to taste

1 teaspoon red pepper flakes

¼ cup minced garlic

⅓ pound ground beef, preferably chuck

⅓ pound lean ground pork

⅓ pound ground veal

Freshly ground black pepper

One 4- to 6-ounce can tomato paste

1 cup dry red wine, such as a merlot or pinot noir

One 14.5-ounce can diced tomatoes, with juices

1 sprig rosemary

12 sprigs thyme

1 large bay leaf

1 pound dried or fresh pasta

2 tablespoons unsalted butter

Grated Parmesan for serving

1. Heat the olive oil in a Dutch oven or heavy-bottomed stockpot over medium heat until shimmering and fragrant. Add the onion, celery, carrot, the teaspoon of kosher salt, and the red pepper flakes and cook until the carrot is softened, 6 to 8 minutes. Add the garlic and cook for an additional 3 minutes.

2. Add the ground beef, pork, and veal and season again with a large pinch of kosher salt and of black pepper. Cook the meat until just cooked through, another 6 to 8 minutes.

3. Add the tomato paste and cook for about 5 minutes to remove the acidity and develop sweetness. Once the mixture begins to stick to the bottom of the pot, add the red wine and stir to deglaze and

scrape up the bits from the surface. Once the wine has almost completely evaporated, add the tomatoes and their juices and bring to a simmer.

4. Once the pot has come to a simmer, lower the heat to maintain the lowest simmer possible. Tie the rosemary and thyme into a bundle with kitchen twine and add to the pot along with the bay leaf. Cover and cook for 2½ to 3 hours until desired thickness or consistency, stirring occasionally to make sure the sauce does not begin to stick to the bottom and burn.

5. Using tongs or a slotted spoon, remove the herb bundle and bay leaf. Season the finished sauce with salt and black pepper to taste. At this point, if desired, the Bolognese may be frozen for future use.

6. Bring a large pot of salted water to a boil and cook the pasta according to the package instructions, until al dente. Make sure the sauce is warm and in a pan large enough to accommodate the sauce and pasta together. Reserving 1 cup of pasta cooking water, drain the pasta in a colander, or scoop the pasta with a spider directly from the water into the sauce. Do not rinse the pasta, since this will rinse away necessary starches that give body to the sauce.

7. If using a colander, add the pasta to the pot of Bolognese sauce. Add the butter and bring the pasta and sauce back to a gentle simmer. Add some of the pasta cooking liquid, if needed. Sometimes with hollow pasta shapes, there will already be enough water to finish the dish.

8. Transfer the sauced pasta to a serving dish and garnish with a generous grating of Parmesan. Drizzle with a fresh tablespoon or two of olive oil, if desired, and serve immediately.

Confetti Vegetable and Goat Cheese Lasagna

RAWSON BROOK FARM

SERVES 8 TO 10

This large, colorful lasagna shows off the bounty of garden vegetables! Although it is a bit of a project, it is rewarding to make for a large party or potluck or even for a week's worth of meals. It can also be cut up into sections after baking and cooling, wrapped tightly, and frozen for future use.

3½ tablespoons extra virgin olive oil, plus more for lasagna dish and pans

3 red bell peppers

3 yellow bell peppers

3½ teaspoons salt

3¼ teaspoons freshly ground black pepper

2 medium zucchini (about 1 pound), cut into ½-inch cubes

2 medium yellow summer squash (about 1 pound), cut into ½-inch cubes

2 Italian eggplants (about 1½ pounds) cut into ½-inch cubes

16 ounces lasagna pasta sheets (can use no-boil)

1 pound spinach

1 pound Rawson Brook chèvre or other soft goat cheese

3 pounds ricotta

1 to 2 tablespoons minced garlic

2 ounces fresh flat-leaf parsley, minced (about 1 cup firmly packed)

2 ounces fresh basil, minced (about 1 cup firmly packed)

2½ cups grated Asiago (about 7½ ounces)

Tomato or pasta sauce, to ladle over finished lasagna (optional)

1. Move a rack to the top of the oven and preheat the broiler. Lightly oil a deep 10-by-15-inch or similarly sized baking dish and set aside. Lightly oil or line with foil two or three rimmed half sheet pans and set aside.

2. Core and seed the bell peppers and cut into quarters. Toss them in a large bowl with 1 tablespoon of the olive oil. Place the pepper pieces, skin side down, on one prepared half sheet pan and sprinkle evenly with 1 teaspoon of the salt, and ½ teaspoon of the black pepper. Turn the pepper pieces over so that they are skin side up and slide the baking sheet into the oven near the top, as close to the broiler as possible. Crack the oven door to watch as they roast. Allow the skins of the peppers to blacken and crack, but do not let the flesh burn. Move the peppers around on the baking sheet, if necessary, to provide exposure to the heat. This should take 15 to 20 minutes. Using tongs, transfer the peppers to a brown paper bag, and close the top of the bag to allow the peppers to steam inside while the other vegetables are roasting. (Be sure to place the bag on something to catch any juices that soak through.)

3. Move the rack to the center of the oven and pre-heat to 400°F. Place the zucchini and yellow squash cubes in the same large bowl as for the peppers and toss with 1 tablespoon of the olive oil, 1 teaspoon of the salt, and ½ teaspoon of the black pepper. Spread onto a separate (or first, if using only 2 pans) prepared half sheet pan.

4. Place the cubes of eggplant into the same large bowl and toss with 1½ teaspoons of the olive oil, ½ teaspoon of the salt, and ¼ teaspoon of the black pepper. Spread on a separate prepared rimmed half sheet pan. Roast both sheets of vegetables for 15 to 20 minutes, until soft. Remove from the oven and allow to cool on the baking sheets.

5. To skin the peppers, transfer from the paper bag to a cutting board, and using your fingers and a small sharp knife, peel the skins off of the flesh. Discard the skins. Cut the peeled peppers into ½-inch dice and set aside.

6. Bring a large pot of salted water to a boil and cook the pasta according to the package instructions. Drain, rinse, and set aside. Be sure to place a clean dish towel or parchment paper between the layers of lasagna noodles so they do not stick together. (If using no-boil pasta, skip this step.)

7. Meanwhile, wilt the spinach. Heat 1 tablespoon of the olive oil in a large skillet over medium heat until shimmering and fragrant. Working in batches if necessary, add the spinach to the skillet and toss gently with 1 teaspoon of the salt. Turn frequently with tongs until the spinach is uniformly wilted. Remove from the heat and set aside to cool to room temperature. Wrap the spinach in paper towels and squeeze out any excess moisture. Chop coarsely.

8. Combine the goat cheese, ricotta, garlic, parsley, basil, and 2 teaspoons of black pepper in a large bowl and beat until smooth with an electric mixer, or use a countertop blender on a low speed. Fold in the chopped spinach until the mixture is fully combined. Set aside.

9. Lower the oven temperature to 350°F. Divide the lasagna sheets equally to make 3 layers. Begin assembling the lasagna in the oiled baking dish by starting with a layer of pasta on the bottom, overlapping each piece of pasta slightly and trimming away any excess to fit neatly in the pan. Spread about a third of the ricotta mixture evenly over the pasta, with ½ cup of the Asiago on top.

10. Spread the zucchini and yellow squash evenly over the top of the cheeses. Layer more pasta sheets over the zucchini and yellow squash, overlapping the pasta slightly and trimming away any excess so it fits neatly over the previous layer. At this point, press gently down on the lasagna to compress the layers evenly together. Spread another third of the ricotta mixture over the pasta and top with an even sprinkling of ½ cup of the Asiago.

11. Scatter the eggplant evenly on top of the cheese. Add another layer of pasta, followed by another gentle compression. Some pieces of pasta may remain unused, depending on the exact size of the baking dish. Spread a final layer of ricotta over the pasta, followed by an even sprinkling of ½ cup of Asiago. Spread the roasted peppers over the top, mixing the reds and yellows together like confetti. Top with the final cup of Asiago sprinkled evenly over the top.

12. Cover the pan loosely with foil and bake for 45 minutes, or until the internal temperature reaches 165°F. Depending on the depth of your pan, you may want to place a rimmed sheet pan underneath to catch any dripping. Remove the foil and bake for an additional 15 minutes, or until the cheese on top becomes slightly golden, the vegetables are soft, and the pasta is sufficiently cooked (if using no-boil). Remove from the oven and allow to rest for 10 minutes before cutting into squares and serving. Offer tomato or pasta sauce alongside the lasagna, if desired, to add tomato flavor and moisture.

Mushroom Ragout over Pasta, Rice, or Polenta

PRAIRIE WHALE

SERVES 2 TO 4

This delicious stew, adapted from Chef Stephen Browning at Prairie Whale in Great Barrington, MA, is thick with mushrooms and just a little au jus to spare. Be sure to use a mixture of mushrooms, including shiitakes if you can, for extra-rich flavor. It is also important to use a low-sodium stock if possible, because the saltiness will become concentrated as the liquid reduces. Serve over pasta, rice, or polenta (see polenta recipe on page 168). If you want to add a protein, this recipe works well with any sausage—pork, turkey, or vegan—but don't choose an overly spicy variety since that will detract from the richness of the mushrooms.

1½ pounds mushrooms, including shiitakes, stemmed, or a mix of varieties, ½-inch diced (about 8 cups)

½ cup plus 2 tablespoons extra virgin olive oil

¾ teaspoon salt, plus more to taste

1 shallot, minced

1 medium onion, diced small

8 ounces pork, turkey, or vegan sausage links (optional)

20 sprigs thyme, tied together with kitchen twine

1 garlic clove, minced

½ cup dry white wine

1 quart vegetable or chicken stock, preferably low-sodium

Freshly ground black pepper

Cooked pasta, rice, or polenta

1. Preheat the oven to 350°F. Place the mushrooms in a large bowl and toss with ½ cup of the olive oil. Spread the mushrooms evenly on a foil-lined rimmed baking sheet and sprinkle with ¾ teaspoon of the salt. Roast for 20 minutes, or until tender and golden brown. Remove from the oven and set aside.

2. Heat 2 tablespoons of olive oil in a 4-quart Dutch oven or a heavy-bottomed stockpot over medium heat until shimmering and fragrant. Add the shallot, onion, and sausage (if using). Sauté until translucent, 5 to 7 minutes, turning the sausage occasionally.

3. Add the thyme bundle and garlic and cook, stirring, for about a minute, taking care not to let the garlic burn. Add the white wine, scrape up any browned bits, and allow the contents of the pot to reduce until nearly dry, 8 to 10 minutes.

4. Add the mushrooms and any accumulated juices and cook for 1 minute. Add the stock and allow to simmer slowly, uncovered. If using sausages, remove from the pot after about 30 minutes, slice into rounds, and return to the pot. Continue to simmer, uncovered, until the liquid in the pot has reduced by half and is slightly thickened, 30 to 60 minutes more (60 to 90 minutes total). Use tongs or a slotted spoon to remove the thyme bundle. Check before adjusting the seasoning, since different stocks vary greatly in saltiness. If necessary, add additional salt and pepper to taste.

5. Serve over cooked pasta, rice, or polenta.

Asian Stir-Fry with Baked Tofu over Rice

BERKSHIRE BOUNTY FARM

SERVES 2 TO 4

The bright orange and red of the carrot and pepper combined with the greens in this dish create a colorful presentation. As with any stir-fry, it is important to have all the vegetables chopped and organized before you begin cooking, which must be done quickly over high heat. Mizuna is a dark, leafy Asian vegetable that can be difficult to find. Any dark, strong-flavored greens can be used, including kale, which should be cut similarly, or arugula leaves, which can be tossed into the pan whole. Try serving this as a main dish with rice—forbidden rice is especially striking—or Asian noodles. Serve without tofu as a side dish with grilled fish or chicken, but either way, definitely consider serving with extra sauce (see Step 1). As Chef Brian Alberg suggests, "keep a stash of sauce in the fridge to add more if the rice steals from the veggies."

1 tablespoon soy sauce (or 1½ tablespoons, if sweet soy sauce is unavailable)

1 tablespoon sweet soy sauce

1 tablespoon rice vinegar

2 teaspoons light brown sugar (only if sweet soy sauce is unavailable)

½ teaspoon sesame oil

2 teaspoons canola or peanut oil, or more if the pan is large

1 teaspoon minced fresh ginger

1 teaspoon minced garlic

⅛ to ¼ teaspoon crushed red pepper flakes (optional)

1 medium carrot, sliced into matchsticks

1 red bell pepper, seeded and sliced into thin strips

1 medium bok choy or 2 baby bok choy (about 3 ounces), stems and leaves sliced separately into ¼-inch ribbons

1 scallion, top and bottom, sliced into ½-inch pieces

2 cups ½-inch-ribboned mizuna from an 8-ounce bunch (see recipe headnote)

7 ounces baked teriyaki-flavor tofu, cut into ¾-inch cubes (optional)

2 tablespoons coarsely chopped fresh cilantro

Zest of 1 lemon

Cooked rice or Asian noodles

1. Combine the soy sauce, sweet soy sauce, and vinegar in a small bowl to make the sauce and set aside. If sweet soy sauce is unavailable, increase the soy sauce to 1½ tablespoons, combine with the vinegar, and add the brown sugar. Whisk until the sugar dissolves. Set aside.

2. Heat a large sauté pan over high heat, add the oils, and heat until shimmering and fragrant. Add the ginger, garlic, and red pepper flakes (if using), stirring rapidly to prevent burning, and cook until fragrant, 30 to 60 seconds.

3. Add the carrot, red bell pepper, and bok choy stems and stir-fry for 2 to 3 minutes, until the vegetables are tender but still crisp. Add the scallion and stir-fry for 1 minute, then the bok choy leaves, and cook until slightly wilted.

4. Add the mizuna, tofu (if using), and the sauce. Stir-fry for 1 to 2 more minutes, until the mizuna wilts. Remove the pan from the heat, fold in the cilantro, and zest the lemon over the top of the stir-fry. Serve over cooked rice or Asian noodles.

Shiitake Mushroom Risotto

DEERFIELD FARM

SERVES 4 TO 6

Risotto is different from other rice dishes in at least two ways. First, it has to be stirred almost constantly to break the starches free from the rice so as to create the creamy texture for which the dish is known. Second, the stock must be at a true simmer before being added to the rice, or the texture will not be as desired.

1 ounce dried shiitake mushrooms (or other dried mushrooms, such as porcini)

4 to 5 cups chicken, beef, or vegetable stock, preferably low-sodium

3 to 4 cups water

3 tablespoons unsalted butter

1 tablespoon extra virgin olive oil, plus more if needed

½ cup finely diced shallot

¼ cup finely diced onion

1½ teaspoons salt

2 garlic cloves, thinly sliced

12 ounces shiitake mushrooms, stemmed and sliced (or oyster, cremini, or a combination)

1½ cups uncooked Arborio rice

½ cup dry white wine

1 tablespoon finely chopped fresh sage

2 tablespoons finely chopped fresh flat-leaf parsley

½ cup grated Parmesan

1 tablespoon fresh lemon juice

¼ teaspoon ground nutmeg

1. Place the dried mushrooms in a small bowl and cover with hot water. Allow to sit for 20 to 30 minutes to rehydrate. They will float, so move them around from time to time so all pieces can absorb water. When hydrated, remove the mushrooms, slice, and set aside. Strain the soaking liquid through a fine-mesh or cheesecloth-lined strainer and reserve.

2. Place the stock and reserved mushroom liquid, plus enough water to bring the total volume of liquid to 8 cups, in a medium saucepan. For ease of access, place the saucepan on the burner behind the pot you will use for the risotto. Bring to a simmer.

3. Heat 2 tablespoons of the butter and the olive oil in a wide-bottomed pot, such as a large saucepan or Dutch oven, over medium heat until shimmering

continued . . .

and fragrant. Add the shallot and onion with ¼ teaspoon of the salt, and sauté until just beginning to brown on the edges. Add the garlic and sauté for another 1 to 2 minutes, being careful not to let the garlic burn.

4. Add the fresh and rehydrated dry mushrooms along with another ¼ teaspoon of salt and sauté until they have released their juices and little moisture remains in the pan. Depending on the moisture of the mushrooms, this may require a bit more oil. Add the rice and stir with the vegetables until just the edges of the rice become translucent. Add the wine and let simmer until completely absorbed.

5. Add the hot stock mixture, 1 to 2 ladlefuls at a time, and adjust the heat to maintain a low simmer. Each time stock is added, it should just cover the rice. Stir constantly, and as the stock mixture gets absorbed into the rice, add more. When one ladleful of the hot stock mixture remains in the saucepan, add the sage to the risotto. Then, add the final ladleful to the rice and stir to combine until it is mostly absorbed. The entire process should take 20 to 25 minutes, until the rice is cooked. The rice should be tender but still have a little bite to it—al dente, and not mushy! You may not need to use all the stock; if there is any left over, it can be saved for another purpose.

6. Remove from the heat and add the remaining teaspoon of salt, remaining tablespoon of butter, and the parsley, Parmesan, lemon juice, and nutmeg, and stir to incorporate before serving. Pass extra Parmesan at the table.

CHEZ NOUS

It's because of Chef Rachel Portnoy that we always have a 5-pound bag of the unhybridized grain einkorn in our refrigerator. (We keep whole grains there to prevent them from becoming rancid.) An einkorn evangelist, she is the pastry chef and, with her husband, Chef Franck Tessier, co-owner of Chez Nous, in Lee, MA. First a confession: The einkorn Portnoy uses—and we use—is local, sort of, purchased through the Heritage Grain Conservancy, growseed.org, in the adjacent Pioneer Valley. Portnoy's route to einkorn, which she's sold us on, as well as on einkorn risotto, and the chef duo's story:

Portnoy grew up in Westport, CT, dreaming of becoming an English professor. While at Wesleyan University, she supported herself with cooking and kitchen jobs, mostly because of the influence of her Nana, her grandmother, a nutritionist who cooked for the family. "I would follow her around," says Portnoy, "this little girl writing down what she was doing, making her give me recipes." Years later, her mother would open an old cookbook and find index cards shoved in the pages, with instructions for chicken à la king and other recipes, in a seven-year-old's handwriting.

True to her passion for books, Portnoy acquired a BA in English and two MAs in English literature. While working as a teaching assistant during her second graduate school stint, her supervisor, a linguist who had been a chef and knew of Portnoy's

cooking background, urged her to check out a culinary career before returning for her PhD. Portnoy was 26, a vegetarian, and didn't want to "deal with meat," so she decided to pursue a pastry diploma at Le Cordon Bleu in London, while supporting herself teaching English.

In 1997, after working for a summer at the Wheatleigh hotel in Lenox, MA, Portnoy applied for and got a job as a pastry chef at the Point, a Relais & Château in Saranac Lake, NY, where she met Tessier, the executive chef. Because of a visa issue—he's a native of Brittany in France—he returned to a previous position at the three Michelin–starred Le Gavroche in London, along with Portnoy, who then ran into a similar problem. They moved back to the United States, got married, and eventually ended up in the Berkshires, partly because of Rachel's fond memories of the area. Portnoy opened Cakewalk, a bakery-café in Lee in 2002, while Tessier became co-chef in the same town at From Ketchup to Caviar, the spot they eventually bought and transformed into the bistro Chez Nous— "our place"—in 2005.

Back to einkorn. A Berkshires-based nutritionist told Tessier to look into eating more digestible high-protein ancient grains to preventatively lower his blood sugar. That led the couple to connect with Eli

Rogosa, who started the Heritage Grain Conservancy in Colrain, MA, and her favorite grain, einkorn. Which in turn led Tessier and Portnoy to create einkorn risotto that just happened to be on the menu the weekend we wrote this profile. (See the Einkorn Risotto with Oven-Roasted Tomatoes and Garlic, page 156.) Portnoy says alternative grains are now part of Chez Nous's offerings 90 percent of the time.

Let's not forget the restaurant also focuses on local, meaning Berkshires-sourced. Tessier gets emails twice a week about product availability from food hub Marty's Local, but Chez Nous still has to buy some of what it uses directly from Berkshire farmers—the new owner of Equinox Farm in Sheffield, for one. And Tessier and Portnoy still go to the Great Barrington farmers' market in season, especially for fruit and corn in August, which they like to select themselves.

Chez Nous also supports local causes. Every Wednesday in January and February, it holds a Community Night, donating 15 percent of the net profit to a different charity each week. "This is all about creating a community experience," Portnoy told the *Berkshire Eagle*, and it comes out of a tradition the pair started nine years ago with special themed menus every Thursday from November to May, including a recent Maple Syrup Night.

Einkorn Risotto with Oven-Roasted Tomatoes and Garlic

CHEZ NOUS

SERVES 4 TO 6

Einkorn is an ancient grain, one not hybridized over time. If you can't find einkorn locally, it can be ordered from Heritage Wheat Conservancy in Massachusetts' Pioneer Valley, at www.growseed .org. A long soak before cooking will soften the grain and help develop its flavor. This recipe, adapted from a menu staple at Chez Nous, is flexible, and can be stretched to cover more servings by topping the risotto with any grilled protein or medley of grilled seasonal vegetables. One variation for preparing the roasted garlic in the recipe: Peel the papery outside skin from a whole head of garlic and cut off the top third horizontally. Drizzle the exposed cloves in the larger portion with the olive oil, add the salt and pepper, and wrap in aluminum foil. Roast at 350°F for an hour. Serve the intact head on top of the risotto for a pretty garnish before squeezing out the roasted garlic.

1½ cups whole-grain einkorn

6½ tablespoons extra virgin olive oil, plus more for pan

1 garlic head

¾ teaspoon salt, plus more to taste

Freshly ground black pepper

1 quart cherry or grape tomatoes, halved

1 tablespoon herbes de Provence

1 large onion, finely diced (about 1 cup)

2 bay leaves

½ cup full-bodied red wine, such as merlot or cabernet sauvignon

3 cups vegetable or chicken stock

½ cup grated Parmesan

3 cups packed baby spinach

1. In a large glass or metal container, soak the einkorn in enough water to cover by 2 inches. Soak for 8 hours prior to cooking. (It is possible to cook this dish without soaking, but it will take longer and may require more liquid.)

2. Preheat the oven to 250°F. Cover a half sheet pan with foil and then oil the foil with olive oil. Lay another large sheet of foil flat on a work surface.

3. Separate the cloves of garlic from the head, peel them, and toss on the foil with 1 tablespoon of the olive oil, ¼ teaspoon of the salt and a sprinkling of pepper. Fold the foil up and over the garlic, making a tidy pouch. Place the foil packet on a corner of the prepared pan.

4. Place the tomatoes in a medium bowl and toss with the herbes de Provence, 2½ tablespoons of the olive oil, remaining ½ teaspoon of salt, and a sprinkling of pepper. Spread the tomatoes on the baking sheet, avoiding the corner where the garlic foil packet sits.

5. Roast in the oven for 1 hour, or until the garlic is soft and caramel colored and the tomatoes are juicy. Turn off the oven, leaving the garlic and tomatoes inside to keep warm until needed.

6. Meanwhile, strain the water from the einkorn grain and set the einkorn aside.

7. Heat the remaining 3 tablespoons of olive oil in a Dutch oven or heavy-bottomed stockpot over medium-high heat until shimmering and fragrant. Sauté the onion until translucent, then add the einkorn and sauté for 1 more minute. Add the bay leaves and the red wine to deglaze the pot, then add enough stock to cover the grain completely, about 2 cups. Bring to a boil and then lower the heat to a low simmer. Cover and cook slowly for 40 to 50 minutes, or more as necessary, stirring every 10 minutes and adding small amounts of additional stock each time the pot is stirred. When the grain is tender and has absorbed all the liquid in the pot, remove from the heat and leave the

cover on to let the grain rest for a few minutes. Einkorn risotto may be slightly crunchier than risotto made with Arborio rice. Remove the bay leaves and season with salt if necessary, and plenty of pepper to taste. Finish the risotto with the Parmesan and keep warm. The spinach can be added after the risotto has finished cooking and allowed to wilt, or see Step 9.

8. When the garlic is cool enough to handle, using a small food processor or pressing with the back of a fork, puree the garlic into a paste.

9. To serve, spread 1 cup of einkorn on the bottom of a warmed dish. Top each portion with ½ packed cup of baby spinach, ¾ cup of roasted tomatoes, and a dab of the roasted garlic puree before serving.

Chili with Chorizo and Butternut Squash

HOLIDAY BROOK FARM

MAKES 3 TO 4 QUARTS CHILI, SERVES 8

This is Chef Brian Alberg's interpretation of Holiday Brook Farm owner Dicken Crane's favorite chili. Chorizo varies by region, but for this recipe, be sure to use the fresh, uncooked kind, removed from its casing if necessary, and crumbled when added to the pot. In place of the meat, you can substitute vegetarian chorizo or another vegetarian sausage, cut into ½-inch pieces. Be aware that three ingredients—chorizo, chili powder, and hot sauce—can vary greatly in terms of heat, depending on the brand, so adjust the amount of chili powder and hot sauce if you prefer less spiciness. As with most chili dishes, it tastes even better the next day.

1 tablespoon extra virgin olive oil

½ cup diced yellow onion

1 cup seeded and diced green bell pepper

1 cup seeded and diced red bell pepper

5 medium garlic cloves, peeled and thinly sliced

1 pound fresh chorizo sausage or vegetarian chorizo or sausage

2 tablespoons chili powder

2 tablespoons ground cumin

1 tablespoon ground cinnamon

2 cups peeled, seeded, and ½-inch-diced butternut squash (about 1 small squash)

1 tablespoon hot sauce (Cholula or sriracha, or other favorite)

Three 15-ounce cans red kidney beans, drained and rinsed

Three 14-ounce cans diced tomatoes, with juices

2 cups chicken or vegetable stock

1 tablespoon salt

2 teaspoons freshly ground black pepper

Fresh cilantro (about ½ cup, chopped), sour cream, and coarsely chopped scallions for garnish

1. Heat the olive oil in a large, heavy-bottomed stockpot or Dutch oven until shimmering and fragrant. Add the onion, bell peppers, garlic, and chorizo and simmer, stirring occasionally, until the vegetables and sausage are cooked through, about 20 minutes.

2. Add the remaining ingredients, except the garnishes, and stir well to combine. Return the chili to a slight boil, stirring occasionally to keep it from sticking to the bottom of the pot. Lower the heat and simmer for 30 minutes more, stirring occasionally. Remove from the heat and allow to cool for a few minutes before serving with the garnishes.

Bean Chili

CARETAKER FARM

SERVES 6

An unusual ingredient for chili—kohlrabi—lends its sweetness and light crunch to this dish. If you can't find the vegetable, broccoli stems can be substituted. Just remove the florets and reserve for another dish, and chop the stems in small pieces before adding to the chili in Step 2 (they don't need roasting). The bulgur adds body and helps make the chili nice and thick.

1 pound whole kohlrabi, peeled and ¼-inch diced
   (about 2 cups)

3 tablespoons extra virgin olive oil

Salt

2 cups chopped onion

3 garlic cloves, minced

2 teaspoons ground cumin

2 teaspoons chili powder

2 tablespoons hot sauce

2 green bell peppers, seeded and chopped

1 cup vegetable stock

Two 28-ounce cans diced tomatoes, with juices

2 cups corn kernels, fresh or frozen and thawed

One 14-ounce can black beans, drained and rinsed

One 14-ounce can red kidney beans,
   drained and rinsed

½ cup uncooked bulgur

Chopped fresh cilantro or sour cream for garnish

1. Preheat the oven to 450°F. Position a rack in the center of the oven. Toss the kohlrabi in a bowl with 1 tablespoon of the olive oil and a sprinkling of salt. Place the kohlrabi in a single layer on a foil-lined rimmed baking sheet and roast in the oven for 15 minutes, stirring once during cooking. When the

kohlrabi has started to soften and has a little color, remove from the oven and set aside.

2. Heat the remaining 2 tablespoons of olive oil in a large stockpot or Dutch oven over medium heat until shimmering and fragrant. Sauté the onion, garlic, cumin, chili powder, and hot sauce in the oil for 5 to 7 minutes. When the onion is soft, stir in the bell peppers and the roasted kohlrabi and sauté for 5 minutes. Add the vegetable stock, tomatoes with their juices, corn, and both types of beans, and bring to a simmer. Cover the pot and lower the heat to maintain the simmer for 20 minutes.

3. Add the bulgur, mixing well, cover the pot, and continue to simmer for 15 minutes, stirring occasionally, to allow the bulgur to soften. Add salt to taste before serving, and garnish with fresh cilantro or a dollop of sour cream.

KRIPALU CENTER FOR YOGA & HEALTH

Kripalu Center for Yoga & Health's dining hall seats 300, and is no ordinary restaurant, as you'll see from the volume and types of ingredients it uses. In 2018, the Kripalu Kitchen served 388,057 meals; chopped 37,825 pounds of carrots, 3,600 gallons of cauliflower, and 13,500 of kale; and prepared 3,075 pounds of chickpeas. When speaking about Kripalu, "restaurant" is sort of a misnomer, although you can drop in for meals and don't have to do yoga or a health workshop. Based in Stockbridge, MA, Kripalu is the largest yoga retreat center in North America, hosting 45,000 guests a year.

While the menu is mostly plant-based, Kripalu fights the perception it only serves vegan/vegetarian food. A recent menu offered Cornmeal Crusted Flounder or Tofu with Roast Poblano Avocado Relish, and BBQ Pulled Turkey or Jackfruit, along with such vegan sides as Harissa Cauliflower and, of course, sautéed kale. (Check out the recipe for Grilled Harissa Cauliflower with Corn and Avocado Relish, page 91.) A sandwich bar offers vegetarian and nonvegetarian fillings—even peanut butter and jelly. "We don't want

to freak people out too much," Executive Chef Jeremy Rock Smith says jokingly.

What this means for farm-to-table, given Kripalu's scale: effort and commitment. Incorporating these values, as well as Ayurvedic practices, into the Kitchen's operation is part of its mission. Smith translates that into a menu emphasizing seasonal, organic—it's 85 to 90 percent—and local where possible, with patrons eating to match their nutrition profile, or dosha. The same tenets ground Smith's recent book, *The Kripalu Kitchen: Nourishing Food for Body and Soul.*

Kripalu buys through food hub Marty's Local and directly from some 15 to 20 farmers and food producers, jockeying between using the hub and working directly, with 20 trucks going in and out every day. "It can be tricky," Smith says. "I have farmers coming at me and they're saying, 'I can give you five tons a week' and I'm like, this will last a quarter of a meal." On the other hand, because Kripalu can handle volume, it is able to absorb bumper crops, such as the call from a farmer who had 200 pounds of organic zucchini. "We need to dump this. We'll give it to you at this price. All right. Cool," Smith says.

Smith does wish small farms would offer more product choice. "We're like, so what's everybody got? Kale, kale, kale. Guys, let's diversify here." But part of the reason there's less range of offerings is that it's easier to grow certain crops, and others have more appealing growing seasons, heading way into late fall. That's kale. In an article in TownVibe.com, Smith jokes that "my children don't know what kale is because I'm told it's not good to bring your work home with you."

We asked Smith how Kripalu guests respond to eating a whole foods, local diet, which for many, is a change from their more conventional regimen. "Honestly, I get people that say, 'My stomach's upset for three days! I'm dying!' It's called fiber," he says with his characteristic humor. Another common reaction

is "I'm not eating as much as I normally would. I feel fuller sooner than I do when I eat at home," again because they're eating a less-processed diet. And as for eating local, he thinks guests feel good to be part of an operation that respects the environment. Kripalu is a longtime composter and all preconsumer veggie scraps are picked up daily by a local farm and used for livestock.

In his own cooking, Smith emphasizes simplicity. Comfort food. Rustic food. "Look at the best food in the world, that's what it was. Country-style peasant. That's kind of what we're doing here." (Check out the Pinto Bean, Butternut Squash, and Corn Curry, page 162.) Smith wants Kripalu guests to be able to go home and cook what they've eaten.

Since Kripalu is a volume cafeteria-style operation, Smith misses using more intricate cheffing skills that smaller establishments would demand. He's a Culinary Institute of America (CIA)–trained chef who had moved to the Berkshires at age 10 and ultimately cooked at many of the area's top restaurants. He started at Kripalu in 2010 as chef de cuisine before becoming its executive chef. "How I envision a meal on a plate is very different from how it comes out on the line, and I'm restricted because it's a buffet." But, he jokes once again, at Kripalu "we garnish with a smile."

Pinto Bean, Butternut Squash, and Corn Curry

KRIPALU CENTER FOR YOGA & HEALTH

SERVES 4

This recipe is adapted from one Chef Jeremy Rock Smith serves at Kripalu Center for Yoga & Health. Canned chickpeas or pinto beans can be substituted for cooked dried pinto beans, if desired, in this hearty vegetable curry. Serve over brown rice.

1 tablespoon coconut oil

¼ cup diced sweet onion

1 cup peeled, seeded, and diced butternut squash (about 10 ounces)

Kernels from 1 ear of corn, or frozen and thawed (about ¾ cup)

1½ teaspoons ground coriander

1½ teaspoons ground cumin

1½ teaspoons garam masala

1½ teaspoons chili powder

1½ teaspoons minced garlic

1½ teaspoons grated fresh ginger

1½ cups diced canned tomatoes, with juices, or one 14-ounce can, with juices

2 cups cooked dried pinto beans, or one 28-ounce can, drained and rinsed

1½ cups coconut milk (one 14-ounce can)

2 tablespoons chopped fresh cilantro, plus more for garnish

½ teaspoon salt

¼ teaspoon freshly ground black pepper

4 lime wedges for garnish

1. Heat the coconut oil in a large, heavy-bottomed stockpot or Dutch oven. Sauté the onion in the oil until translucent. Add the squash and sauté for 5 to 7 minutes, until "al dente," as Smith says. Add the corn and cook for 2 more minutes.

2. Add the coriander, cumin, garam masala, and chili powder and sauté for 1 minute. Add the garlic and ginger and sauté until fragrant, about 1 minute. Add the tomatoes with their juices, beans, and coconut milk and simmer over low heat for 20 to 25 minutes, until the squash is soft.

3. Add the cilantro and adjust the seasoning with the salt and pepper. Serve over rice, with a sprinkling of cilantro on top, and a lime wedge on the side of each plate for garnish.

PRAIRIE WHALE

The day Prairie Whale's minuscule first order from global food distributor Sysco pulled up in an 18-wheeler on Main Street outside the Great Barrington, MA, restaurant, was the day owner Mark Firth dug his heels in on buying local. "This is not gonna work." His accomplice in all things local, Chef Stephen Browning, echoes, "We had a heart attack when the truck actually showed up."

The pair fiercely promote buying local because it strengthens community and regional self-reliance. When we ask Firth why the home cook should use locally sourced ingredients, he says, "You want the deep answer? You fix tires and you go to the farmers' market and that's the person whose tires you just fixed. Now, you're buying his vegetables. It's the whole package. Keeps the economy in the town." In fact, local farmers are often seen dining at Prairie Whale. "They get a farmers' discount. They eat their own food, which is great," he says.

The duo are also all things farm-to-table, but again, both agree that the phrase is losing its meaning. "You can't be opening cans," Firth says. As a restaurateur, first in Brooklyn, "we just went to the farmers' market, made friends with the farmers, then they delivered straight to us and that was it. It wasn't a word. There was no bandwagon to get on; we were just doing our thing. And Steve's from the same school as me." For Browning, sourcing from local farms is the only way he can guarantee the best ingredients, which, he says, is not a fad. "Exactly," says Firth, emphasizing that the true "fad" is the decades we've been cooking with "bad ingredients and chemicals."

Firth grew up in Zambia, where his family indeed ate canned food from China because of a trade deal between the Zambian and Chinese governments. He eventually moved to the United States and, according to the *New York Times*, "helped define the Brooklyn dining scene of the aughts" as a cofounder of Diner and Marlow & Sons. He then bought an 82-acre farm in Monterey, MA, permanently moving in 2011 with his wife, Bettina Schwartz, and kids. Firth thought he'd farm, but when he realized "I would have gone bust in a year or two," he started Prairie Whale, first named Bell & Anchor, alluding to Herman Melville, who penned *Moby Dick* in the Berkshires. "We needed the table to go with the farm," Firth told the *Times*. The CIA-trained Browning, who had worked for Firth in Brooklyn, followed him to Massachusetts.

To buy locally and cook fresh necessitates a certain amount of "winging it," but Firth and Browning delight in the opportunity. What gets picked today shows up on the menu that same day or the next. Even a dish Browning shared with us, which we've called Local Braised Beans (page 164), came with instructions for improvising.

Firth and Browning mention the two usual suspects that hamper even the most dogged, farm-to-table proponents: lack of breadth and volume of ingredients available. "We get a lot of tomatoes but we don't get snap peas," Firth said when we first spoke. "Finding local asparagus in quantity is almost impossible. I know it's hard because I grow it at the farm and I get 10 a day for two weeks." But just recently, he told us that "change is afoot! A lot of farmers are specifically asking us what we are short of and making an effort to grow those things." It helps that Firth sources some of Prairie Whale's ingredients from his own farm, although he says that he's a "small cog" in the larger wheel of farms they use. The other deterrence to local sourcing is the realities of restaurant pricing. While Firth is happy to pay farmers he likes for what Prairie Whale needs, he can't take on an ingredient that pushes a menu price over the top. He compliments Browning: "I've never worked with a chef like Steve who nails his food cost every month."

Local Braised Beans

PRAIRIE WHALE

SERVES 8 TO 10

Prairie Whale's chef Stephen Browning says any bean can be used in this adapted recipe but he often uses either of two local varieties, Vermont Cranberry or Marfax. What makes this savory dish so delicious, aside from using fresh local beans, is slowly braising them. And, consistent with Browning's emphasis on improvising when cooking, he notes, "it is a great dish to add seasonal produce from the farmers' market or CSA that people don't know what to do with, peppers, Swiss chard, kale. I would like to encourage people to cook with ingredients that are in season together because that alone is usually enough to bind them, and beans are a great neutral way to do that. Use mushrooms as well. I can't think of anything that doesn't go with beans or mushrooms."

1 large onion, trimmed, peeled, and quartered

1 tablespoon extra virgin olive oil

3 garlic cloves, minced

1 pound dried cranberry, cannellini, or pinto beans, or a bean of your choice, rinsed and picked over for grit

1 cup peeled and 1-inch-diced carrots

1 cup 1-inch-diced celery

10 sprigs thyme, tied together with kitchen twine

¼ to ½ teaspoon red pepper flakes (optional)

5 cups vegetable stock, plus 1 cup more if needed

Salt and freshly ground black pepper

½ cup chopped fresh herbs, such as thyme, parsley, tarragon, or oregano

1. Place an oven rack in the highest position in the oven. Preheat the broiler. Coat the onion with 1½ teaspoons of the olive oil, place on a foil-lined, rimmed baking sheet, and slide under the broiler.

Allow the onion pieces to become lightly charred, turning as needed with tongs to get good color on all sides. Remove from the oven and set aside to cool. When cool enough to handle, cut into 1-inch pieces.

2. Move the rack to the middle or lower part of the oven and set the oven to bake at 300°F.

3. Heat the remaining 1½ teaspoons of olive oil in a large Dutch oven or other large, oven-safe, lidded pot over medium heat. When the oil is shimmering and fragrant, add the garlic and sauté until lightly golden, 1 to 2 minutes. Add the dried beans and stir to coat in the garlicky oil.

4. Add the onion, carrot, celery, and bunch of thyme to the pot of beans. If desired, add the red pepper flakes for a spicier dish. Add 5 cups of stock to the pot and stir to combine. Cover the pot and bring to a low simmer over medium heat. When a low simmer has been reached, stir the beans in the pot to redistribute and transfer the covered pot to the oven.

5. Cook the beans in the oven for 45 minutes, stirring the pot every 15 minutes so that all the beans get redistributed at regular intervals. As the beans cook, if it looks as if they need a little more liquid or if they start to stick to the bottom, add the remaining cup of stock. The beans should be close to done after 45 minutes, but if they are larger in size or have been stored for a long time, they may require additional time in the oven, as long as 90 minutes or more. To check for doneness, see whether the beans have smooth skins, and taste a few to test whether they are tender and cooked through but not mushy. If the beans are not quite done, stir to redistribute in the pot and continue to cook for 15-minute intervals, checking repeatedly for doneness. Taste for seasoning and add salt and pepper to taste.

6. When the beans are done, remove from the oven and leave the covered pot to rest for 30 minutes. This will allow the beans to soak up more liquid. Use tongs to take out the thyme bundle, add the chopped fresh herbs, and stir to combine. Serve warm.

White Bean Dip

GOOD DOGS FARM

SERVES 6 TO 8

Serve this hummus-like dip with vegetables, points of grilled bread, or crackers. It's lighter and less dense than the traditional version made with chickpeas.

A little more than 1 cup (7 to 8 ounces) dried navy beans or other white bean; 1 pound cooked beans; or two 15-ounce cans of beans

1½ teaspoons salt, plus more to taste

¼ cup chopped scallions, green and white parts (about 2 scallions)

¼ cup fresh lemon juice

2 tablespoons packed coarsely chopped fresh cilantro

¼ teaspoon ground cumin

1 garlic clove, peeled

⅛ teaspoon freshly ground black pepper

6 to 8 tablespoons extra virgin olive oil, or enough to make the dip smooth and light

1. If using cooked or canned beans, skip to Step 2. Rinse the dried beans and pick over carefully for grit. Place the beans in a 1-gallon heavy-bottomed stockpot or a Dutch oven and add enough water to cover the beans by 3 inches. Add ½ teaspoon of the salt and bring the beans to a boil over medium-high heat. Then, cover the pot, lower the heat, and simmer for 90 minutes, or until the beans are tender and cooked through, adding water to the pot if necessary. Drain the beans through a colander and allow to cool slightly. Weigh out 1 pound of cooked beans to use in the recipe.

2. If using canned beans, drain and rinse thoroughly before weighing out 1 pound.

3. Using a blender, food processor, or an immersion blender and a bowl, puree the cooked beans, scallions, lemon juice, cilantro, cumin, garlic, and pepper. Add the remaining 1 teaspoon of salt if using dried beans, but salt to taste, especially if using canned beans. (Canned beans already contain sodium, although rinsing them before using will reduce the amount.) Start by adding 4 tablespoons of the olive oil slowly in a thin stream through the opening of the processor lid with the processor running, and continue to add more until the paste is smooth and dip-like. Taste for consistency and add more olive oil through the lid with the processor running if a thinner consistency is desired. Adjust the seasoning, if necessary.

POULTRY AND FISH

WHEN PIGS FLY FARM

Andy Snyder, co-owner with his wife, Sandy, of When Pigs Fly Farm in Sandisfield, MA, tells a story about his off-farm job as a crew leader for a tree company. It also gives insight into how his work outdoors inspires him. He was at his synagogue in Pittsfield, MA, where he and his family have been congregants for four generations, listening to the rabbi who said he was biking on the Rail Trail and moved by a magnificent sunrise. He stopped to say a prayer. "It really struck home when he said that," Andy says, "so I walked up to him after synagogue and said, 'Tell me the prayer. Because I feel the exact same way every day when I go to work. I mean, the outdoors is my office.'" The rabbi shared the prayer with Andy, who says that he and his crew now say it when they get to work. "Everybody says, 'You know, what a great idea.'"

Sandy offers a similar anecdote. When she is outside weeding, "all of a sudden the Saturday Sabbath service runs through my head."

Andy and Sandy *are* the farm. One daughter is at college studying foreign languages; the other about to study chemical engineering. Andy's full-time off-farm work leaves a lot in his wife's hands, but his schedule is less daunting than when we first met them. Andy used to sleep from 6 p.m. to midnight, leaving the house at 1 a.m. for his first job, picking up newspaper bundles in Chicopee, MA, and dropping them off in Great Barrington for other carriers. He'd get back by 7 a.m. to drive a school bus. Then, he'd farm. He did it for three or four years, but said he was a "zombie." "If you're a small family farm," he says, "it is impossible to make it work just farming. And, God knows, we tried for 10 years."

His wife grew up in a Polish family that grew much of their own food. Stuffed cabbage was a favorite, and Sandy, who loves cooking, suggested using collard greens instead to fold up meat, rice, and roasted vegetables. (See the beef and vegetarian versions of Stuffed Collard Greens Golabki-Style, page 196.) Andy, a college biology major, landed an internship with a professor who had a Shrewsbury, MA, farm in the '70s that

whetted his interest. After college, he was doing science research when the government cut funding; he moved back with his parents and worked in their Pittsfield hardware store. The couple married in 1992 and started looking for land, knowing they'd like to farm. When they bought their 16 acres in '94, Andy told himself, "when I hit 50, it's now or never." He quit his job as a hardware store manager in Great Barrington.

When Pigs Fly gives off an informal, welcoming vibe. It is a diversified organic and sustainable produce farm, and the only one we visited that raises peacocks (they use the feathers to make Christmas wreaths). There are no fields, just sections of plants growing in a compact area. When we visited, different varieties of kale surrounded a low-lying rock wall. Kohlrabi grew in the middle. Their farmstand at the end of the driveway along with their 15-person CSA are the primary sales outlets, the Snyders having decided that 15 years of displaying at farmers' markets was enough.

When we visited, the couple raised chickens, Muscovy ducks, and Narragansett turkeys but gave them up temporarily. "We've had birds for 20 years and the ground was getting totally depleted," Andy says. "We sold off the flocks last fall, and are letting the ground go fallow this year to recoup." Even in the Torah, he says, again tying farming to his spirituality, it says that land should lie fallow every seven years. "We're a little late."

Another important principle for Sandy and Andy: keeping their prices low. He says they haven't changed since they started farming, except for eggs. "Our theory is that organic doesn't have to be expensive. We're not catering to rich people here. Everyone has the right to have great food at a reasonable price. If they can't afford it, we give them a break."

Andy is optimistic about the future of small farms, and thinks supermarkets are cooperating, offering more local produce. Consumers are also coming around, realizing the value of local food. "If you buy green beans at our stand, you'll buy them the same day they were picked," Sandy says. An egg they sell is only a day or two old compared to ones at the supermarket, which Andy says can be up to 30. "They're still safe to eat, but crack both open and the farm yolk is bright orange, the one from the supermarket is yellow."

Chicken Cacciatore with Polenta

WHEN PIGS FLY FARM

SERVES 4 TO 6

A belly-warming recipe for a crisp fall day, this braised chicken cacciatore pairs well with polenta, for which a recipe is included. The rustic Italian chicken dish perfectly showcases bell peppers at their peak flavor. Many farmers sell whole chickens that will need to be cut into pieces for this recipe, but purchased chicken parts from the store also work.

One 4- to 5-pound chicken, or the equivalent in chicken pieces

1 teaspoon salt, plus more to taste

½ teaspoon freshly ground black pepper, plus more to taste

2 tablespoons extra virgin olive oil, plus more if needed

1 red onion, thinly sliced into half-moons

2 large green bell peppers, seeded and thinly sliced

2 large red bell peppers, seeded and thinly sliced

1 pound fresh mushrooms (button, cremini, or any favorite), sliced

4 large garlic cloves, minced

One 28-ounce can diced tomatoes, with juices

2 cups chicken stock

2 tablespoons chopped fresh flat-leaf parsley

⅓ cup chopped fresh basil leaves

Polenta:

2 cups chicken stock

1 cup whole milk

1 cup white or yellow cornmeal

2 tablespoons unsalted butter, cut into several pieces

Salt and freshly ground black pepper

1. If using a whole chicken, begin by cutting it into 8 pieces, or ask the butcher to do this. To break down a whole chicken, cut off the leg quarters and divide into drumsticks and thighs. Cut off the wings close to where they meet the rib cage. Cut out the back, and with the chicken skin side down, pry open the chest, so that the underside of the sternum is exposed. Cut through the rib bones on either side of the sternum to make two separate breast pieces. Cut each of the breast pieces equally across the middle, parallel to the rib bones. (If using chicken pieces, cut each breast in two as well.) This should make up 2 drumsticks, 2 thighs, and 4 breast pieces in total. Save the back, wings, and sternum for a future batch of chicken stock. Season the chicken pieces with the salt and black pepper and set aside.

2. Heat the olive oil in a large, heavy-bottomed stockpot or large Dutch oven over medium heat until shimmering and fragrant. Sauté the red onion, bell peppers, mushrooms, and garlic, stirring frequently, until lightly caramelized, 8 to 10 minutes. Transfer to a bowl and set aside.

3. Using tongs, and working in batches if necessary, place the chicken pieces in the pot, skin side down, and brown until the skin is crispy and golden. Turn the pieces over and brown on the other side. If working in batches, transfer the first pieces to a plate, and add a tablespoon more oil, if necessary, to brown the next batch of chicken. A dark crust, called a fond, will appear on the bottom of the pot. When all the chicken pieces are browned on both sides, set aside on the plate.

4. Add the tomatoes and chicken stock to the pot and gently use the edge of a wooden spoon to deglaze the fond from the bottom of the pot. Return the chicken pieces and any accumulated juices to the pot and simmer for 15 minutes. Return the

vegetable mixture to the pot along with the parsley and basil and stir to combine. Cover and simmer for 1 hour, stirring periodically to prevent the sauce from sticking. If the sauce is not reducing enough, adjust the lid to cover partially, or remove the lid entirely for part of the cooking time until the sauce reaches your desired consistency. Taste for seasoning and adjust with salt and black pepper, if needed.

5. When the chicken is done simmering, start the polenta: Bring the chicken stock and milk to a boil in a medium saucepan over medium-high heat. Using a whisk to keep the liquid moving constantly, add the cornmeal in a thin stream to avoid clumping. Still whisking constantly, lower the heat and simmer for 10 to 15 minutes. It may be more practical to switch from the whisk to a wooden spoon as the polenta thickens. When the polenta is the consistency of thick mashed potatoes, it is ready to come off the heat. Finish the polenta by mixing in the butter and salt and black pepper to taste.

6. To serve, scoop ½ cup of the polenta into a dish or bowl, and place one or two pieces of chicken on each. Top with a heaping ladleful of the vegetables and sauce from the pot. Serve hot.

Garlic Chicken

WILDSTONE FARM

SERVES 4 TO 6

This oh-so-savory roasted chicken is perfect to cook in winter when its aroma fills the house, uplifting spirits dampened by the cold.

2 tablespoons extra virgin olive oil, plus more for pan

One 3½- to 4-pound chicken

1 garlic head (10 to 15 cloves)

Zest and juice of 1 lemon

1 teaspoon kosher salt, plus more to sprinkle

8 sprigs thyme

4 sprigs rosemary

1 sweet onion, peeled and quartered (about 5 ounces)

1. Preheat the oven to 425°F. Lightly oil a 9-by-13-inch roasting pan that will fit the chicken comfortably. Lightly oil a rack that fits inside the roasting pan or create a rack out of a few thin coils of tightly rolled aluminum foil. This roasting rack will help keep the chicken up out of the juices as it cooks.

2. Rinse the chicken in cold water, inside and out, and pat dry with paper towels. Place the chicken, breast side up, on the rack in the roasting pan.

3. Break apart and peel each garlic clove. Mince or crush them through a garlic press into a small bowl. Mix the garlic paste with the lemon zest and juice, and salt and set aside. Remove half of the thyme and rosemary leaves from their stems, chop finely, and set aside in a pinch bowl, about 1 tablespoon total.

4. Gently fold back the wings of the chicken behind its shoulders, tucking them in. Press hard to massage and pinch the skin all over to create space between the meat and the skin. When the skin can be pinched away from the meat easily, take a small knife and make a slit at the edge of each side of the breast. Slide your fingers between the skin and the meat to create a small pocket. Using your fingers, push some of the garlic mixture into the pocket between the skin and the meat, and coat the meat under the skin. Make a similar slit in the skin of each thigh, and push more of the garlic mixture into the slits, using your fingers. Rub all over the outside of the chicken's skin with any remaining garlic mixture, and pour any remaining liquid from the mixture into the cavity of the chicken. Drizzle the skin on the outside with the 2 tablespoons of olive oil, and sprinkle with the chopped thyme and rosemary plus salt to taste.

5. Place the onion quarters and the whole thyme and rosemary sprigs in the cavity of the chicken, being careful not to overstuff. Using a length of kitchen twine, with the chicken breast side up, tie the ends of the legs together.

6. Roast the chicken in the oven for 15 minutes, then lower the oven temperature to 350°F and roast for 20 minutes per pound (70 to 90 minutes), basting the chicken in its own juices at least twice during this time. The chicken should be done when the drumsticks jiggle or move easily and the skin is crisp and golden brown. A meat thermometer inserted at the thickest part of the thigh should read at least 165°F.

7. Remove the chicken from the oven and allow to rest for 15 minutes before carving. Serve the delicious juices on the side for each person to pour over his or her serving.

CHEF BRIAN ALBERG, THE RED LION INN AND MAIN STREET HOSPITALITY

Chef Brian Alberg characterizes his cooking style as "simple," one that lets "the ingredients speak for themselves." A true voice and supporter of the Berkshire farmer—he was president of local agriculture advocate Berkshire Grown and on its board for years—he says, "Don't take a beautiful carrot in season and cover it with curry. It loses a sense of the terroir of where it grew."

Alberg candidly admits that chefs are often stereotyped as having a "holier-than-thou attitude," but we can't imagine someone farther from that image, more approachable, more collaborative, than he is. Vice president of culinary development for Main Street Hospitality, Alberg oversees the group's restaurants at the Red Lion, which it owns and where he served as executive chef, Hancock Shaker Village's Seeds Market Cafe, Eat on North at Hotel on North, the Tap House at Shaker Mill, and off-premise catering. He'd prefer to give chefs he works with accolades rather than himself. Alberg is in turn grateful to his mentors, the late Jean Morel, owner of the former L'Hostellerie Bressane in Hillsdale, NY, and Brad Wagstaff and

Leslie Miller, former owners of The Old Inn On The Green, New Marlborough, MA, where he served as executive sous chef after graduating from the CIA, the youngest in his class. Alberg says Berkshire chefs he knows "care more about shedding light on the region than on an individual property because it benefits all of us."

He is a fierce proponent not only of area farmers but of the region and its traditions. He left the Old Inn to become an executive chef in Westchester County, NY, then jumped to the Connecticut shore's Saybrook Point Inn. But the pull of his roots—Copake, NY—led him back to the Berkshires. He says he treasures the region's beauty and while Old Saybrook was right on the ocean, "I missed the link between chefs and food and farms and family . . . When I went to Old Saybrook, I could get fish but it wasn't a huge spot for local vegetables. I missed the collaboration."

When he started cheffing in the '80s, farm to table was not exactly the credo of the times. His orientation at first was about cooking "cool California stuff," and

trucking in wild mushrooms and truffles. Now, Alberg couldn't be keener on bolstering area farms, concerned that if the Berkshire landscape changes from agricultural to blacktop the region will lose its visitors. "I've always tried to go the extra mile to ensure that farms stay farms. If that means buying a little extra at a little higher price, it's worth it. And spending time to make that happen is invaluable." Ultimately, Alberg envisions the Berkshires not only as a cultural mecca but a food magnet as well.

Toward that end, as the Red Lion's executive chef, the position that lured him back in 2004, Alberg was set on both maintaining its status as a local icon and upgrading its offerings as it jumped into a new century. On the one hand, he told the *Berkshire Edge* that "the Red Lion has its own history and persona, and I would never dream of taking turkey or prime rib or apple pie off the menu," yet he is on top of culinary trends. As *Edible Berkshires* wrote, "with tattoos, piercings and a love of motorcycles, Alberg might not be the most likely face of a quintessentially New England inn, but he has nevertheless become synonymous with the Red Lion's sterling reputation beyond the Berkshires," a position he helps to cement with repeated appearances at the James Beard Foundation in New York City.

We can't end without mentioning Alberg in another Berkshire culinary role, specifically as a founding chef of the Railroad Street Youth Project in Great Barrington, which gives at-risk youth the opportunity to explore culinary arts under the tutelage of a professional chef. Over 10 years, Alberg says, the project has probably touched 100 kids, about 20 of whom have continued in the field. But for all the participants, he says, "it teaches them camaraderie, respect, attention to detail."

It's intriguing to think that one can spend hours discussing recipes with someone and still uncover biographical tidbits. To wit: (1) Alberg attended nursing school for two winters as his backup plan; and (2) if he weren't a chef, he would be a woodworker. On the other hand, he's probably not leaving the food industry anytime soon. If there's any doubt, his plethora of food tattoos—carrots, a pig, even the abbreviation "USDA"—attest to that. And it's also unlikely he's ditching the Berkshires, given yet one more tattoo: "413," the county's area code.

Chicken Pot Pie

THE RED LION INN

SERVES 4 TO 6

This traditional chicken pot pie with carrots, parsnips, and green peas, is adapted from a recipe by Chef Brian Alberg, former executive chef of the venerable Red Lion Inn. Try using parsnips that have been through a few cold snaps outside in the early winter since these will be noticeably sweeter than those harvested in the fall. This is also a great recipe for using leftover cooked chicken.

3 cups chicken stock, plus more if needed

1 pound boneless, skinless chicken breasts (2 to 3 breasts), or 2 cups cubed cooked chicken

6 tablespoons unsalted butter, plus more for baking dish

¼ cup all-purpose flour

2 tablespoons minced fresh sage, or 2 teaspoons dried

Salt and freshly ground black pepper

1 cup peeled and small-diced carrot

¾ cup peeled and small-diced parsnips

1 cup small-diced onions

1 cup frozen peas

1 frozen puff pastry sheet, enough to cover a 7-by-11-inch baking dish, thawed

1 large egg

2 tablespoons whole milk

1. Pour the chicken stock in a large stockpot and bring to a boil over medium-high heat. Then, place the chicken breasts in the hot stock and immediately lower the heat to maintain a constant simmer. Cover the stockpot and gently simmer the breasts until cooked through, about 20 minutes.

2. Meanwhile, make the roux for the sauce. Melt 4 tablespoons of the butter in a large saucepan over medium heat. Whisk in the flour and half of the sage. Cook, whisking frequently, until slightly golden in color and the consistency of very wet fine sand, 4 to 5 minutes. Remove from the heat.

3. Remove the stockpot from the heat. Using tongs or a slotted spoon, remove the breasts from the stock, reserving the stock, and place on a plate to cool until safe for handling.

4. Preheat the oven to 350°F. Set an oven rack in the center of the oven. Butter the bottom and sides of a 7-by-11-inch baking dish or other baking dish with a capacity of 2 quarts.

5. When the chicken is cool, dice into ½-inch pieces (this should yield about 2 cups) and set aside.

6. Measure the reserved stock in a 4-cup measuring cup. Add enough additional stock to bring the volume up to 3 cups total.

7. Using a wire whisk to keep the roux moving constantly, slowly add the 3 cups of chicken stock, ¼ cup at a time. At first, the sauce will clump together, but continue to whisk constantly and add the stock slowly until the sauce becomes smooth. Return the saucepan to medium heat and simmer until thickened, 5 to 7 minutes, whisking frequently so the sauce does not stick to the bottom. Remove from the heat, taste, and add salt and pepper as needed.

8. Melt the remaining 2 tablespoons of butter in a large skillet. Add the carrots, parsnips, and onion and sauté gently, stirring occasionally, until the vegetables are tender and the onion is translucent, 8 to 10 minutes. Remove from the heat.

9. Add the diced chicken and the remaining sage to the skillet and mix gently. Add the peas, stirring gently to combine. Add salt and pepper to taste. Pour the chicken mixture into the prepared baking dish and spread evenly into the corners. Pour the sauce on top and spread evenly.

10. Unroll the puff pastry. If it is not big enough to cover the baking dish, gently use a rolling pin to stretch it until the right size is achieved. Carefully lay the puff pastry over the top of the baking dish to cover all the filling. Pinch the edges of the pastry along the rim of the dish to seal the chicken mixture inside. With a sharp knife, carefully cut three X-shaped slits into the top of the puff pastry so that steam can escape from the filling as it cooks.

11. Prepare an egg wash by beating together the egg and milk in a small bowl. Brush the egg wash all over the puff pastry, avoiding any exposed filling. Not all of the egg wash will be used.

12. Place the dish in the center of a foil-lined, rimmed baking sheet. Place in the center of the oven and bake for 35 to 40 minutes, until the puff pastry is golden brown on top, and the filling is bubbling.

13. Remove from the oven and allow the pot pie to cool for 20 minutes before serving, so that the filling and gravy can thicken. Use a sharp knife to cut through the pastry topping and a spoon to ladle the filling into serving bowls.

Aloo Gobi (With or Without Chicken)

HAWK DANCE FARM

SERVES 4 TO 6

This hearty and flavorful dish is a beloved vegetarian staple from India that the Hawk Dance farmers love to make (without chicken—they're vegan!). For those who want a little more protein, substitute 2 cups of the potatoes with chicken or "vegetarian" chicken.

- 1 tablespoon extra virgin olive oil
- 1 serrano chile, stemmed, seeded, and sliced into half-moons
- 2 garlic cloves, minced
- 1 tablespoon grated fresh ginger
- 2 teaspoons ground coriander
- 2 teaspoons ground cumin
- ½ teaspoon ground turmeric
- 2 cups 1-inch-diced boneless, skinless chicken breast, or "vegetarian" chicken (optional)
- 1 small head cauliflower, stem and florets cut into 1-inch pieces (about 4 cups)
- 2 to 2½ pounds Yukon Gold potatoes, peeled and cut into 1-inch cubes (4 to 6 cups)
- 1½ cups water
- 2 teaspoons kosher salt
- 2 limes, 1 zested, the other cut into thick wedges for serving
- 3 tablespoons chopped fresh cilantro

1. Heat the olive oil in a large, heavy-bottomed stockpot or Dutch oven over medium heat until shimmering and fragrant. Add the serrano chile and sauté for 1 to 2 minutes, then add the garlic, ginger, coriander, cumin, and turmeric, stirring briskly and constantly to bring out the oils in the spices, watching closely to keep from scorching.

2. Add the chicken (if using) and stir to coat fully with the spices. Allow the chicken to cook for 10 minutes, just enough to get a little color on the edges of the meat.

3. Add the cauliflower and potatoes—the amount of the latter depends on whether you are using chicken or not, as discussed in the headnote—and stir, coating with the spices. Deglaze the pan with the water and mix in the salt. Cover the pot and simmer until the vegetables are tender, and the chicken (if using) is fully cooked, about 15 minutes.

4. The sauce should thicken and reduce and coat all the pieces of vegetable and chicken. If not, simmer, uncovered, for an additional 5 to 10 minutes, until the sauce has thickened. Sprinkle with the lime zest and cilantro and stir them into the sauce. Serve in a bowl with a lime wedge for a nice acidic kick.

SQUARE ROOTS FARM

When we last caught up with Michael Gallagher, owner of Square Roots Farm in Lanesborough, MA, with his wife, Ashley Amsden, he was delivering eggs to Guido's Fresh Marketplace, Berkshire Mountain Bakery, and the Berkshire Food Co-op. We told him we purchased his eggs at Guido's. Which location? he asked. In Pittsfield, we answered, and said, "Please don't run out."

We aren't alone. "People are getting used to the idea that there is a difference in food quality, that not every egg is the same, that some may be better for you," says Gallagher. The Square Roots website links to a *Mother Earth News* test favorably comparing pasture-raised eggs with USDA nutritional data for the commercial kind, the former with less cholesterol and saturated fat, more vitamins A and E, beta-carotene and omega-3s.

Aside from in stores, Gallagher says you can find his eggs—and his other products—at farmers' markets, through an online ordering system for pickup at Square Roots, self-serve at the farm, and through CSA-like shares.

Just because we're customers, let's not fixate on eggs. The 185-acre farm is now entering its 10th year and primarily sells pasture-raised pork, chicken, Thanksgiving turkeys, and 100 percent grass-fed beef. Gallagher and Amsden also grow vegetables for sale at farmers' markets, using organic practices. (At home, Gallagher and Amsden say they make a lot of chicken stock, which they use to flavor everything from rice to soup. Check out the recipe for Chicken Soup, Three Ways, page 77.) Chickens and turkeys are processed in their on-site state-inspected processing unit.

The farm's name gives a clue about Gallagher's first career step. He grew up in nearby Cheshire, MA, and graduated from Williams College, majoring in Russian and biology, with an almost-completed third major, math. In high school, he baled hay for a Lanesborough, MA, farmer who worked nights as a secu-

rity guard; Gallagher internalized the message that it wasn't possible to make it farming. When he graduated, he taught math in the Mississippi Delta, looking for something he felt was important and would produce immediate results. Instead, "when I was supposed to be grading tests, I was thinking about what I was going to do when I was out." While in the South, though, he found examples of people who did make farming work. Gallagher returned to the Berkshires and then spent two years apprenticing on diversified, organic farms in New York and Vermont. And that's where his life intersected with Amsden's: at Maple Wind Farm in Huntington, VT, where she was an apprentice as well.

After farming leased land in Clarksburg, MA, they moved to Lanesborough to start Square Roots, which they bought under an Agricultural Preservation Restriction (APR). "I don't see myself burning out here as I did when teaching in Mississippi. We work just as hard but more variables are under my control," Gallagher says. "There are definitely days when nothing seems to be going right or you've already been going for 12 hours, and can see you have at least four to go. You wonder, like 'what am I doing here exactly?' But I think most of the time, we feel pretty good about what we've chosen."

Opting to locate their farm in Lanesborough, he says, "we were conscious we weren't going to target tourists. We were more interested in providing food for people who live and work here." Compared to other regions in the country, Gallagher thinks that the Berkshires is in a good space, with a population willing to think more about where their food is coming from. On the other hand, he occasionally worries that interest in local food may have peaked. "On some days, it makes me think, like, 'how can we change the grocery store experience to reach all the people who aren't going to go anywhere else?' and on other days, I think we have to approach that question differently. Instead, we have to try to chip off another small fraction of the people who only shop at the grocery store, and get them to try something else. So, I don't know what the right answer to that is."

Grilled Turkey Breast Paillard

SQUARE ROOTS FARM

SERVES 6 TO 8

These thin, quick-grilling pieces of turkey breast are so versatile—as a weeknight meal served with rice and some grilled vegetables, or as the hearty center of an oversize sandwich. Be sure to use fresh herbs since their tender texture is better than dried.

2 pounds whole boneless turkey breast, skin removed

2 tablespoons finely chopped fresh basil leaves or fresh rosemary

1 teaspoon salt

½ teaspoon freshly ground black pepper

Zest of 1 lemon

Juice of ½ lemon

1 tablespoon extra virgin olive oil, plus more for grill

1. If possible, have a butcher cut and pound the boneless turkey breast into ½-inch-thick cutlets. Otherwise, if the turkey breast has a large tender attached to the underside, gently separate the tender from the main part of the breast. Remove the tendon from the tender with the edge of a sharp knife and set aside. Slice the turkey breast across the grain into 1-inch-thick slices. Center a slice of the turkey inside a large, resealable bag and place it flat on the counter. Pound the fillet to ½ inch thick with a rolling pin or meat mallet, or the back of a heavy iron skillet. Repeat for each of the turkey pieces, including the tender.

2. Once all the turkey has been pounded thin, lay the pieces in a single layer on a foil-lined, rimmed half sheet pan. Sprinkle one side of the turkey pieces evenly with half of the basil, salt, pepper, and lemon zest, and drizzle with half of the lemon juice and olive oil. Turn and repeat with the remaining seasonings, and rub into both sides. Let rest for about 30 minutes on the counter.

3. While the turkey is marinating, heat a grill to medium-high. Use tongs to rub a bunched-up paper towel covered with olive oil over the grate, to help keep the turkey from sticking. Place each piece of turkey flat on the grill and cook for 2 minutes. With the tongs, gently turn each piece 45 degrees and cook for another 2 minutes to mark the meat and help the protein cook more evenly. Then, turn each piece over and cook for another 2 minutes. Mark it again on this side by turning each piece by 45 degrees and let cook for a final 2 minutes. Grill heat varies tremendously, so keep a close watch to ensure that the turkey does not overcook. It should be firm to the touch, but not hard. The internal temperature at the thickest part should read 165°F on an instant-read thermometer, though it can be difficult to use a thermometer on such thin slices of meat. Transfer the turkey pieces to a platter and let rest for 5 minutes before serving.

THE DREAM AWAY LODGE

We're spoiled since we live in the same neighborhood—or more precisely—near the same 18,000-acre forest—as the Dream Away Lodge in Becket, MA, and are what you call "regulars." Many a time we've walked through the screened porch door with an antique sweatbox lying alongside, hung out in the room to the right to catch a set by singer-songwriter Bobby Sweet, and turned left into the bar where actor and owner Daniel Osman, the maestro, producer of everything that goes on at Dream Away from dinner to music to weddings, sits. He checks us in. Behind him is an ornate gilt-framed picture of Marilyn Monroe, sans clothes.

When Osman bought Dream Away in 1997, he says, "we hadn't invented local yet." His concern then was respecting the venue's "history, nostalgia, community, the things that Dream Away represents." (It was reputed to be a brothel and speakeasy during the Great Depression.) It eventually became obvious to Osman that local food and farming had to be part of Dream Away's continuing story. But with a global menu. "Amy's [Chef Amy Loveless] and my interests are too far flung internationally to be cooking Yankee pot roast all the time," he quips. "Wonderful food grown locally can be turned into anything. You know, it's kind of divine." (See Crispy-Skin Salmon, page 180.)

Osman says Loveless knows every farmer within 50 miles of her West Stockbridge home. That includes, for example, the Hudson Valley, where she sources stone fruit—it's one zone warmer than the Berkshires, Loveless says. (See the recipe for German Plum Kuchen, page 204.) She is thrilled "this locavore thing has opened up in the Berkshires and that more chefs are devoting themselves to this." She's equally as delighted at "the reclamation of small farms," which she saw as "a lost art for years."

Loveless herself is a Berkshires native and grew up in a family that picked fruit and planted vegetables. Her mom was "a very good cook" who once cheffed for

Norman and Molly Rockwell. Amy says her parents "kept succumbing to my desire for things like cows for my birthday."

When she lived on her own, she planted a vegetable garden and berry bushes, but then grew too busy to take care of them, especially when she owned Suchele Bakers in Lenox. "It was a constant source of frustration and finally it dawned on me that I was not from that tribe—I'm a hunter-gatherer," she says. "I can have other people take care of those plants much better than I can, and I can fetch and use them. It's a much calmer relationship with food." She laughs.

She tends not to go to farmers' markets because she's usually working, but also finds "it's much more fun to go to the farm and hang with the farmer." What really has cut down on her driving is ordering from

Marty's Local, a newish food distributor that connects local farms and producers to restaurants.

Loveless ended up at Dream Away after knowing Osman for years and planned just to help him temporarily. "We had too much fun working together, so she got stuck," says Osman. For Loveless, "it was really kind of interesting to spread my wings a bit more ethnically and see that it was exciting to the clientele." Their menu spans world cuisine and changes seasonally. "Part of it has to do with keeping the interest of both the public—and the kitchen," she says. Customer preferences also change, based on the season. Osman remembers an egg salad from a Republic of Georgia recipe that sold fabulously in the spring but didn't move in the fall. "Hard-boiled eggs are a spring thing. Who knew?" he says. Loveless finds fall a terrific time to cook, with great root vegetables, kale, chard, squashes. And apples. "You know, I like to play with that sweet-savory combination of fruit engaged with food," she says.

To end with one little idiosyncrasy about Dream Away (there's plenty). If you want tea or coffee, you need to cross to the back of the restaurant and serve yourself from a station set up with random, nonmatching mugs—little matches anyway at Dream Away—and a few daintier teacups. "Why do you have to get your own coffee? Because you gotta get up, you gotta work the room, you gotta interact with people," Osman explains. "If you just want to go out to dinner, choose a nice beige-walled, white tablecloth restaurant where nobody will notice you."

Dining at Dream Away is what Osman repeatedly calls "reality dinner theatre." "There's a lot going on. And you get to be part of it." And eat really good local food.

Crispy-Skin Salmon

THE DREAM AWAY LODGE

SERVES 4

Sweet and sour with the familiar flavors of Vietnamese cuisine, this dish, known as Ca Chien Sot Ca Chua, is traditionally served with jasmine rice, thick slices of cucumber, and a generous sprig of mint. Chef Amy Loveless loves experimenting with international cuisine while still using local ingredients.

1½ to 2 pounds salmon fillet, skin on,
    cut into 4 portions

¾ cup water

½ cup Vietnamese or Thai fish sauce
    (Three Crabs or Squid brand, if possible)

2 large garlic cloves, peeled

¾ cup sugar

¼ teaspoon freshly ground black pepper

3 tablespoons canola or sunflower oil

1½ cups small-diced fresh tomato (local red or
    heirloom mixed colors)

½ cup thinly diagonally sliced scallion, green and
    white parts

Cooked jasmine rice for serving

1 cucumber, cut into thick slices

4 big sprigs mint

1. Preheat the oven to 500°F. Keep all the ingredients close at hand, as this recipe moves quickly.

2. Run your finger across the top of the salmon pieces, searching for pin bones. If you feel them under your fingertips, use a set of tweezers or a very sharp knife and your fingernails to gently pull these tiny bones out of the salmon.

3. Place the water, fish sauce, garlic, sugar, and pepper in a blender. Blend until the garlic is liquefied and the liquid is somewhat foamy. Pour the sauce into a jar and set aside to allow the foam to settle. Once settled, scrape off any foam and measure 1 cup for this recipe. Store the remainder in a glass jar in the refrigerator for up to 2 weeks.

4. Heat a large, heavy-bottomed, oven-safe skillet (preferably cast iron) over high heat. Add the canola oil and heat until almost smoking. Carefully, so as not to burn yourself with spattered oil, lay each piece of salmon, skin side down, in the hot pan, not touching each other. Fry over high heat for about 1 minute, just to crisp the skin.

5. Transfer the entire pan to the oven and bake for 8 to 10 minutes, until the salmon is done to medium; there will still be a bit of give when the salmon is touched. Remove from the oven—be careful of any hot pan handles—and with a set of tongs and a spatula, carefully transfer each fillet portion to a dinner plate, turning it skin side up for serving.

6. Return the pan with the hot oil to high heat on the stovetop. Carefully, watching out for spattering, add the diced tomato and stir briefly with a large spoon. Quickly add the scallion, stir briefly again, then add 1 cup of the fish sauce mixture. Bring to a boil and cook for about 30 seconds. Remove the pan from the heat and spoon equal portions of the sauce around each fillet portion on the dinner plates (a little over ½ cup of sauce per serving). Serve with jasmine rice, and garnish with fresh cucumber and the sprigs of mint.

THE OLD INN ON THE GREEN

The Old Inn On The Green couldn't be a more perfect property to own for a Williams College history major—that's Chef Peter Platt—and a former head gardener of the historic New England farm Hancock Shaker Village, his wife, Meredith Kennard.

Platt and Kennard bought the 1760s stagecoach relay in New Marlborough, MA, with its three candlelit dining rooms, each with a fireplace, in 2005. He had been the executive chef there for three years after serving in the same position for 12 years at Wheatleigh in Lenox, MA. The accolades have poured in, from *Yankee Magazine* to Zagat.

Platt is pretty low-key about any hoopla. We spoke to him and his wife on a Sunday in February before the dinner service and were struck by how laid back the two of them were. Especially for a Le Cordon Bleu–trained chef who had worked in some fairly formal places, including the Parker House in Boston. We asked if they meditated. "See me in the third week in July," Platt responds. "I'd probably tell you to go away."

No wonder. Their responsibilities go well beyond running an award-winning inn with a restaurant and lodging. They also own a full-service catering company plus the Southfield Store, a coffee shop/café by day that also serves dinner half the year. Add to that: Jacob's Pillow Dance Festival in Becket, MA, partnered with Platt and Kennard to provide their culinary offerings, starting in summer 2018.

We were also struck by Platt's interest in promoting farm-to-table in the region as well as his collegiality. He is on the board of Berkshire Grown. He's happy other chefs succeed, including some who've worked for him and started their own establishments. "They're my best friends," he says. "It's good to have a place to go on your day off," he told WAMC Northeast Public Radio. Or when neighboring farm-to-table restaurant Cantina 229 first opened and ran out of tomatoes for their Taco Tuesday, Platt and Kennard brought over a case. "You're traveling in a small circle," Kennard

says. "And there's no press scrutiny here that creates tension among chefs. There's no reviews," says Platt.

As a small, or not so small, business owner himself, Platt is aware of the pressures facing farmers he deals with as he works to bring farm-to-table dining to his entities. In the past, "when you used to have generations of farmers," he says, "there was a lot of knowledge passed on from father to son—or mother to daughter." For new farmers, there's so much to learn in such a short period and every year the growing season is different. And, farming is not just about growing and raising food, says Kennard. It's about making a living, she says, and here's where Berkshire Grown's workshops on the business of farming can be helpful.

Platt finds it promising that supermarkets are catching on to farm-to-table and selling what local farmers offer. He tells the story of looking for a sweet butternut squash that sold out at the farm he was buying from. But then, he says, "there they are at the Big Y. It's just before Thanksgiving and I need these squash.

The display says the farmer's name. I asked the guy at Big Y, 'Can you get me some of these?' 'Yeah, I think so.' 'I need six cases.' The next morning, I get a call saying, 'I have your six cases of squash.'"

When Platt and Kennard first bought the Old Inn, they thought they would farm some of the land themselves, but quickly realized they couldn't do it. Now they have a number of raised beds where they grow herbs and edible flowers to use in the restaurant, but acknowledge it doesn't make sense to plant their own tomatoes and more common crops. "I enjoy gardening things I can't find elsewhere," says Kennard.

Platt and Kennard are also committed to respecting the life of the animals they use and not wasting, even plants. Kennard tells the tale of famed Napa Valley chef Thomas Keller who, it is said, trains new chefs to slaughter, skin, and dress a rabbit. "He does it to teach respect for what it took to get that rabbit to the plate. You know what you went through and what the rabbit went through."

It bothers Platt that, unlike the most famous French chefs who took pride in using everything, he has colleagues, particularly in cities where meal prices are high, who will "use one piece of a green bean." Platt is grateful for the influence of his English-born mother: "She grew up through the war, and they would save their eggs every week so they could make a cake."

Pan-Seared Massachusetts Striped Bass

THE OLD INN ON THE GREEN

SERVES 4

This elegant showstopper of an entrée will dazzle your guests. Much of the prep work in this recipe, adapted from Chef Peter Platt of The Old Inn On The Green, can be done ahead of time, so you can just cook the fish and plate it right before serving. If you can't find Massachusetts striped bass, any lean, firm-textured fish, such as grouper or sea bass, can substitute.

4 heirloom tomatoes, preferably of different colors

¼ cup plus 1 tablespoon extra virgin olive oil

1 cucumber, peeled, seeded, and quartered lengthwise

24 pitted Kalamata olives, cut into slivers

1 tablespoon sherry vinegar

¼ teaspoon kosher salt, plus more for sprinkling

⅛ teaspoon freshly ground black pepper, plus more for sprinkling

Four 6-ounce fillets Massachusetts striped bass, scaled, skin on, or other lean, firm-textured fish

3 tablespoons grapeseed or canola oil

1 head Bibb lettuce, separated into leaves

1 tablespoon balsamic vinegar, preferably aged

½ cup fresh purple or green basil leaves

1. Prepare a large bowl of ice water and set aside. Bring a pot of water to a rapid boil. Meanwhile, score the tomatoes on the bottom with a paring knife by making a shallow X through the base into the skin. Lower the tomatoes into the boiling water and cook for about 30 seconds. Remove the tomatoes with a slotted spoon and place in the ice water to stop the

cooking process. After about a minute or two, the tomatoes should be cool enough to handle and the skin will peel off easily. Cut each tomato into wedges, and remove and discard the seeds and the inside flesh. Cut the remaining outer walls of tomato into diamonds or other attractive shapes and place in a medium, nonreactive bowl (such as stainless steel, glass, ceramic, or enamel-coated).

2. Slice the cucumber quarters diagonally into ¼-inch-wide strips. Heat 1½ teaspoons of the olive oil in a medium sauté pan over medium-low heat until shimmering and fragrant, and sauté the cucumber slowly until soft, about 5 minutes. Let cool slightly and add to the tomatoes. Add the olives to the tomato mixture and set aside.

3. Prepare a dressing by combining ¼ cup of the olive oil, the sherry vinegar, the kosher salt, and ⅛ teaspoon of the pepper in a small measuring cup and set aside.

4. Preheat the oven to 350°F. Score the skin of the fish in a crosshatch pattern with a sharp knife to prevent curling, and season both sides with salt and pepper. Heat the grapeseed oil over medium heat in an oven-safe sauté pan large enough to hold all the fillets without crowding.

5. Place the fillets in the oil, skin side down, and cook until the skin begins to brown and become crispy, 3 to 5 minutes. Transfer the pan into the oven to finish cooking. The total cooking time could be as short as 8 minutes or up to 20 minutes, depending on the thickness of the fish and the temperature of the pan on the burner. The fillets should feel firm but not hard, and be opaque through the middle.

6. While the fish is in the oven, heat the remaining 1½ teaspoons of olive oil in a medium sauté pan over medium heat and cook the lettuce leaves quickly with a sprinkling of salt and pepper until just wilted. Pat the leaves dry with a paper towel. Just before serving, pour the dressing over the tomato mixture and toss to coat.

7. To plate the dish, arrange the lettuce leaves on four plates, fanning them out flat so they overlap slightly. Place one cooked fillet atop the lettuce in the center of each plate. Spoon the tomato mixture around the fillets and drizzle the balsamic vinegar over the top. Garnish with the basil leaves and serve immediately.

Diver Scallops with Cauliflower

JOHN ANDREWS FARMHOUSE RESTAURANT

SERVES 4

Adapted from a recipe by Chef Dan Smith of John Andrews Farmhouse Restaurant, this dish can be the centerpiece of an elegant meal, but it can come together easily enough to serve on a weeknight. The scallion oil can be made ahead and stored in the refrigerator to cut prep time. Look for fresh dry sea scallops at the store; larger than bay scallops, they are more suitable for an entrée portion. Of course, source the vegetables and dairy locally, if possible.

1 cup plus 2 tablespoons extra virgin olive oil, plus more for baking sheets

1 bunch scallions (7 to 9 scallions), rinsed and slightly trimmed of their roots

1½ teaspoons kosher salt, plus more for seasoning scallops and leeks

1 medium head cauliflower, trimmed and cut into florets

2 garlic cloves, minced

2 large leeks

4 ounces pancetta, chopped

½ cup heavy cream

¼ cup grated Parmesan

1 tablespoon chopped fresh flat-leaf parsley

24 large diver sea scallops

continued . . .

1. Move a rack to the highest position in the oven and turn on the broiler. Set another oven rack in the center of the oven. Lightly oil two rimmed half sheet pans.

2. Toss the scallions in a large bowl with ½ teaspoon of the salt and 2 tablespoons of the olive oil. Lay out the whole scallions on one of the prepared half sheet pans and broil in the oven on the highest rack until lightly charred and tender, about 3 minutes. Remove from the oven and allow to cool.

3. Adjust the oven temperature to bake at 400°F. Using the same bowl as for the scallions, toss the cauliflower with the garlic, ¼ cup of the olive oil, and 1 teaspoon of the salt. Spread the cauliflower on the second half sheet pan and bake on the center oven rack for 30 minutes, or until tender and lightly browned in places. Remove from the oven and set aside.

4. While the cauliflower is roasting, use a blender to puree the scallions with the remaining ¾ cup of olive oil. This should make about 1 cup of scallion oil. Set aside. Whatever is not used for this recipe can be stored in the refrigerator in an airtight container for 1 week.

5. Trim and clean the leeks: Remove and discard the toughest dark green leaves and the root ends, leaving only the white and light green parts. Slice them down the center lengthwise to make two long halves. Wash carefully in cold water while fanning the leaves apart to remove any fine grit. When clean, shake off any extra water and slice across into half-moon shapes about ½ inch wide. Place the leeks in a large saucepan with a pinch of salt and ½ cup of water. Cover and simmer over medium heat for 10 minutes. Remove the lid and cook, stirring gently, until tender and most of the liquid in the saucepan is reduced.

6. Render the pancetta in a small saucepan over medium heat until brown and crispy, about 7 minutes. Drain the fat and add the pancetta to the leeks. Add the roasted cauliflower to the leek mixture. Bring the mixture to a simmer and stir in the cream. Stirring gently, cook until the cream has reduced to coat the cauliflower, about 7 minutes. Stir in the Parmesan and the parsley, and keep warm while the scallops cook.

7. Rinse the scallops under cold water and pat completely dry. Lay out in a single layer on a plate. Inspect for any that might have the side muscle on them, and if so, pull this little rectangle of slightly tougher tissue away gently with your fingertips. Season with a sprinkling of salt on each side. Heat a stainless-steel or cast-iron pan large enough to hold the scallops in a single layer, over medium-high heat until the pan is hot. Use a pair of tongs to place the scallops gently in the pan. Sear for 1 to 2 minutes on each side, turning carefully by loosening from the pan with a spatula and then turning with the tongs. They should have a nice golden color on each side and feel firm when pressed.

8. Divide the scallops among the serving plates and place a heap of the cauliflower mixture on the side. Drizzle scallion oil over each plate and serve.

MEAT

Lamb Ragu

MOON IN THE POND FARM

SERVES 4 TO 6

This easy, extraordinarily fragrant one-pot meal can be served with rice or potatoes, over pasta, or with warm, buttered artisanal bread to dip in the juices. Like most braised dishes, this ragu tastes even better when served a day or two after it is made.

2 pounds lamb shoulder or leg, trimmed of fat and ¾-inch diced

1¼ teaspoons salt, plus more to taste

½ teaspoon freshly ground black pepper, plus more to taste

2 tablespoons extra virgin olive oil

1 onion, diced (about 1 cup)

2 tablespoons finely chopped garlic

2 cups lightly packed chopped kale or other dark hearty green, such as escarole

1 cup beef or chicken stock

6 sprigs fresh thyme

One 28-ounce can diced tomatoes, with juices

One 15.5-ounce can cannellini beans, drained and rinsed

4 fresh basil leaves, chopped (about 2 tablespoons)

2 tablespoons chopped fresh flat-leaf parsley

1. Preheat the oven to 350°F. Season the lamb on all sides with 1 teaspoon of salt and the pepper.

2. Heat the olive oil in a large, heavy-bottomed ovenproof stockpot or a Dutch oven over medium-high heat until shimmering and fragrant. Working in batches to prevent overcrowding, brown the lamb pieces on all sides. Using tongs or a slotted spoon, transfer to a plate or bowl and set aside.

3. Add the onion to the pot with ¼ teaspoon of the salt and sauté, stirring often, until soft and translucent, 5 to 7 minutes. Add the garlic and cook, stirring constantly, until fragrant and golden, 1 to 2 minutes. Return the lamb pieces to the pot with any accumulated juices, add the kale, and stir until wilted, 1 to 2 minutes. Pour in the stock and, using a wooden spoon, scrape the bottom of the pot gently to release any browned bits. Tie the thyme springs into a bundle with kitchen twine. Add the tomatoes, beans, thyme bundle, basil, and parsley to the pot and stir to combine.

4. Bring to a simmer, cover, and place in the oven to bake for 1 hour. Check every 20 minutes or so and add a small amount of additional stock or water if the ragu is beginning to stick to the bottom. The ragu can be left in the oven for a longer period if a thicker or more deeply flavored ragu is desired.

5. Remove the thyme bundle from the ragu and taste for seasoning, adding salt and pepper, if necessary, before serving.

NORTH PLAIN FARM AND BLUE HILL FARM

Sean Stanton's farm setup is complicated. He describes his enterprise as one farm with two names in multiple locations. First, he farms on land his parents owned. That's North Plain Farm. Then, he runs Blue Hill Farm, where his dairy is located and he keeps other livestock. That's land that belongs to the Barber family, including Dan Barber, chef and one of the owners of Blue Hill Restaurant and Blue Hill at Stone Barns in New York. Altogether, Stanton farms about 300 acres of which he owns about 130 on 13 parcels, which he says, as crazy as it sounds, works for a livestock farmer because there's less equipment.

Land is expensive to buy in the Berkshires; it's less expensive, Stanton says, to lease through owners who want to keep property but don't want to farm it themselves. The quandary for farmers who don't own their land is that they want to improve soil health and increase production, but it's counterintuitive to invest in acreage they can't control.

Stanton's—and his wife, Tess Diamond's—signature products are grass-fed beef, pork, chicken, eggs, and heirloom tomatoes. They sell raw milk from the farm, and pasteurized milk when there's enough produced. Half of what the couple raises and grows

is used by the Blue Hill restaurants. The rest is sold through the farm store at 342 North Plain Road, in Great Barrington, MA; at the Great Barrington Farmers' Market; and to local chefs and retailers.

When he started farming 18 years ago on his 7-acre family parcel, Stanton was one of the few local egg suppliers, but now, he says, there are at least four at the Berkshire Food Co-op. He'd like to sell his meat, chicken, and pork through the same retail outlets, but the margins are too tight. His animals eat costly certified or transitional organic feed and slaughtering them is expensive ($400 for a pig at the small New England slaughterhouse he uses, Eagle Bridge Custom Meat & Smokehouse, compared to the $20 or $30 he says it costs big processors). Large producers that slaughter 10,000 pigs a day rather than the 20 or fewer at the facility Stanton patronizes, take advantage of economy of scale, but their lower prices also result from what he argues is the inhumane way they structure the workday for those who do the killing. "We talk about animal rights all the time. When you go to these places and see the kinds of jobs [workers are] doing for 8 or 10 hours a day, it's as much a human rights issue as an animal welfare issue." At Eagle Bridge, people work a variety of jobs throughout the day. "They might be killing in the morning, cutting in the afternoon. You're not on an assembly line where you're cutting one section of each pig that comes through and then moving it to the next person."

We asked Stanton for advice for new farmers, and he emphasized that networking is essential, attending conferences, Berkshire Grown events. "I didn't start farming with the connection to Blue Hill. That happened later," he says. Forging relationships like that and also finding chefs that care is essential, although he acknowledges it may be increasingly difficult because of greater competition, including from nearby Pioneer Valley, MA, and Vermont. (That's not all bad, he says. It creates awareness that there's a market for items the Berkshires is not producing.)

In a former life, Stanton chaired the Select Board in Great Barrington, although he recently decided not to run for reelection, choosing instead to devote more time to farming. But his experience in government makes him appreciate Massachusetts' commitment to supporting agriculture. He notes, for example, that there are dairy farms in business because of the state's tax credit, and while it doesn't affect him because of his small output, "for farms that are producing millions of gallons of milk, it's a huge impact on their ability to stay in business."

The couple are not heavy meat eaters themselves. But that's not to suggest that meat farmer Stanton is against eating meat: He feels strongly that for the planet, people should eat less meat but of higher quality, the kind he and his colleagues profiled in this cookbook produce. If you ask him what he'd most like to eat for dinner, his answer: a good, grass-fed steak. (He'll certainly eat a less luxurious London broil, of course, since he'll use all of the animal.) What is particularly gratifying to him is when customers he knows don't have a tremendous amount of discretionary income choose to buy his meat, because they value what they eat.

Grilled Grass-Fed Top Round London Broil

NORTH PLAIN FARM AND BLUE HILL FARM
LEAHEY FARM

SERVES 4 TO 6

London broil refers to the technique of leaving a thicker cut steak in a marinade for some time before cooking it with high heat. As Chef Brian Alberg notes, "this is a wonderful preparation for under-rated cuts that are not as popular as the tender cuts, such as tenderloin, New York strip, or rib eye." He adds that "I like to use cuts like flat iron, hanger, skirt, top round, chuck, et cetera. Choosing these cuts is not only more economical, but also pays respect to the animal as a whole and not just as a 'piece of meat,' so to speak." Grass-fed meat cooks faster than commercially raised beef, so be sure not to overcook it, or the steak may become rubbery. Again, Alberg notes, "we have become accustomed to the tender cuts we find in supermarkets. . . . Grass-fed beef can be tender but it needs to be cooked with the care and respect that it was raised with."

2 tablespoons red wine vinegar

¼ cup extra virgin olive oil, plus more for grill

1 teaspoon salt

1 teaspoon freshly ground black pepper

1 tablespoon minced fresh garlic

2 tablespoons chopped rosemary

2½ pounds top round steak

1. Mix together all the ingredients, except the steak, in a shallow baking dish that is the size of the meat. Pat the steak dry with a paper towel and lay it into the marinade, turning to make sure it covers both sides and massaging the marinade gently into the beef. Cover the dish with plastic wrap and allow it to rest in the refrigerator for 2 to 4 hours or more, turning the steak once during the resting period.

2. About 30 minutes before cooking, remove the dish from the refrigerator to allow the meat to come to room temperature. It is important that this happens before grilling or searing, so as not to shock the muscle, which makes the meat tough. Right before cooking, remove the meat from the marinade and pat dry again.

3. While the beef is resting, preheat a grill to high, or if using an oven broiler, place an oven rack at the highest point in the oven and turn on the broiler. A grill pan over high heat on the stove will also work. Paint the grill, broiling pan, or grill pan with olive oil to help prevent sticking. If using the broiler, slide the broiling pan with the steak on it under the flame and leave it for 6 minutes before flipping to cook for 6 minutes on the other side. Otherwise, lay the beef down on the grill (or grill pan) and let sear for 2 to 3 minutes untouched. Then, rotate the beef 45 degrees on the same side, and let it sear for another 2 to 3 minutes, which "marks" the meat and helps it cook evenly. Next, turn the steak over onto a new section of the grill as it will be hotter. Let it cook for 2 to 3 minutes before rotating 45 degrees and then cook another 2 to 3 minutes. Depending on the thickness of the meat and the temperature of the grill, the steak might be done in as little as 10 minutes, so be sure to check the internal temperature early enough so as not to overcook. Using an instant-read meat thermometer, the internal temperature should read 120°F for rare, and 130°F for medium rare to medium.

4. Transfer the steak to a platter and allow to rest for 10 minutes, during which time the meat will continue to cook. This will also help keep the juices in the meat when slicing. Slice thinly against the grain and serve.

LEAHEY FARM

The Leahey Farm story is one of determination, of a family insistent on keeping its dairy farm alive. It is also one of evolution, with the most recent chapter unfolding in the last year.

Phil Leahey's family has owned and operated the Lee, MA, farm since 1889, milking 30 to 40 cows daily until it stopped producing dairy in 1972. The farm continued raising livestock and crops. In 2013, Phil and his wife, Jen, who returned to Lee to farm full-time, received financing to build a small dairy processing plant, adding milk once again to the farm's repertoire of pasture-raised heritage cattle, the Milking Devon cow, Tamworth hogs, turkeys, chickens, and goats, and selling at the farmers' market in Great Barrington and to local stores and restaurants.

Phil and Jen had met working at the New England Heritage Breeds Conservancy. What Phil really wanted to do was ensure the survival of his family farm. Jen was willing to join him in that endeavor.

Jen: "We are very stubborn people. We're holding the line. We have something unique."

Phil: "Since I've grown up here, the farm next door is condominiums. It is built up to our property line. I'm fifth generation. I feel like digging in my heels a bit more. It's not always rainbows and unicorns."

That's when they decided to add dairy and started producing small-batch pasteurized, unhomogenized milk, and yogurt.

A note about their choice of breeds. By choosing heritage breeds, Phil told *Edible Berkshires*, "we're supporting biodiversity of livestock. To preserve those animals, they need to be raised." The couple worked to educate the community about the importance of buying their 90 percent pasture-raised meat, with its benefit to the environment and consumer health compared with animals finished in feedlots, given hormones, antibiotics, and other drugs. But people have to perceive a benefit between healthier food and communities and buying more expensive beef and milk. It was hard for Phil and Jen to get the price they needed for their meat. Jen: "Everybody wants the good cut,

and then you end up with a freezer full of hamburgers that nobody wants to pay $11 a pound for." They stopped raising beef cattle in 2017, producing meat only for themselves.

The profit margin on the milk was also small, says Jen. And it was tough to keep bottling. They had to make a decision about business priorities. "We're a grass-fed based farm," she says. "So, if you're trying to graze animals for meat, that's going to compete with the cows that need to graze to get energy to make milk. We only have so much open land." That's when they heard that Sidehill Farm in Hawley, MA, was looking for dairy farms to help grow its yogurt business.

So, in this most recent incarnation of Leahey Farm, Phil and Jen are out of bottling milk, they're certified organic, they've increased their dairy cow herd, and ironically once yogurt makers themselves, are selling milk to yogurt producer Sidehill. (See the recipe for Balsamic Stone Fruit over Yogurt, page 29.) The arrangement also enables Phil to keep his family farm

going. He runs the dairy (with support from his dad, retired veterinarian James Leahey). The other post-script is that Jen started a nonprofit, Nature Matters. Using the farm, she offers educational programs to teach kids about live animals and the outdoors.

Even though the Leaheys no longer sell grass-fed meat, we'd like to end with a morsel from Phil on how best to cook it. Grass-fed beef needs delicate treatment, he counsels. Thaw frozen grass-fed cuts slowly, and bring them to room temperature before grilling. "You've allowed the meat to relax instead of taking it from extremely cold to extremely hot." He says to take

it off the heat source and let it sit for a few minutes because it will keep cooking. (Grass-fed beef needs less cooking time, so check earlier than usual to see whether it's done.) He recommends protracted marinating for tougher cuts. Take a London broil, he says, which can either be a top round or shoulder. He optimally marinates it for 24 hours, and serves it medium rare. A grass-fed beef steak is gourmet, Phil says. "I think a lot of people throw it on (the grill) while they're drinking beers, take it off, and think it's going to be awesome. But if you're going to do that, you're going to be disappointed."

CAFEADAM

Adam Zieminski, owner and operator of cafeADAM, in Great Barrington, MA, with his partner Sylwia Orczykowska, has cooked all over the globe, starting in Housatonic, MA, and finishing before returning here, at a couple of two Michelin–starred restaurants in the UK and Manhattan. We're sure that if Adam chose to stay in Europe or New York, he could have done so, and as Berkshires promoters ourselves, admire that he came back. To be precise, he worked at Wheatleigh in Lenox, MA, before opening cafeADAM in 2006, with its modern European cuisine and reliance on local ingredients.

Zieminski himself couldn't be more "local." As his bio on the restaurant website says, "Adam is truly Berkshire Grown!" (The wordplay here: Zieminski was on the organization's board for about three years.) Born in Housatonic, his family is four generations in this area; his great-grandparents ran a dairy farm in Cheshire, MA, where Zieminski spent time when it was still operating. When Zieminski was young his mom owned a bakery, introducing him to food through the business, which included helping her scoop out cookie dough and eating batter. At age 13, Zieminski decided to become a chef. He graduated from Monument Mountain High School in 1994 and managed to

cook at the Seranak and Highwood Dining Clubs at Tanglewood, the former Federal House in South Lee, MA, and Bistro Zinc in Lenox, MA, before heading off to get a BA (on full scholarship) in culinary arts at Johnson & Wales University in Rhode Island.

It's clear Zieminski is committed to locally sourced ingredients. His website is a photo gallery of past and present purveyors. As a guest on WAMC Northeast Public Radio, he extolled the taste of local carrots,

which he told host Ray Graf can't compare even to organic ones from the supermarket. Zieminski pulled out two mystery carrots and asked his host to taste each and pick his favorite. We listened to Graf chomp on air before he chose the one grown about 10 miles from cafeADAM as opposed to the commercial sample. Zieminski was triumphant.

Zieminski gets his local produce by ordering from farmers who send emails and newsletters about what they offer that week, and then deliver. When we first spoke to him in 2014, he told us that rather than farmers offering the usual zucchini and peppers, "if you're contracting with restaurants, give me buckwheat shoots, shiso, things that are hard to find." He is heartened by how much the situation has improved. Just the other day, MX Morningstar Farm, in Claverack, NY, called to tell him about "celtuce." Zieminski told us it was so exotic that even he had to look it up, discovering it's a lettuce popular in China and Taiwan.

He cooks with the season, telling WAMC that not only do ingredients change, but so do the methods; for example, braising is popular in winter and early spring. Spring is all about sprouts, ramps, pea tendrils. He likes seafood, even if the Berkshires is not on the coast, with his current menu reflecting a long-standing favorite, New England–based bouillabaisse, and scallops (which he has in some form year-round). Half of the menu is classic, half rotates based by season. For a profile on the BerkShares website (that's a local currency), he says that in the summer, he likes ingredients to speak for themselves. "Local farms are at their peak and everything is so fresh it's like a Garden of Eden. We do a lot more chilled foods, raw food…. Very light, easy-to-digest dishes, with crisp white wines and rosés."

Zieminski is also a cheerleader for the Berkshires as a locus for more enlightened eating. "Everyone has a garden; everyone knows what fresh vegetables taste like; everyone has gone apple and strawberry picking. It's ingrained into Berkshire culture. There's a very high level of food consciousness here."

Braised Beef Shanks with Eggplant and Scarlet Runner Beans

CAFEADAM

SERVES 6 TO 8

This recipe, adapted from Chef Adam Zieminski of cafeADAM, pairs braised beef shanks with buttery eggplant and an uncommon bean called the scarlet runner. Although these extra-large beans can be ordered online, great northern beans can substitute. The braising time may be long, but the prep work is not overly burdensome, and the end result is worth the wait. Serve this comfort food with polenta, rice, or mashed potatoes.

1 tablespoon extra virgin olive oil

1 teaspoon kosher salt, plus more to taste

½ teaspoon freshly ground black pepper, plus more to taste

1 to 1½ pounds grass-fed beef shanks, crosscut with the bone at the center

2.5 ounces bacon, diced small

1 eggplant, partially peeled and ½-inch diced

2 medium onions, diced

5 celery ribs, ½-inch diced

3 medium carrots, peeled and ½-inch diced

½ medium fennel bulb, ½-inch diced

5 garlic cloves, minced

1½ tablespoons minced fresh flat-leaf parsley, plus 2 tablespoons chopped for garnish

1 tablespoon minced fresh rosemary

1½ teaspoons fresh thyme, minced

1 tablespoon minced celery leaves

½ cup dry white wine, such as chardonnay or pinot grigio

½ cup Worcestershire sauce, plus more to taste

1 cup dried scarlet runner beans or
   great northern beans

3 cups veal, beef, or chicken stock,
   heated to a simmer

2 medium heirloom tomatoes, diced

1. Heat the olive oil in a 2-gallon Dutch oven or similar heavy-bottomed saucepan over medium heat until shimmering and fragrant. Combine the salt and pepper in a small pinch bowl and sprinkle evenly over both sides of the shanks. Working in batches if necessary to prevent overcrowding, brown the shanks until they have a dark brown crust on both sides, 8 to 10 minutes total. Transfer to a plate.

2. In the same pot, sauté the chopped bacon until the fat is mostly rendered, about 2 minutes. Add the eggplant, onions, celery, carrots, and fennel and sauté until all are slightly softened. Add the garlic, 1½ tablespoons of the parsley, and the rosemary, thyme, and celery leaves and continue to sauté for 5 minutes. Deglaze the pot with the white wine and Worcestershire sauce, using a wooden spoon to scrape any browned bits from the bottom of the pot.

3. Add the dried beans to the pot and mix into the vegetables. Nestle the shanks in the vegetables, avoiding overlap if possible. Add the heated stock to the pot and pile the tomatoes on top of the shanks. Put the lid on the pot and simmer gently, adjusting the heat level as necessary, until the beans are soft and the meat falls off the bone, 4 to 5 hours, stirring gently a few times during cooking. If the liquid is not reducing, set the lid askew or remove entirely for the second half of the simmering time.

4. Using tongs, remove the bones from the pot and place on a small plate. If the marrow is still present in the center of the bone, push it out with a small spoon onto the plate and discard the bone. Eat the marrow immediately as a cook's treat, or press it into a paste with the back of the spoon and mix it back into the pot.

5. Season the braise before serving, if necessary, with additional salt, pepper, and a splash of the Worcestershire sauce. Break up the meat into smaller pieces as needed for portioning. Sprinkle with the chopped parsley for garnish.

Stuffed Collard Greens Golabki-Style

WHEN PIGS FLY FARM

SERVES 4 TO 6

Golabki are Polish cabbage rolls filled with minced meat, onions, and cooked rice and smothered with a savory tomato sauce. In this recipe, collard greens are used instead of the traditional cabbage wrapper, and a touch of curry powder gives this version an unexpected twist. Different types of curry, or even different brands of the same type, can vary in spiciness, so be sure to add it gradually to your taste. The meat can be replaced with an all-vegetable filling, highlighting the best of the summer garden, or even with a vegan ground beef substitute.

2 tablespoons extra virgin olive oil, plus more for pan and if needed

2 tablespoons chopped garlic

One 28-ounce can diced tomatoes, with juices

2 cups chicken or vegetable stock

½ cup chopped fresh flat-leaf parsley

¼ cup chopped fresh basil leaves

8 large collard leaves, stemmed

½ large onion, finely diced (1 to 1½ cups)

8 ounces ground beef or vegan substitute, or 3 cups eggplant, zucchini, and/or fennel, peeled and finely chopped

8 ounces ground pork, or for a vegan version, 1 cup mushrooms, finely chopped

1½ cups cooked rice

1 to 2 tablespoons Madras or other favorite curry powder

½ teaspoon salt, or to taste

¼ teaspoon freshly ground black pepper, or to taste

1. Preheat the oven to 350°F. Lightly oil a 9-by-13-inch baking dish with olive oil.

2. Make the golabki sauce: Heat 1 tablespoon of the olive oil in a large, heavy-bottomed stockpot or Dutch oven over medium heat until shimmering and fragrant. Sauté 1 tablespoon of the garlic until fragrant, about 1 minute. Add the tomatoes with juices, stock, ¼ cup of the parsley, and the basil. Bring to a boil, then lower the heat and simmer for 20 to 30 minutes. Remove from the heat and set aside.

3. Meanwhile, prepare an ice water bath in a large bowl. Boil water in a large pot and blanch the collard greens until pliable, about 5 minutes. Remove the leaves and shock them in the ice water bath.

4. Heat the remaining tablespoon of olive oil in a large sauté pan or skillet over medium heat until shimmering and fragrant. Cook the onion, stirring occasionally, until soft and translucent, about 5 minutes. Add the remaining tablespoon of garlic and cook until fragrant, about 1 minute. If you are substituting vegetables or vegan ground beef, add now and cook until the mushrooms have yielded their moisture. The vegetable mixture may require an extra tablespoon of olive oil. Remove from the heat and let cool.

5. Combine the raw ground meat (or cooked vegan substitutes) and cooled onion with the cooked rice, curry powder, salt, pepper, and 1 tablespoon of the parsley. If using meat, heat a small amount of oil in a small sauté pan and cook a teaspoon of the mixture first. Taste the cooked meat filling or the vegan mixture and check for seasoning, adding more curry powder, salt, or pepper as needed.

6. Pour some golabki sauce about ½ inch deep into the bottom of the baking dish.

7. To fill and roll, blot each collard leaf dry with a paper towel, then lay on a flat surface. Place a heaping ⅓ cup of the filling in the middle of each leaf. Gently, because the leaves can tear easily, start

with the stem end and roll up, tucking in the edges, burrito style, as you go. As each roll is completed, place, seam side down, in the baking dish.

8. When the greens have been rolled and arranged in the baking dish, top with the remaining sauce and bake for 1 hour. If using meat, the internal temperature should reach 165°F. Allow the rolls to rest for 10 minutes before serving, and garnish with the remaining 3 tablespoons of parsley.

Braised Pork Shoulder

CLIMBING TREE FARM

SERVES 4 TO 6

This hearty braise can be made a day ahead and reheated since it only gets better with additional time to let the flavors develop. Serve over rice or egg noodles.

1 tablespoon extra virgin olive oil

2 tablespoons unsalted butter

2 pounds pork shoulder, cut into 1-inch pieces

1 teaspoon kosher salt

1 teaspoon freshly ground black pepper

4 ounces bacon, cut into ½-inch pieces

2 garlic cloves, thinly sliced

1 small onion, ½-inch diced

2 carrots, ½-inch diced

2 celery stalks, ½-inch diced

One 15-ounce can diced tomatoes, with juices

¼ cup Madeira wine

2 cups stemmed chopped kale

¼ cup chopped dried porcini mushrooms

1 sprig rosemary

1 quart chicken stock

1. Heat the olive oil and butter in a large, heavy-bottomed stockpot or a Dutch oven over medium-high heat until the butter has melted. Season the pork on all sides with salt and pepper. In batches, brown the pork on all sides until golden, 3 to 5 minutes per side. Transfer with tongs to a plate to rest.

2. Add the bacon to the pot and sauté until the fat has mostly rendered off, about 5 minutes. Add the garlic, onion, carrots, and celery, tossing with the pan juices until fully coated and slightly softened, 5 to 8 minutes. Add the tomatoes with juices and the pork and bring to a boil. Lower the heat to medium and allow to simmer, uncovered, stirring occasionally so it does not stick to the bottom, until most of the liquid is gone, 30 to 40 minutes.

3. Deglaze the pot with the Madeira, loosening any bits stuck on the bottom with a wooden spoon. Add the kale, dried mushrooms, rosemary, and chicken stock, stirring to combine. Simmer uncovered until the pork is tender, 30 to 45 minutes. The sauce should reduce a little and coat the meat.

CLIMBING TREE FARM

Schuyler and Colby Gail of Climbing Tree Farm, in New Lebanon, NY, started with a Noah's Ark of farm animals, but now they're pretty much down to one kind—pigs. This is the story of happy-to-be-farming-but-conscious, ex-vegetarian pig farmers who raise animals instinctually, using regenerative agricultural practices. That's a mouthful, but give us a second and we'll parse this.

When they started, the two were almost farming newbies. Schuyler, from Williamstown, MA, apprenticed at Caretaker Farm, which primarily grows vegetables, while Colby grew up in the west, and although his grandparents owned a farm, he didn't learn the business. When they came back to this area after college, they first farmed unused acreage with a barnyard Schuyler's grandmother owned in Berlin, NY, land that her family had lived on for over 100 years. After six years of searching for their own land, in 2011, with the help of the Columbia Land Conservancy, they bought 20 acres in New Lebanon and leased another 300-plus. As Colby says, pigs need space. Especially

those allowed to express their natural instincts, who freely roam the woods as their forebears did, and need to move every few days to forage food. What it means to raise pigs instinctually, says Schuyler, is "looking at the world through a pig's eyes."

The couple didn't begin as pig farmers. In fact, they started out as vegetarians, or mostly Schuyler, since she had eaten that way since childhood. When they had kids, they debated whether to raise them similarly and felt that farming livestock to provide meat for the family was a compromise. They started with sheep, and added 50 laying hens that produced so many eggs, they started selling them. Eventually that number increased to 500 hens, which Schuyler says grew out of control. The hens destroyed their garden and snuck into the house when the door was open. They also found that washing 450 eggs a day wasn't fun, and winnowed the brood to a dozen, mostly for their own food.

The Gails did find they were good at raising pigs, although they embraced it with great ethical wariness. As Colby says, "we're taking lives for our consump-

tion and that's not something to be taken lightly." His wife can't imagine eating an animal without knowing where it comes from, writing in her blog that people always ask whether it disturbs the Gails to slaughter. "It's sad every time," she answers. "These are living things (some of whom are extremely cute and/or animals that we have known since the moment they were born) and we choose to kill them. When killing animals we care about becomes nonchalant and fails to stir our emotions, then we will know we need to stop raising animals for meat. We respect our animals in life and we are thankful for them in death."

The Gails raise between 75 and 120 pigs a year, mostly selling whole animals to restaurants. The animals live on grass and in the woods year-round, in moveable sections of fence. Unlike pigs bred to be reared in confinement, heritage pigs are efficient foragers. They also graze on pasture covered with healthy, palatable foraging crops that the Gails plant. (Schuyler bristles at the term *pasture-raised*. What they're shooting for, she says, is really "regenerative agriculture. *Pasture-raised* doesn't necessarily mean

that there's anything good to eat or that the land is staying healthy. *Regenerative* means leaving the land healthier than when we started.")

What their pigs munch on matters—their meat takes on the flavor of what they eat. Each season, Schuyler says, produces a different "terroir," using the term from viniculture. A pig slaughtered in late fall may have an acorn and apple flavor. A pig slaughtered in summer will taste more like grass. Winter pigs will have eaten more grain. Despite raising pigs, the Gails are not big meat eaters, with their favorite pork dish, slow cooked pork shoulder. (See the recipe for Braised Pork Shoulder, page 197.)

The Gails are happy farming. "I feel we're doing a good job making the product that we make," Schuyler says. "And there's a puzzle every day, so it feels like an intellectual job." She is also optimistic about their customer base. "I see more people wanting to eat the kind of food that small farms grow," but notes that consumers still aren't willing to pay its true cost, except for millennials, who she observes seem to spend a higher percentage of their income on food.

Maple-Cured Pork Tenderloin

IOKA VALLEY FARM
EAST MOUNTAIN FARM

SERVES 6 TO 8

Medallions of grilled pork tenderloin are a great summer dish. A side of summer tomatoes or sweet corn along with a few gently grilled new potatoes help to complete the meal. Be sure to purchase 1-pound pork tenderloins, rather than a whole pork loin. Juniper berries, so popular in European cooking, are less common in recipes in the United States. If you cannot find any at a local retailer, it is worth seeking them out online for their distinctive flavor. This dish needs an overnight brining period, so plan ahead.

4 pork tenderloins (about 4 pounds total)

½ cup pure maple syrup

1 cup water

¼ cup kosher salt

¼ cup sugar

2 celery stalks, diced

1 carrot, diced

½ onion, diced

1 tablespoon juniper berries

2 bay leaves

1 sprig rosemary

Extra virgin olive oil for grilling

Freshly ground black pepper

1 tablespoon finely chopped fresh rosemary

1. Lay the pork tenderloins flat in one layer in a glass or other nonreactive rectangular dish.

2. Combine the maple syrup, water, salt, and sugar in a medium bowl and stir until the salt and sugar have dissolved. Add the celery, carrot, onion, juniper berries, bay leaves, and rosemary sprig. Taste to make sure the flavor is evenly balanced between salty and sweet, but not too salty. Pour over the pork, being sure to tuck the bay leaves and the rosemary sprig down underneath the level of the liquid or between the pork pieces. Cover and refrigerate overnight, turning occasionally.

3. Preheat a grill to medium-high. Remove the pork from the brine and discard the brine. Gently blot the pork dry with paper towels. Brush with the olive oil on all sides. Sprinkle with pepper and chopped rosemary.

4. Grill the pork, turning at regular 3-minute intervals, until medium done or until a meat thermometer inserted into the center of the pork reads 160°F, 20 to 35 minutes, depending on your grill. Be sure to begin checking the internal temperature early so that it does not overcook. Remove from the grill and allow to rest for 5 minutes on a plate, loosely covered with foil.

5. Slice ½ to ¾ inch thick for serving, and drizzle with any accumulated juices from the resting period.

DESSERTS AND BREADS

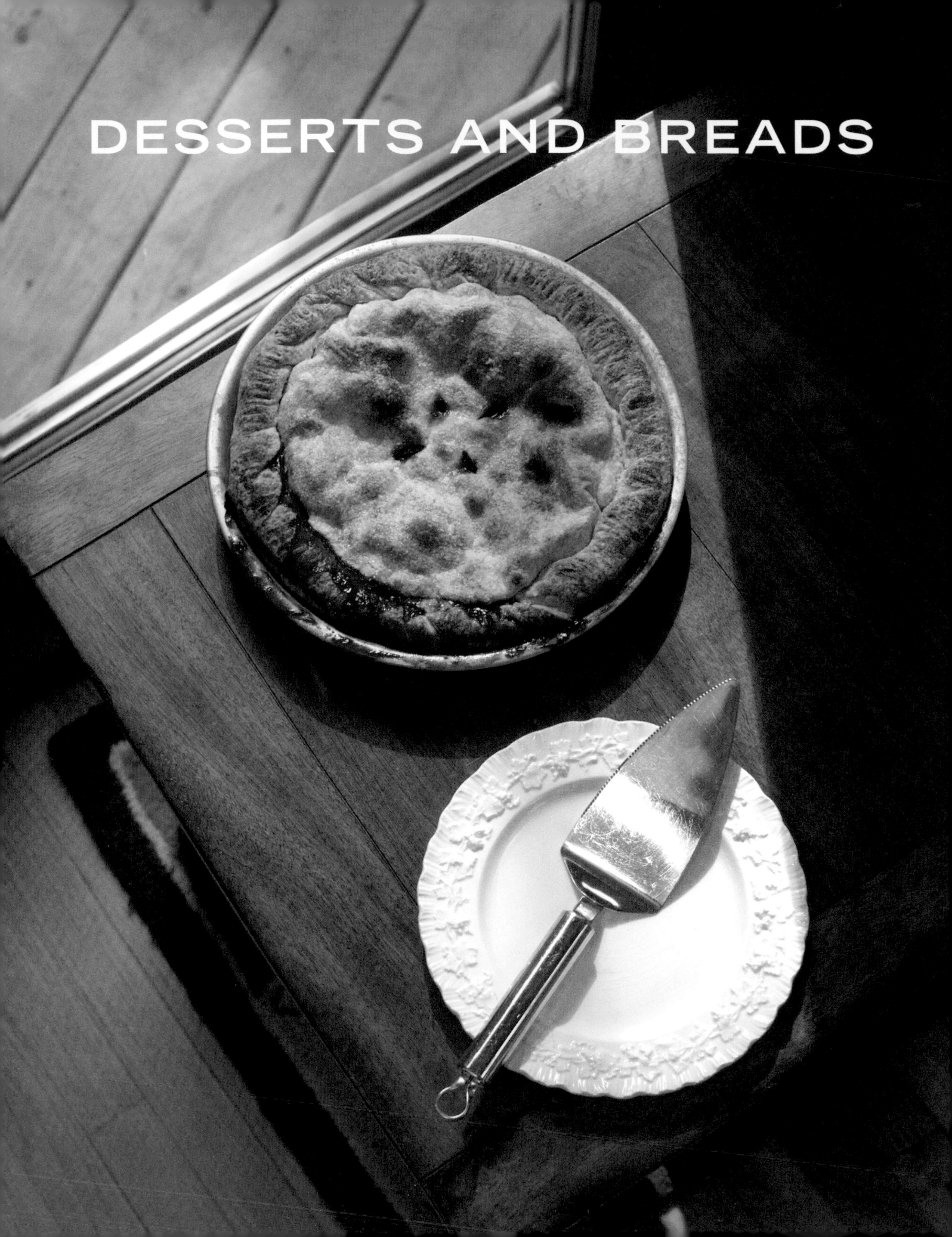

Warm Cranberry Cobbler

MICHAEL BALLON, OWNER OF THE FORMER
CASTLE STREET CAFÉ

SERVES 4 TO 6

Most of us eat cranberries once a year on Thanks-giving, which is a shame, said Chef Michael Ballon, owner of the former Castle Street Café. After all, they are the official berry of the Bay State. Folks like cranberries sweetened before eating them, which is why sugar is prominent in the following recipe, adapted from Ballon, for warm cranberry cobbler with caramelized walnuts. The walnuts add texture and autumn color.

1 tablespoon unsalted butter, melted,
    plus more for baking sheet

2¼ cups sugar, plus more for sprinkling

¾ cup walnuts, coarsely chopped

1 cup water

12 ounces whole cranberries, fresh or frozen
    (about 3 cups)

Grated zest of 1 orange

Pinch of ground nutmeg

Pinch of ground cinnamon

1 cup all-purpose flour

1 tablespoon baking powder

1 large egg, lightly beaten

Vanilla ice cream or whipped cream for serving

1. Preheat the oven to 350°F. Butter an 8-inch square baking pan and set aside. Lightly butter a baking sheet, or for easier cleanup, cover with aluminum foil, then butter the foil. Set aside.

2. Heat ½ cup of the sugar on a small saucepan over medium heat, stirring constantly with a wooden spoon, until the sugar softens and starts to caramelize. When the caramel is golden brown, add the nuts to the pan, stirring to coat them all over with the caramel. Remove from the heat and spoon the caramelized nuts onto the baking sheet, spreading them out in a single layer so they are not clumped together. Set aside to let cool.

3. Bring the water and 1 cup of the sugar to a boil in a medium saucepan over medium-high heat and add the cranberries, orange zest, nutmeg, and cinnamon. Reduce heat and simmer for about 7 minutes, or until the berries start to burst. Remove from the heat and let cool for 5 minutes. Measure half of the berries into a food processor, or use an immersion blender and a medium bowl, and coarsely puree. Combine the pureed berries with the remaining berries in the saucepan and set aside.

4. Using a fork, combine the flour, the remaining ¾ cup of sugar, and the baking powder and egg in a medium bowl until the mixture is the consistency of cornmeal.

5. To assemble the cobbler, fill the prepared baking pan with the cranberry filling, spreading evenly into the corners. Scatter the caramelized walnuts evenly over the fruit. Sprinkle the flour mixture evenly on the top, then smooth the surface gently with your fingers or the back of a spoon. Drizzle evenly with the melted butter, then sprinkle the cobbler with a little more sugar.

6. Bake for 30 minutes, or until the top starts to turn golden brown. Serve with vanilla ice cream or whipped cream.

German Plum Kuchen

THE DREAM AWAY LODGE

MAKES 2 KUCHEN

About this recipe, Chef Amy Loveless of The Dream Away Lodge says, "The first time I ate this kuchen was when my best friend's German grandmother baked it for a family dinner. She did a plum and elderberry kuchen that I will never forget! She was one of those grandmothers who never wrote down recipes. I asked to make this kuchen with her so I could learn and get it written down." This kuchen, or "cake" in German, says Loveless, may seem like it's a lot of fruit, but "that's the point. Really the ratio of batter to fruit should be almost 50/50; the batter is just there to hold the fruit together!" Kuchen may be made with other stone fruits, including peaches, sweet or sour cherries, apricots, or nectarines. And, the recipe can be easily halved to make one kuchen.

Cooking spray or unsalted butter for pans

1½ cups all-purpose flour

2 teaspoons baking powder

1 teaspoon kosher salt

6 large eggs

2 large egg yolks

1 cup canola or sunflower oil

1¼ cups sugar, or more if desired

Zest of 1 lemon

½ teaspoon almond extract

½ teaspoon vanilla extract

1¾ to 2 pounds purple or red plums, pitted and cut into quarters or eighths (40 to 48 pieces total)

1. Preheat the oven to 400°F and spray or butter two 8- or 9-inch round cake pans. (Loveless notes that the batter may also be spread thinly on a rimmed sheet pan, which is what her friend's grandmother did.)

2. Sift together the flour, baking powder, and salt into a medium bowl. Whisk together the eggs, yolks, oil, 1 cup of the sugar, and the lemon zest, and almond and vanilla extracts in a large bowl. With the whisk, stir the wet ingredients into the dry until just incorporated. Do not overmix.

3. Pour equal amounts of batter into each pan and arrange the plum pieces in circles around the edges and in the center of each cake. The plum pieces should be touching as much as possible, and will sink into the batter, but that is fine.

4. Sprinkle the tops of the kuchen liberally with the remaining ¼ cup of sugar, or more if desired, and bake for about 30 minutes, or until the tops are golden and the center of the cakes spring back when touched. Remove from the oven and let cool in the pans on a wire rack. Serve at room temperature directly from the pans.

THE BERRY PATCH

Dale-Ila Riggs, who with her husband, Don Miles, owns the 235-acre Berry Patch, in Stephentown, NY, says that when there's a question about farming, she (and Miles) look to science for the answer, not to a philosophy or set of principles like "we're an organic farm." They are looking for information, for scientific studies, including research conducted on their farm, to guide the pair to the best possible way to farm pesticide-free.

Their issue with organic: A lot of organic farmers spray a lot, says Riggs. "Organic berries right now are one of the most heavily sprayed crops in the country because of the spotted wing drosophila [a fruit fly]. There's only one organic pesticide that is effective and you can only use it for two applications before you have to rotate to something else. And there isn't an effective something else to rotate to. That's where I'm going with science, rather than saying, 'Oh, you know, I'm an organic grower, so this is my only option.'"

The Berry Patch has become a national leader in pesticide-free berry farming, after Riggs found and studied a nonchemical way to combat the dreaded drosophila, which swooped across the region and hit the farm in 2012. She tested the use of fine mesh netting to protect her blueberry bushes, partnering with Greg Loeb, a Cornell entomology research specialist, and even started a company, Berry Protection Solutions, with Miles to market the product and educate farmers on healthy options for protecting crops.

As scientists themselves, Riggs and Miles come naturally to this approach. Riggs worked for almost 10 years for the Cornell Cooperative Extension in Albany before the couple decided to start the Berry Patch in 1995, selling their first strawberries in '97. Riggs has a BA in plant science and international agriculture and an MA in horticulture and adult ed from Oregon State, which is where she met fellow student Miles, who has a background in botany, soil science, and public health. He worked as a NYS Department of Health scientist while farming part-time before finally quit-

ting his day job to join Riggs. They grow 52 weeks a year—here again, science is their friend—selling at the Troy Waterfront Farmers' Market on Saturdays and to restaurants. They offer a free choice CSA that allows their 40 members to purchase in their farm store, open to the public, selling berries, melons, fresh-cut flowers, and more than 40 types of veggies plus local foods. (About the only thing they don't grow are standard root vegetables.) Berries—strawberries, blueberries, and raspberries—are Riggs's passion. She says they're a great product to sell since there are fewer berry growers. Miles adds, "a zucchini sign just doesn't do what a strawberry sign does."

And all this with no pesticides if possible, includ-

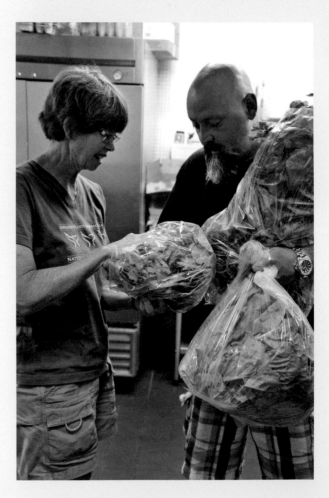

ing organic ones. But Riggs says it is a disservice to the health of consumers and to agriculture in general when people start saying, "this production method is a healthy way to do it," and if it's not done this way, it's unhealthy. "We need more people eating fresh fruits and vegetables, not being paranoid and scared about what they're putting in their mouths," she says.

In 2019, Riggs and Miles started a partnership with Michelle Todd and Autumn McManus of M&A Farm in Petersburgh, NY, to run their store, adding to Berry Patch offerings what they grow and raise: vegetables, pork, and chicken. In their newsletter, Riggs and Miles say "old farmers never retire, just plant less," and the couple plan to scale back, planting on 2 rather than 8 acres because they'd like to have a summer Sunday off, possibly a vacation. The other issue lurking behind their decision is the severe worker shortage that makes it difficult to run an operation requiring the amount of hand labor they need. "Americans will not do this work," Riggs says, recalling how a few years ago she hired two 16-year-old sisters to work in the farm store. They asked for more hours, and Riggs offered berry picking and tomato harvesting, which matched their availability. "I had this long list of jobs that were not out in the hot sun hoeing all day. I got an email from their parents saying their daughters were not available for farm work."

From a policy issue to a practical tidbit: We'd like to end with this advice from Riggs on picking and choosing strawberries. Small strawberries taste better, she says, even though consumers like the way the larger ones look. Later-season berries, which are smaller, are the ones with a higher sugar content.

Blueberry Crisp

THE BERRY PATCH

SERVES 6 TO 8

Warm blueberry crisp, fresh from the oven and topped with a slowly melting scoop of ice cream, makes a scrumptious dessert. Try tiny wild blueberries or fat, juicy ones from the farm. Smaller berries make a denser filling, whereas larger ones release their juices and create a more liquid base for the crisp on top. If using granola in this recipe instead of oats, make sure the brand used doesn't add any more sweetness than desired.

Unsalted butter for baking dish

Topping:

8 tablespoons (1 stick) unsalted butter

½ cup packed light brown sugar

1½ cups whole wheat flour

1 cup rolled oats or granola (such as BOLA from Great Barrington, MA)

Filling:

2 pints blueberries, washed and picked over for stems

½ cup granulated sugar

Zest and juice of 1 lemon

2 tablespoons cornstarch

1. Preheat the oven to 350°F. Lightly butter an 8-inch square baking dish. Place the dish on a foil-lined half sheet pan to catch any drips.

2. Prepare the topping: Melt the butter in a small saucepan over medium heat. Combine the brown sugar, whole wheat flour, and rolled oats in a medium bowl. Add the butter to the dry ingredients and stir to combine. Set aside.

3. Prepare the filling: Gently but thoroughly combine the blueberries, granulated sugar, lemon zest and juice, and cornstarch in a large bowl. Pour the berry filling mixture into the prepared baking dish and crumble the topping evenly over the fruit. Pack the topping down gently with the back of a large mixing spoon until uniformly thick.

4. Bake for 1 hour, or until the fruit is bubbling and the topping is golden. Transfer to a wire rack and let rest for 10 minutes before serving.

Sweet Piecrust

MAKES A DOUBLE PIECRUST

This easy recipe makes the perfect pastry container for any sweet pie filling.

2½ cups all-purpose flour

1 teaspoon salt

½ pound (2 sticks) unsalted butter, cut into pea-size pieces, plus more for pie plate

2 tablespoons sugar

½ cup ice water, or more as needed

1 pound dried beans, if blind-baking the bottom crust

1. Blend the flour, salt, butter, and sugar in a food processor until a granular mixture is achieved. With the processor running, gradually add the cold water through the opening of the processor lid until the dough balls up. It may not require all the water, but if it does not come together after using all of it, add 1 more teaspoon at a time. This should only take a few minutes from start to finish. Do not overmix.

2. Remove the dough from the processor and divide into two equal portions. Form each piece into a thick disk, wrap in plastic, and chill in the refrigerator for at least 30 minutes. (The dough can be held for a day or two in the refrigerator, or frozen for 4 to 6 weeks.)

3. Follow your recipe instructions for rolling and filling.

4. If the recipe does not specify a particular way to roll the dough, lightly flour a work surface and a rolling pin and roll out one piece of the dough into a wide circle, about ⅛ inch thick and about 12 inches in diameter for a standard pie plate. Adjust for a larger pie plate.

5. Lightly butter the pie plate, then carefully transfer the bottom crust circle to the pie plate, either by rolling the dough partially up onto the rolling pin so that half of the crust is supported by the pin and the other half hangs down, or by folding the dough into quarters. Unroll or unfold the crust into the pie plate and press gently on the bottom and sides. Trim any crust overhang according to the recipe instructions.

6. Most fruit pies benefit from blind-baking the bottom crust before assembling, to prevent the crust from getting too soggy, although it is not absolutely necessary. To blind-bake the bottom crust, preheat the oven to 325°F. Lay a piece of parchment paper over the bottom crust and fill with the dried beans to weigh the crust down and prevent it from puffing up. Bake for 15 minutes, or until lightly golden. Remove the parchment and beans from the crust, and save the beans to use again for blind-baking.

7. Return to the work surface, reflouring if necessary, and roll out the top crust in the same way as the bottom crust. Once the pie has been filled, move the top crust as described earlier to cover the pie. Seal the edges of the pie and cut vent holes according to the recipe instructions.

Apple Pie

RIISKA BROOK ORCHARD

SERVES 8

Different varieties of apples have specific uses: Some are great as storage apples, others are better for baking or to make cider, and some are best just eaten out of hand. Make this pie more interesting by choosing a variety of apples instead of using only one type.

1 recipe Sweet Piecrust (page 207), or store-bought

7 cups tart apples, peeled, cored, and thinly sliced (6 to 7 apples)

1 cup sugar, plus more for garnish

1 teaspoon ground cinnamon, plus more for garnish

1 teaspoon ground nutmeg

½ teaspoon salt

2 tablespoons instant tapioca

2 tablespoons unsalted butter, cut into small pieces

1. Roll out the pie dough for the lower crust and use it to line the bottom of a 9-inch pie pan, allowing the crust to hang over the edges of the pan by about ½ inch. If desired, blind-bake according to the Sweet Piecrust recipe instructions, page 207.

2. Preheat the oven to 400°F. Place the pie pan on top of a foil-lined half sheet pan to catch any drips.

3. Toss the apples with the sugar, cinnamon, nutmeg, and salt in a large bowl.

4. Sprinkle the tapioca evenly over the piecrust in the bottom of the pie pan. Add the apple mixture and dot the top with the butter.

5. Cover with the top crust and crimp the edges of the crusts together with the back of a fork to seal. Cut four steam vents in the top of the pie. If there is extra crust, try cutting out apple or leaf shapes to decorate the top. Add a little water to the back of the shapes and gently press down onto the crust. Sprinkle the top of the pie lightly with mixed sugar and cinnamon.

6. Transferring the pie pan along with its half sheet pan to the center rack of the oven, bake the pie for 45 to 60 minutes, until the crust is golden and the juices are bubbling, watching to make sure the crust does not burn. Remove from the oven and allow to cool for at least 15 minutes before serving.

RIISKA BROOK ORCHARD

There's a cute headline in an article on Riiska Brook Orchard in the *Sandisfield Times*: "APPLES ON THE TREES, IT TAKES A LOT OF RIISKAS." It couldn't be truer. Riiska Brook is a family farm and orchard run by third- and fourth-generation Riiskas (and sometimes fifth, when third-generation orchard founder Bill Riiska says his grandchildren are around).

Bill's grandfather, Matty Riiska, started a dairy farm on the property in 1913, paying about $1,300 for it. Matty's son took it over and then his son, Bill, ran it for a few years until he was drafted into the Vietnam War. "The last time we had cow's milk out here was in 1965," Bill says. Only much later, in 1990, did he start the orchard, on 25 of the farm's 155 acres. But this bare-bones sketch of the farm's history doesn't give the full sense of the Riiska imprint on this south-

eastern part of Berkshire County. Matty emigrated from Finland to the area with two brothers. According to the *Sandisfield Times*, so many relatives and friends followed that the sermon accompanying the town's Congregational Church dedication in 1909 was delivered in Finnish. When the descendants of the three brothers spread to other parts, Bill's father remained. After Vietnam, where Bill was wounded in the recapture of Hue, he eventually became a logger. But in 1990, along with his wife, Barbara, he returned to the farm at the request of one of their six children, Bethany. A friend of Bill's suggested he plant apple trees on the property—he was loath to restart dairy farming—but found that the fruit did well on the crest of the hill where the property sits, which he attributes to its higher altitude than surrounding areas. Bill started with 500 trees. Sadly, Barbara Riiska died in February 2018, but we were lucky to speak with her shortly before her death. She told us "you don't tell my husband to plant some apple trees. He wound up planting 2,500."

Bill is pretty picky about when to open up the orchard for picking, the bulk of their business. He starts with Macs and Cortlands, moves into Galas, and eventually offers 10 varieties but doesn't open to the public until the apples are ripe. As he told the *Sandisfield Times*, "apples have to hang on the trees and fill up with water and sugar and everything they need. If you pick them too soon, all that is interrupted. You want to sell people apples they'll like, or they won't come back." The farm is not organic, but Bill says he sprays minimally and only for insects (not for color, he emphasizes). Besides pick-your-own apples, Riiska sells pick-your-own blueberries in July, and pumpkins, homemade raw cider, jams, and other items in the Apple Shack.

Bill still logs in addition to running the orchard, but now with Barbara's death, is relying more on his two daughters, Suzanne Riiska Avery and Bethany Riiska Perry, and their extended families to manage the business. We spent a long time talking to Barbara about her suggestions for using the orchard's apples. She was a huge applesauce maker, which she cooked without sugar because of a diabetic granddaughter. Our recipe (page 100), inspired by Riiska Orchard, can be made with or without sugar. Barbara also suggested that using different varieties of apples in a pie "makes the best pie in the world," inspiring our recipe on page 208.

Riiska is not only a farm run by family but for families. Barbara told us that parents would ask whether their children could pick apples. She would reply, "Of course, you can. Go out, taste an apple, and if you like it, fine, pick them." She told the *Berkshire Eagle* that the trees are kept short so kids can better reach the fruit. This welcoming philosophy suggests that the Riiskas feel their orchard offers the public something besides the fruit they grow. For Barbara herself, it was her "healing place." She recounted that when her eldest daughter died, Bill would take her every evening around the orchard in a golf cart. "You couldn't stay angry with the world and see the beauty out there," she said. But Barbara was not the only one moved by the orchard's loveliness. She told the story of a couple with two small children who came to the orchard every Sunday. The husband would walk the rows while his wife sat at picnic tables with their two children playing nearby. It turns out they had a second home in the area and the husband, who had worked two blocks away from the 9/11 site in New York City and lost friends in the attacks, also found it his healing place.

Blueberry Pie

MOUNTAIN PASTURE FARM

SERVES 8

Honey takes on a supporting role as a sweetener in this charming blueberry pie, while the brightness of the lemon helps bring out the freshness of summer fruit. Be sure to let the pie fully cool after baking; otherwise, the warm fruit filling won't hold together when cut and served.

1 recipe Sweet Piecrust (page 207), or store-bought

1 cup light brown sugar

2 tablespoons local honey

6 tablespoons instant tapioca

Zest and juice of 1 lemon

¼ teaspoon salt

2 quarts blueberries, picked through for stems

2 tablespoons unsalted butter, melted

2 tablespoons granulated sugar for sprinkling

1. Roll out the pie dough for the lower crust and use it to line the bottom of a 9-inch pie pan, allowing the crust to hang over the edges of the pan by about a half inch. If desired, blind-bake according to the Sweet Piecrust recipe instructions, page 207.

2. Preheat the oven to 350°F. Place the pie pan on top of a foil-lined half sheet pan to catch any drips.

3. Combine the brown sugar, honey, tapioca, lemon zest and juice, and salt in a large bowl. Mix well, then add the berries and toss to coat.

4. Add the berry mixture to the bottom crust in the pie pan and even out with the back of a spoon. Roll out the top crust and place over the berries. Fold the overhang of the bottom crust up and over the top around the edges and crimp in place with the back of a fork to seal the crust, or otherwise seal as desired.

5. Brush the top of the pie with the melted butter and sprinkle the granulated sugar over the top. Cut four steam holes in the top. Transferring the pie pan along with its half sheet pan to the center rack of the oven, bake for 60 to 75 minutes, until the berry filling is bubbling and steam is venting from the pie, watching to make sure the piecrust does not burn. Remove from the oven and allow to cool fully before cutting and serving.

Strawberry Pie

THE BERRY PATCH

SERVES 8

Strawberry season in the Northeast is fleeting, yet the fruit abundant. There's no better way to celebrate strawberries in New England than in this pie with its signature addition of bourbon.

1 recipe Sweet Piecrust (page 207), or store-bought

2 quarts strawberries (about 3 pounds), hulled and halved; larger berries can be cut into quarters

Zest and juice of 1 large orange

½ cup sugar, plus 2 tablespoons for sprinkling

3 tablespoons cornstarch

2 tablespoons good bourbon

½ teaspoon salt

1. Roll out the pie dough for the lower crust and use it to line the bottom of a 9-inch pie pan, allowing the crust to hang over the edges of the pan by about a half inch. If desired, blind-bake according to the Sweet Piecrust recipe instructions, page 207.

2. Preheat the oven to 400°F. Place the pie pan on top of a foil-lined half sheet pan to catch any drips.

3. Combine the strawberries, orange zest and juice, ½ cup of the sugar, and the cornstarch, bourbon, and salt in a large bowl. Let the filling macerate at room temperature for 30 minutes to allow the berries to yield their juices.

4. Without pressing down on the berries, strain the accumulated juice into a small saucepan. Simmer over medium heat until thickened, whisking continually, 2 to 3 minutes once the mixture reaches a simmer. Pour the thickened sauce over the macerated berries, stir to combine, and allow to cool.

5. Pour the filling into the pie dish and smooth with the back of a spoon or a rubber spatula. Roll out the upper crust and place on top of the filling and fold the lower crust overhang over the upper crust and seal together by crimping with the tines of a fork.

6. Cut a small vent hole in the center of the pie. Sprinkle the remaining 2 tablespoons of sugar evenly over the pie. Transferring the pie pan along with its half sheet pan to the oven, bake for 45 to 60 minutes, until the crust is golden brown and the filling is bubbling, watching to make sure the piecrust does not burn. Remove from the oven and allow to cool fully so the filling can thicken.

Dutch-Style Strawberry Rhubarb Pie

THE BERRY PATCH

SERVES 8

This crumb-topped variation on a familiar pairing, combining the sweetness of strawberries with the tartness of rhubarb, will become a new favorite. If using local or another granola in this recipe instead of rolled oats, which can make the pie more interesting, make sure the brand used doesn't add more sweetness than desired.

If you make the full Sweet Piecrust from this cookbook or use a store-bought one, you'll have a second crust for another pie.

¾ cup plus 2 tablespoons all-purpose flour, plus more for dusting

½ recipe Sweet Piecrust (page 207), or store-bought

1 large egg

1 cup granulated sugar

½ teaspoon orange extract

½ teaspoon vanilla extract

14 ounces fresh rhubarb, cut into ½-inch pieces (about 3 cups)

2 pints fresh strawberries, hulled and sliced (about 4 cups sliced)

½ cup packed light brown sugar

¾ cup granola (such as **BOLA** from Great Barrington, MA) or rolled oats

Zest of 2 oranges

8 tablespoons (1 stick) cold unsalted butter, cut into pea-size pieces

1. Preheat the oven to 350°F, and set an oven rack in the center of the oven. On a lightly floured surface, using a lightly floured rolling pin, roll out the pie dough to ⅛ inch thick. Line a 9-inch pie pan with the rolled dough. Place the pie plate on a foil-lined half sheet pan to protect the oven from drips.

2. Beat the egg in a large bowl. Add the granulated sugar, 2 tablespoons of flour, and orange and vanilla extracts and mix until smooth. Fold in the rhubarb and strawberries, making sure the fruit is fully coated. Pour into the piecrust, using a rubber spatula to scrape the contents of the bowl fully into the crust.

3. Combine the remaining ¾ cup of flour with the brown sugar, granola, and orange zest in a medium bowl. Use two knives to cut the butter into little pieces into the dry ingredients. The same result can be achieved by pressing down on the butter pieces with the back of a fork. Once the butter has been cut into the flour enough to make it crumbly, sprinkle the mixture over the fruit in the pie plate.

4. Transferring the pie pan along with its half sheet pan to the center rack of the oven, bake for 60 to 70 minutes, until the pie is golden brown and bubbling. Remove from the oven and allow to cool on a wire rack for at least 30 minutes before serving.

Kabocha Squash Cake with Maple Butter Drizzle

JOHN ANDREWS FARMHOUSE RESTAURANT

SERVES 10 TO 12

This wonderful gluten-free dessert, adapted from Chef Dan Smith of John Andrews Farmhouse Restaurant, is more like a soufflé—light and airy, yet full of flavor. Despite the cake's ethereal texture, winter squash plays a starring role, accompanied by the fresh sweetness of maple syrup. If kabocha is unavailable, butternut squash may be used as a substitute (but it's more flavorful with the former).

Cake:

½ pound (2 sticks) plus 2 tablespoons unsalted butter, cut into 1-inch pieces, plus more for pan

2½ pounds kabocha squash, peeled, seeded, and 1-inch diced (about 4 cups)

½ cup heavy cream

6 large eggs

½ cup pure maple syrup

¼ cup cornstarch

¼ cup sugar

Maple Butter Drizzle:

¼ cup pure maple syrup or honey

8 tablespoons (1 stick) unsalted butter, cut into 1-inch pieces

¼ to ½ teaspoon freshly ground black pepper

1. Preheat the oven to 325°F. Set an oven rack in the center of the oven. Wrap foil around the bottom of a 9- or 10-inch springform pan to prevent leaks. Lightly butter the sides and bottom of the pan, and cut a circle of parchment paper to line the bottom. Place the prepared springform pan in a larger roasting pan.

2. Steam the squash in a pot with a steamer insert, until tender and easily pierced with a fork, 8 to 10 minutes. Drain and set aside to cool to room temperature.

3. Gently warm the butter and cream together over low heat in a small, heavy-bottomed saucepan until the butter is just melted. Do not allow it to simmer. In a separate pot or tea kettle, bring water to a boil to use in Step 7.

4. Separate three of the eggs.

5. Working in batches, in a blender or food processor, puree together the squash, cream mixture, maple syrup, three whole eggs plus three egg yolks, and the cornstarch until smooth and no lumps of squash remain. Combine the batches in a large bowl.

6. Whip the remaining three egg whites in a large bowl with an electric mixer, adding the sugar slowly in a thin stream while the mixer runs, and scraping down the sides of the bowl with a rubber spatula. Beat until soft peaks form. Gently fold the egg whites into the puree until no white streaks or lumps remain. Pour the batter into the prepared springform pan.

7. Transfer the roasting pan along with its springform to the center rack of the oven. Carefully pour the boiling water into the roasting pan so that the water comes about halfway up the outside of the springform pan. This will create a bain-marie, in which a cake pan is set in a larger roasting pan surrounded with hot water, creating a gentler, more uniform heat for cooking custards, such as this cake. Bake for 90 minutes, or until the top is golden and center is set.

8. Remove from the oven, carefully lift the springform pan out of the roasting pan, and set it on a wire rack to cool. After a few minutes, remove the foil and run a thin knife around the inside of the pan, and loosen gently to remove the springform ring. Leave the cake on the base of the pan for cooling. Once the cake has reached room temperature, and firmed up a little, gently run a knife or a thin spatula

under the parchment paper to separate it from the pan base, then slide it gently onto a serving platter.

9. While the cake is cooling, prepare the maple butter (if using): Gently warm the maple syrup in a small, heavy-bottomed saucepan over low heat. When warm, whisk in the butter until melted and season to taste with pepper. Serve the cake slightly warm or at room temperature, drizzled with maple butter.

Maple Cheesecake with Pecan Topping

IOKA VALLEY FARM

SERVES 10

Decadent and flavorful, this beautiful maple cheese-cake is crowned with a pecan caramel topping. Per-fect for a party, it's best made the morning of or the day before you plan to serve it, since a nice long rest in the refrigerator will help it firm up. If you prefer the graham cracker crust to go up the sides of the pan, just double the amounts given for the crust and you will have enough.

Unsalted butter for pan

Crust:

4 tablespoons (½ stick) unsalted butter

1½ cups graham cracker crumbs (about 11 to 13 whole graham crackers)

2 tablespoons pure maple syrup

Filling:

1 vanilla bean, or 1 teaspoon vanilla extract

2 pounds cream cheese, at room temperature

1 cup pure maple syrup

4 large eggs

2 tablespoons freshly grated lemon zest (from about 2 large lemons)

½ cup heavy cream

Topping:

1 cup coarsely chopped pecan halves

6 tablespoons unsalted butter

½ cup dark brown sugar

¼ cup heavy cream

Pinch of salt

1. Preheat the oven to 350°F and set an oven rack in the center of the oven. Lightly butter the bottom and sides of a 9-, 10-, or 11-inch springform pan. Cut a circle of parchment paper to line the bottom of the pan.

2. Prepare the crust: Melt the butter in a large saucepan over medium heat, but do not allow it to brown. Remove from the heat and stir in the graham cracker crumbs and maple syrup. Allow to cool enough to touch comfortably with your fingers. Press the mixture into the bottom of the pan on top of the parchment paper, creating an even thickness, and pressing the mixture just over the seam around the bottom.

3. Prepare the filling: If using, slice the vanilla bean lengthwise down the center. Using a small spoon or the flat side of the knife, scrape the tiny black vanilla seeds out of each side of the bean. Carefully collect the seeds in a small bowl and set aside.

4. By hand, in a large bowl with a wooden spoon, or using an electric mixer and a large bowl or a stand mixer fitted with the paddle attachment, beat the cream cheese until soft and smooth, scraping down the sides of the bowl as necessary. Add the maple syrup and beat, scraping the bottom and sides of the bowl to incorporate all the cream cheese. Some small lumps of cream cheese may remain at this stage. Add the eggs gradually, one at a time, and

continued . . .

beat to incorporate evenly. Add the vanilla bean seeds or vanilla extract, lemon zest, and heavy cream and beat until just incorporated.

5. Set the springform pan in the center of a foil-lined rimmed baking sheet to prevent any leaks from dripping. Pour the filling into the crust and smooth with a spatula. Transfer the springform pan along with its baking sheet with the cheesecake to the middle of the oven. Bake for 60 to 90 minutes, which will depend on the size of your pan, until the cheesecake is set on the sides and is still slightly jiggly in the center, checking periodically to make sure the top does not burn and loosely covering with foil if necessary. Remove from the oven and place the pan on a wire rack on the counter. The cheesecake will firm up as it cools to room temperature. Be sure that the cake is fully cooled to room temperature before covering the pan with foil and chilling in the refrigerator for at least 6 hours or overnight.

6. Prepare the topping: Toast the pecan pieces in a small skillet over medium heat, stirring frequently, until slightly browned and fragrant, 5 to 7 minutes. Nuts can burn very quickly, so watch carefully. Remove the pan from the heat and set aside to cool.

7. When almost ready to serve, combine the butter and brown sugar in a medium saucepan and cook over medium heat, stirring constantly, until smooth. Stir in the cream and salt and allow to come to a boil. Simmer just until slightly thickened, stirring constantly to avoid sticking, about 5 minutes, then add the pecan pieces, stirring to coat. Remove from the heat and let cool slightly, but not so much that it becomes difficult to spoon over the cheesecake.

8. Remove the cheesecake from the refrigerator, run a thin knife around the pan to help release the sides, and ease the ring over the top of the cheesecake. Cut the cheesecake with a sharp knife, and spoon the warm pecan caramel over the top of each slice.

HIGH LAWN FARM

Perhaps the ultimate praise for High Lawn Farm, Lee, MA, comes from Bjorn Somlo, chef/owner of Nudel restaurant in Lenox, MA, himself an icon of Berkshire farm-to-table dining. "If I could imagine how to sum up their business it would be to say they are a pillar of what the farm-to-table movement is all about." High Lawn Farm milk is what our adult children grab from the dairy case at Guido's Fresh Marketplace—for them, it is synonymous with local.

High Lawn is a small dairy—about 350 Jersey cows, of which 120 are milked—with an unusual family pedigree. The Wilde family has owned High Lawn since 1935, but what is unique is that second-generation owner Marjorie Field Wilde, who died in 1997, descended from railroad tycoon Cornelius Vanderbilt through her mother, Lila B. Field, one of the original owners. Even with this distinguished lineage, dairy farming in New England isn't easy. But General Manager Roberto Laurens says the current generation plans to preserve it as a small-scale family farm.

High Lawn is the last Berkshire County dairy to process its own milk and deliver finished products, ranging from skim, low-fat, whole, and chocolate milk to half-and-half, heavy cream, and butter to ice cream and even seasonal eggnog. They also just began to produce artisanal cheeses. High Lawn is ubiquitous in the Berkshires, selling to local markets, cafés, high-end restaurants, and regional supermarket chains, and even farther afield, including to Whole Foods Market in Massachusetts and educational institutions.

The farm is a major booster of Jersey cows and their milk and has found a huge advocate in Laurens. When we asked what differentiates High Lawn milk, he says, "It's the Jersey cow." Wilde herself became known as a breeder of this small brown cow from the Channel Islands. "Mrs. Wilde did it by eye," Laurens told the *Berkshire Eagle*. "She would say that a cow is great, so we're going to breed that

cow with that bull." According to High Lawn, the breed's milk is more nutritious, producing 20 percent more calcium and 17 percent more protein per unit of feed than average cows. The breed—and Laurens would agree—produces a richer-tasting milk. He says he can detect when High Lawn butter is used in a croissant and vouches for the fact that its skim milk tastes like another dairy's whole milk. He also finds it more digestible. "Some people believe they have lactose intolerance and sometimes it's just that they have a hard time digesting the milk. I am one of them. So, I learned with the Jersey milk here, that I actually can drink it without any trouble." As further testament to the digestibility of Jersey cow milk, he says he has no problem eating High Lawn ice cream.

The farm is proud of the purity of its products. At High Lawn, with its 1,500 acres, over half wooded, the Jerseys have plenty of fresh grass to graze on and almost all their winter feed comes from High Lawn's own corn and hay fields. No GMO seed is used nor harmful pesticides. High Lawn calls its milk natural, and artificial hormone-free. The website describes happy cows with waterbeds to sleep on, udders cleaned with every milking, and a greater life expectancy. Because of the difficulty finding people to work on a dairy farm—it's a hands-on, intensive job—Laurens purchased the Lely Astronaut robotic milking system. It runs 23 hours a day, seven days a week, and almost wholly frees humans—those hard-to-get farmworkers—from the milking process. But, it also allows High Lawn Farm cows to choose to get milked when they are ready.

Laurens also finds the Jersey cow behaviorally exceptional, comparing the gentle cow to pet dogs. "All cows in general are curious but Jerseys want to go over to you, lick you, push you."

An agronomist engineer from Colombia, Laurens was recruited in 2002 and is so invested in what the farm produces that he says "this is probably going to be my last job." (Also, to be truthful, he says, "I am not the one that wants to be working at 80 years old!") "It's fun here, because when I was working just with cows, you concentrate on one piece. When you work with production, storage, distribution, customers, your stress increases but your passion does also."

Chocolate Ganache with Dried Cranberries

HIGH LAWN FARM

SERVES 10 TO 12

These small ganache squares, using High Lawn Farm dairy products, are so rich and elegant! The dried cranberries may be replaced by any other favorite dried fruit, chopped into small pieces. If you can find them, tiny dried wild blueberries work exceptionally well.

14 ounces semisweet chocolate chips (about 2 cups)
1 cup High Lawn Farm heavy cream
1 teaspoon vanilla extract
2 tablespoons unsalted butter
½ cup dried cranberries, or other chopped dried fruit

1. Cut a wide strip of parchment paper to line a 9-inch square baking dish, allowing the paper to come up and overhang two opposite sides of the pan.

2. Place the chocolate chips in a medium bowl.

3. Bring the cream and vanilla to a boil in a small saucepan over medium to high heat, then remove from the heat. Pour over the chips and mix quickly, and as the chocolate melts down, add in the butter and stir until smooth. Fold in the cranberries and pour into the prepared pan. Place in the refrigerator for at least 1 hour. Do not put into the freezer as a shortcut since this will cause the butter to separate from the ganache.

4. Once the ganache is set, remove from the refrigerator and run a sharp knife along the sides without parchment paper. Use the overhanging parchment paper to lift the ganache gently out of the pan and place on a plate or cutting board. Invert the ganache over a large platter or clean, dry cutting board.

continued . . .

5. Starting from one corner, carefully pull the parchment paper off the top of the ganache. Warm a sharp knife in hot water, wipe dry, and cut the ganache into small pieces, about 1½ by 3 inches. This is a very rich dessert, so one piece is typically enough for a serving. The ganache is best served slightly cold—make sure it doesn't start to get too soft or melt—either by itself or with sweetened High Lawn Farm whipped cream, or drizzle with caramel or a fruit puree.

Carrot Cake with Cream Cheese Frosting

HAVEN CAFE & BAKERY

SERVES 20 AS A LAYER CAKE

This handsome carrot cake, adapted from owner Shelly Williams of Haven Cafe & Bakery, makes a magnificent party-size dessert. The cake also freezes well, so that a smaller, single-layer version can grace the table one evening while the other layer, unfrosted, can hibernate, ready to be plucked from the freezer for a last-minute dessert.

Neutral oil, like canola, for pans

Cake:

**1½ pounds carrots, peeled and cut into
    1-inch pieces (about 5½ cups)**

4 cups all-purpose flour

1½ teaspoons baking powder

1½ teaspoons baking soda

1½ teaspoons salt

1 tablespoon plus ½ teaspoon ground cinnamon

½ teaspoon ground cloves

¾ teaspoon ground cardamom

¾ teaspoon ground allspice

2 cups canola oil

1¾ cups granulated sugar

1 cup packed dark brown sugar

6 large eggs

1 tablespoon vanilla extract

1½ cups drained crushed pineapple

2 cups unsweetened desiccated grated coconut

Frosting:

**1 pound (4 sticks) unsalted butter, at room
    temperature**

1½ pounds cream cheese, at room temperature

3½ cups powdered sugar

1½ teaspoons vanilla extract

⅛ teaspoon salt

2 cups chopped pecans or walnuts (optional)

1. Preheat the oven to 325°F and oil two 9-inch square or round cake pans with canola oil. Cut a piece of parchment paper to fit into the bottom of each pan.

2. Prepare the cake: Add water to a large saucepan fitted with a steamer basket, keeping the water below the basket. Bring the water to a boil over high heat. Place 3¼ cups of the carrots in the steamer basket and cover the saucepan. Steam until soft, about 20 minutes, checking the water periodically to make sure it has not boiled away. Transfer the steamed carrots to a food processor and puree. Use a rubber spatula to scrape the carrot puree into a large glass measuring cup and set aside to cool. There should be about 1½ cups of carrot puree.

3. Fit the food processor with a shredding blade attachment and shred the remaining carrots. This should make about 2 cups of shredded carrots.

4. Sift the flour, baking powder, baking soda, salt, cinnamon, cloves, cardamom, and allspice into a medium bowl and set aside.

continued . . .

5. Using an electric mixer with a very large bowl, cream together the canola oil and both sugars, scraping down the sides of the bowl frequently with a rubber spatula.

6. Combine the eggs and vanilla in a small bowl and add to the batter gradually, about one-quarter at a time. Mix on medium speed until well combined. The mixture will thicken a bit at this stage. One ingredient at a time, mixing well between additions, add the carrot puree, grated carrots, crushed pineapple, and coconut to the batter.

7. Slowly add the flour mixture to the batter and mix on medium-high speed for about 1 minute to combine thoroughly. Remove the beaters from the batter and tap on the rim of the bowl to get any shredded carrots off the beaters. Scrape down the sides of the bowl and mix a few times to keep the carrots from clumping together.

8. Pour the batter into the prepared cake pans, dividing the batter evenly between the two pans. Set the cake pans into the middle of the oven and bake for 50 minutes. Test for doneness by inserting a skewer into the center of a cake until the skewer comes out clean, adding more baking time in 5-minute increments as needed. If more baking time is needed, cover the cake with foil as it continues to bake. When the cakes are done, remove from the oven and set the pans on a wire rack to cool to room temperature.

9. While the cakes cool, prepare the cream cheese frosting: With an electric mixer fitted with the paddle attachment, beat the butter until light and fluffy, about 5 minutes. Add the cream cheese and beat until fully incorporated and no lumps remain, scraping down the sides of the bowl frequently with a rubber spatula. Add the powdered sugar, ½ cup at a time, beating between each addition. This will help keep the sugar from puffing up and out of the bowl onto the counter. Add the vanilla and salt to the frosting and beat well to incorporate, until light and fluffy.

10. Run a thin knife around the edge of the cooled cakes in the pan and gently turn one cake out of the pan, top side down, onto a serving plate. Peel off the parchment paper. Using a spreader or a rubber spatula, thinly frost the sides and top of the cake to create a crumb coat that will be the base layer of the frosting, to seal the cake and keep any loose crumbs from getting mixed into the next, thicker layer of frosting.

11. If making only one layer of the cake, frost this first cake thickly over the crumb coat on the sides and top as desired. Wrap the second, unfrosted cake tightly in several layers of plastic wrap, label, and freeze for future use. Place the remaining cream cheese frosting in an airtight container, label, and freeze for future use. If making a two-layer cake, proceed to the following step.

12. Spread a thicker layer of frosting over the crumb coat only on the top of the first layer. Carefully turn the second layer of the cake out of the pan, top side down, onto a plate that is large enough to hold it. Peel off the parchment paper. Using your hands and a large spatula, carefully flip the second layer of cake so that the flat bottom meets the frosted top of the first layer. Gently push the top layer around a little to center it over the bottom layer.

13. Spread a thin crumb coat of frosting all over the sides of both layers, as well as on the top of the second layer of the cake, filling in any cracks between the two layers with frosting and creating a smooth, flat surface to seal the cake. Once the crumb coat is applied, cover the sides and top of the cake with a thicker layer of frosting. If you would like to add chopped nuts, scatter them over the top of the frosted cake. Store the cake in the refrigerator to allow the frosting to firm before serving.

HAVEN CAFE & BAKERY

Pardon us in advance for mixing yoga and meditation nomenclature. For Shelly Williams, a former yoga teacher and now owner of Haven Cafe & Bakery, Lenox, MA, her mantra for her restaurant is "flavor," and if we could add just a few more words, "ingredients matter most," as in the need to source the best, preferably local and organic. As Williams told the *Berkshire Edge*, "if you don't start there, all the techniques you master won't make it right. You need to have 100 percent commitment to your ingredients."

Williams never expected to be a restaurateur, although starting Haven is not so far-fetched, given that she worked in restaurants in Washington state, albeit in the front of the house. It was a chef at a Spokane restaurant, Luna, who influenced her greatly, a "genius with food, bar none." Her flavors were extraordinary and so was her commitment to buying the best ingredients, so much so that years later, Williams can recall the local handmade tofu the restaurant purchased from "Tofu Phil," and each layer of a signature grilled tofu Napoleon. Working at Luna underscored for Williams the primacy of flavor.

From Washington, Williams came to Kripalu for yoga teacher training, ended up working there, running its store, teaching yoga, and then marrying and having children. Once again, she fell into the food business, agreeing to cook a few dishes for a couple hosting a 50-person party in Richmond the day after Christmas. First, they just wanted her to bake lasagna, then added beef tenderloin to the list. Which led to a guest asking her to cater another party, this time for 150. Eventually, Williams realized she needed a professional kitchen and bought what is now Haven, opening in July 2008 and selling coffee, scones, and pastries. Then, she added breakfast. And then lunch. It was exhausting and a learning experience for someone who had never worked a restaurant line. "Every day, we ran out of eggs," Williams recalls. "At the end of August, I was going to get eggs and I was so tired, a front of the house guy had to drive me. I said to him,

'Can we not go back?' 'You have to go back,' he says. 'You're the owner.'"

Which leads us back to Williams's emphasis on flavor and sourcing local. She tells the story of how she once hired an excellent cook with an institutional food background. He couldn't understand why she didn't buy precut butternut squash, opting instead for whole fresh ones from a local farm. "Shelly," he said, "It would be much easier. It's the same product." She told him it was definitely not. But one day he had an epiphany and realized that the squash cut from scratch actually released moisture. That's what you lose when you buy the precut, Williams told him. To her, spending more money on the best ingredients is worth it, and she says, "all things being equal, I'd like to give my money to people I know and respect—to the local farmer—to the person that shares my values." She'll buy local over organic, and acknowledges that many area farmers can't afford certification but grow sustainably. She buys organic sugar, flour, steel-cut oats, and polenta, but not olive oil. "Things like that, I go more on flavor than strictly organic."

True to her principles, Williams buys eggs from a regional farm with "happy, free, chickens"; milk from High Lawn Farm in Lee, MA; yogurt from Sidehill Farm in Hawley, MA (where Leahey Farm in Lee, MA, sells its milk); fruit from The Berry Patch in Stephentown, NY. We asked how she keeps her price point down. "My numbers aren't as good as other restaurants but I don't care because—this is where yoga comes in—if I fail, it'll be because I'm doing what I believe in, not because I lowered my standards."

Farm Camp Brownies

HAWTHORNE VALLEY FARM

MAKES 10 TO 12 BROWNIES

Brownies are a perennial treat for chocolate lovers. Here, jazzing up a Hawthorne Valley Farm camp recipe with chocolate chips, orange zest, and walnuts is well worth it!

½ pound (2 sticks) unsalted butter, at room temperature, plus more for baking dish

1 cup unsweetened cocoa powder

¼ cup canola oil

1¾ cups sugar

4 large eggs

1½ teaspoons vanilla extract

1 scant cup all-purpose flour

½ cup chocolate chips (optional)

½ cup chopped walnuts (optional)

1 tablespoon zested orange peel (optional)

1. Preheat the oven to 350°F. Lightly butter a 7-by-11- or 9-by-9-inch baking dish.

2. Combine the cocoa and canola oil in a medium bowl to make a thick paste. Be sure to mix completely to eliminate any lumps.

3. Cream together the butter and sugar in a large bowl until light and fluffy. Add the eggs, one at a time, beating in each egg to integrate fully. Beat in the vanilla. Using a rubber spatula, scrape the cocoa mixture into the butter mixture and continue to beat until combined. Stir in the flour, and any optional ingredients.

4. Spread the batter in the prepared baking dish, smoothing the top with a rubber spatula or the back of a large spoon. Bake for 35 to 40 minutes, until a toothpick inserted in the center comes out clean.

5. Remove from the oven and allow to cool in the pan for at least 30 minutes before cutting the brownies from the pan. Cut into squares and serve.

Indian Pudding

THE RED LION INN

SERVES 12 TO 14

Chef Brian Alberg, former Red Lion executive chef, notes that Indian pudding is among the oldest of New England desserts and many consider it the best. Early New Englanders baked it on Saturday in the same oven as baked beans, cooking for 10 hours. Then, it was served for supper—dished up in a soup plate and drowned in thick, sweet cream. What follows is, as Alberg puts it, "the very old, very New England, the very Red Lion Inn version, which fortunately takes only two hours in the oven." Indian pudding is best if made a day before it is eaten.

8 tablespoons (1 stick) unsalted butter, plus more for baking dish, or cooking spray

6 cups milk (do not use skim)

¾ cup cornmeal

⅔ cup molasses

2 large eggs

3 tablespoons ground cinnamon

1 tablespoon ground ginger

1 cup peeled, cored, and thinly sliced apple

½ cup dried cranberries

Vanilla ice cream or whipped cream for serving

1. Preheat the oven to 300°F. Butter the bottom and sides of a 2½- to 3-quart shallow baking dish or spray with cooking spray.

2. Combine 5 cups of the milk and the butter in a large saucepan, of at least 3- to 4-quart capacity, and bring to a boil over medium-high heat, watching carefully so it does not boil over.

3. Meanwhile, whisk the remaining 1 cup of milk with the cornmeal in a medium bowl, stirring well to avoid lumps. Once the milk reaches a boil, lower the heat, add the cornmeal mixture, and continue to stir, again to avoid lumps. Cook for 20 minutes over low heat, stirring slowly so the mixture does not burn or stick to the bottom of the saucepan. Remove from the heat.

4. Mix together the molasses, eggs, cinnamon, and ginger in a medium bowl. Slowly pour the molasses mixture in a thin stream into the thickened cornmeal mixture, whisking constantly, until thoroughly blended together. Pour this mixture into the prepared baking dish and bake for 1 hour.

5. Remove the dish from the oven and scatter the sliced apple and dried cranberries over the top of the pudding. Using a rubber spatula, gently fold them into the pudding, making sure the fruit pieces are evenly distributed. Return the dish to the oven and bake for 1 hour more, or until a tester inserted into the center comes out clean.

6. Remove from the oven and allow the pudding to rest for at least 1 hour before serving. Use a large serving spoon to scoop the pudding from the baking dish into serving dishes. Serve warm or at room temperature, topped with vanilla ice cream or whipped cream.

Pumpkin Crème Brûlée

IOKA VALLEY FARM

SERVES 8

Rich and creamy, these individual-size desserts are topped with caramelized sugar that cracks satisfyingly when tapped with the back of a spoon. Although they can be finished under the broiler, the best results are achieved by using a kitchen torch to melt the ginger sugar coating. If you cannot find fresh pumpkin, canned pure pumpkin puree is an acceptable substitute. Be aware, however, that the moisture and consistency is different and the crème brûlée may not set as firmly with canned puree.

1 pie pumpkin (about 2½ pounds),
   or 1½ cups canned pure pumpkin puree
   (not pumpkin pie filling)

1 tablespoon extra virgin olive oil,
   plus more for half sheet pan

4 cups heavy cream

1½ tablespoons vanilla extract

¼ teaspoon salt

½ cup light brown sugar

6 large egg yolks

½ cup granulated sugar

2 teaspoons finely grated fresh ginger

1. Preheat the oven to 350°F. Lightly oil a half sheet pan and set aside. Assemble eight ramekins on a baking dish or roasting pan and set aside.

2. Cut the pumpkin in half and scoop out the seeds and pulp. The seeds can be saved for toasting or discarded. Coat the inside and cut edges of the pumpkin with the olive oil and place, cut side down, on the prepared half sheet pan. Roast in the oven for 30 minutes, or until the pumpkin flesh is very soft. Remove from the oven and allow to cool to room temperature, then scoop out the soft pumpkin flesh from the rind and puree in a blender, food processor,

or in a bowl with an immersion blender. Reserve 1½ cups of the pumpkin puree for the crème brûlée.

3. Combine the cream, vanilla, salt, pumpkin puree, and brown sugar in a medium saucepan and bring to a gentle boil over medium heat.

4. Whisk together the egg yolks and ¼ cup of the sugar in a large bowl until smooth and creamy yellow in color. Temper the yolks with the hot pumpkin mixture by slowly adding ¼ cup of the mixture to the yolks. Whisk constantly to bring the eggs up to a warm temperature slowly and carefully to avoid lumps. Add another ¼ cup of the hot mixture while whisking the yolks, and then add another. Repeat, using ¼-cup measurements of the hot mixture and whisking all the time, until the mixture is incorporated into the yolks as a custard in the large bowl.

5. Divide the custard equally among each of the ramekins. Place the ramekins in the baking dish. Create a hot water bath by carefully pouring boiling water into the baking dish around the outside of the ramekins without getting any water into the custard. The water should rise halfway up the sides of the ramekins. Place the baking dish in the oven and bake until the custards are set, about 30 minutes. Remove from the oven, take the custard ramekins out of the hot water bath, and allow to cool to room temperature before chilling them in the refrigerator for at least 1 hour or overnight.

6. When ready to finish with the burnt sugar topping, mix ¼ cup of the granulated sugar and grated ginger together in a small bowl. Sprinkle the ginger sugar evenly over the tops of the cold crème brûlées and caramelize with a kitchen torch. Alternatively, place the sugared ramekins directly under the broiler just until the sugar mix begins to caramelize, which can be quick depending on your broiler. If using the broiler, try not to leave the custards under the broiler any longer than necessary since they will warm up and the custard will become less firm. Allow the hot sugar on top to cool slightly before serving.

Rosemary Popovers

THE RED LION INN

MAKES 6 POPOVERS OR 9 SMALL ONES

Light, puffed, crispy on the outside, and fragrant with rosemary, these popovers, from Brian Alberg, former executive chef of The Red Lion Inn, are a big hit with the brunch or luncheon crowd. They are simple to make, and the recipe will double easily if more are needed. Be sure to allow the ingredients for the batter to come to room temperature before mixing, which will make for better popovers. If you can, it's best if you prepare the batter the day before and let it rest in the refrigerator overnight. You can use the popover batter right from the refrigerator. If you have a source for rendered duck fat, that will enrich these rolls with a distinctive flavor and aroma.

1 cup whole milk

2 large eggs, lightly beaten

2 cups rendered duck fat (canola oil will work if duck fat is not available)

1 cup all-purpose flour

1½ teaspoons kosher salt

1½ tablespoons fresh rosemary, or 2½ teaspoons dried, finely chopped

1. About an hour before mixing the batter, measure out the milk and leave on the counter along with the eggs to bring them to room temperature.

2. Preheat the oven to 400°F. Place a nonstick 12-muffin tin on a foil-lined rimmed half sheet pan. If using a smaller tin, you may need to prepare a second one.

3. To allow the hot air from the oven to circulate freely around each popover, fill every other muffin well in the tin with about ⅓ cup of the duck fat so that when the popovers puff, they will not be next to one another and touch. It is not necessary to be exact about the amount, but be sure it is close to

⅓ cup. Place the half sheet pan along with its muffin tin in the oven for 10 minutes to allow the fat to melt and get hot.

4. Whisk together the flour, salt, eggs, milk, and chopped rosemary in a large bowl, taking care not to overmix. The consistency may be slightly runny.

5. Remove the muffin tin and baking sheet from the oven, and using a ⅓-cup measure, pour the batter into the wells where the duck fat has melted almost to the top. The batter will also reach almost to the top, causing some duck fat to spill over the sides, but that is fine. As the popovers rise and bake, more melted duck fat will run off onto the sheet pan; it can be discarded later.

6. Return the baking sheet and muffin tin to the oven. Bake for 33 to 40 minutes, until the popovers are well risen and browned. Remove the half sheet pan and muffin tin from the oven and if popovers are sticking at all, use a rubber spatula to gently pry them out of the pan. Serve hot.

Parsnip (or Carrot) Bread

HANCOCK SHAKER VILLAGE

MAKES 1 LOAF

This quick bread adapted from Chef Brian Alberg, who oversees food operations at Hancock Shaker Village, can also be made with carrots.

11 tablespoons unsalted butter, plus more for pan

1 cup sugar

1½ cups all-purpose flour

1 teaspoon baking soda

1½ teaspoons ground cinnamon

1 teaspoon ground ginger

1 teaspoon salt

2 cups peeled, trimmed, and finely grated parsnips (about 4) or carrots (about 6)

½ cup dried cranberries, chopped

2 large eggs

1. Preheat the oven to 350°F. Grease an 8-by-4-inch loaf pan with butter and line the bottom with a piece of parchment paper. Melt the butter and sugar together in a medium saucepan over medium-low heat until the sugar has dissolved. Remove from the heat and set aside to cool to room temperature.

2. Combine the flour, baking soda, cinnamon, ginger, salt, grated parsnips, and dried cranberries in a medium bowl.

3. Beat the eggs into the cooled butter mixture in the saucepan, then whisk until fully incorporated. Add the wet ingredients to the dry and mix together.

4. Pour the batter into the loaf pan and bake for 45 to 60 minutes, until a toothpick inserted in the center comes out clean. Remove from the oven and allow to cool in the pan for 15 minutes. Slide a thin knife around the outside edges of the loaf and invert to remove the loaf gently from the pan. Allow the loaf to cool fully on a wire rack before serving.

Pumpkin Bread

HANCOCK SHAKER VILLAGE

MAKES 1 LOAF

This sweet yet hearty pumpkin bread, adapted from a recipe by Chef Brian Alberg, is delicious with breakfast, at teatime, or heated and topped with ice cream for dessert.

8 tablespoons (1 stick) unsalted butter, melted, plus more for pan

1 cup all-purpose flour

¾ cup rye flour

1 tablespoon ground cinnamon

1½ teaspoons ground ginger

1 teaspoon salt

1 teaspoon baking soda

½ cup granulated sugar

1 cup light brown sugar

¼ cup water

2 large eggs, lightly beaten

1 cup pure pumpkin puree, either fresh from a roasted pumpkin or canned (do not use pumpkin pie filling)

1. Preheat the oven to 350°F. Lightly butter the bottom and sides of an 8-by-4-inch loaf pan and line the bottom with parchment paper.

2. Combine both flours and the cinnamon, ginger, salt, and baking soda in a medium bowl until incorporated. Combine the sugars, melted butter, water, eggs, and pumpkin in a large bowl until fully blended. Add the dry ingredients to the wet and fold together gently. Do not overmix, or the batter will become starchy and tough.

3. Once the batter has barely come together, pour into the prepared loaf pan and place in the oven. Bake for 50 to 70 minutes, until a toothpick inserted in the center of the loaf comes out clean. The length

of baking time may depend on the amount of moisture in the pumpkin puree.

4. Remove from the oven and place on a wire rack to cool. Gently run a thin knife around the edges of the bread before it cools, to loosen from the sides of the pan. Allow to cool for 20 minutes in the pan. Gently tip the pan over and ease the bread out carefully so as not to tear the loaf. Allow to continue to cool on the rack before peeling off the parchment paper and serving.

Apple Bread

RIISKA BROOK ORCHARD

MAKES 1 LOAF

When apples are abundant in the fall, this bread makes a tasty and seasonal treat. For a heartier loaf, use all whole wheat flour, or experiment with half whole wheat and half all-purpose. Try the bread toasted for breakfast or as an after-school snack.

Unsalted butter for pan

2 large eggs

1 cup plus 2 tablespoons sugar

½ cup pure maple syrup

2 cups peeled, cored, and diced apple

2 cups whole wheat flour, or 1 cup whole wheat
   flour plus 1 cup all-purpose flour

1 teaspoon salt

1¼ teaspoons baking powder

1 teaspoon ground cinnamon

1. Preheat the oven to 350°F. Lightly butter an 8-by-4-inch loaf pan and line the bottom with parchment paper.

2. Beat together the eggs, sugar, and maple syrup in a large bowl. Add the apple, tossing to coat.

3. Combine flour, salt, baking powder, and cinnamon in a medium bowl. Add the dry ingredients to the apple mixture and stir until it just comes together in a thick batter. Pour the batter into the prepared loaf pan.

4. Bake for 45 minutes. Cover the loaf pan loosely with aluminum foil, and continue to bake until a toothpick inserted in the center comes out clean, about 15 minutes more. Do not overbake.

5. Remove from the oven and take off the foil. Allow the apple bread to cool in the pan for 10 minutes before removing to cool completely on a wire rack.

Chocolate Chip Zucchini Almond Bread

MIGHTY FOOD FARM

MAKES 2 LOAVES

This moist and sweet vegan quick bread is ideal for brunch or dessert. Without eggs, the magic of leavening comes from the chemical reaction between the vinegar and the baking soda. Often nicknamed "war ration cakes," this baking technique may have been developed during World War II, when eggs and dairy products were hard for home bakers to obtain. This recipe makes two loaves, one for now and one to freeze for later.

½ cup canola oil, plus more for pans

3 tablespoons finely ground almonds

½ cup water

½ cup applesauce

1 tablespoon apple cider vinegar

2 cups sugar

2 cups grated zucchini (about 1 medium)

2 teaspoons vanilla extract

3 cups all-purpose flour

2 teaspoons ground cinnamon

1 teaspoon ground ginger

1 teaspoon baking soda

¼ teaspoon baking powder

½ teaspoon salt

1 cup finely chopped almonds (optional; see Step 3)

1 cup chocolate chips or vegan chocolate chips (optional; see Step 3)

1. Preheat the oven to 325°F. Lightly oil two 8-by-4-inch loaf pans with canola oil and line the bottoms with parchment paper.

2. Combine the ground almonds and the water in a food processor or blender and blend until thick and creamy. While the blade is running, add the canola oil, applesauce, vinegar, and sugar through the opening of the lid and blend until smooth. Pour the liquid into a large bowl and stir in the zucchini and vanilla.

3. Combine the flour, cinnamon, ginger, baking soda, baking powder, and salt in a separate bowl. Add the chopped almonds and chocolate chips (or add only one or the other, rather than both). Stir the dry mixture into the zucchini mixture, folding carefully to avoid clumps.

4. Divide batter evenly between the prepared loaf pans. Bake for 60 to 75 minutes, until a toothpick inserted in the center comes out clean. Allow the breads to rest in the pans for 15 minutes before turning out onto a wire rack to cool.

Glazed Blueberry Lemon Bread

MOUNTAIN PASTURE FARM

SERVES 8

The lemon and maple flavors bring out the sweetness of the blueberries in this luscious quick bread. It's great for a breakfast sweet, a dessert, or to perk up a coffee break or afternoon snack.

Bread:

½ pound (2 sticks) unsalted butter, at room temperature

1 cup all-purpose flour

¾ cup whole wheat flour

1½ teaspoons baking powder

½ teaspoon salt

¾ cup sugar

2 large eggs

2 tablespoons lemon zest (from about 2 lemons)

2 tablespoons fresh lemon juice (from 1 to 2 lemons)

¼ cup pure maple syrup

2 cups fresh blueberries

Glaze (optional):

Juice of 1 lemon (about 2 tablespoons)

½ cup sugar

1. Preheat the oven to 325°F. Use 1 tablespoon of the butter to generously butter the bottom and sides of a 9-inch metal loaf pan.

2. Prepare the bread: Combine both flours, baking powder, and salt in a medium bowl.

3. Using an electric mixer, cream together the remaining butter and the sugar until smooth and light-colored. Add the eggs, one at a time, beating

well after each addition. Add the lemon zest and juice and beat to mix in fully.

4. Mix in flour mixture, alternating with the maple syrup, beating well on low speed between each addition, beginning and ending with the dry ingredients.

5. Using a rubber spatula, gently fold the blueberries into the batter. Try to distribute the berries evenly throughout. Fill the prepared pan with the batter and smooth the top with the rubber spatula.

6. Bake for 65 to 75 minutes, until the bread springs back when lightly pressed in the center. Watch the bread carefully so the top does not burn. If the bread needs additional baking time and is beginning to burn, cover with aluminum foil. Remove from the oven and allow to cool fully on a wire rack. Run a knife with a thin blade around the edges of the pan and gently loosen the bread. Carefully turn out the bread upside down onto a plate and then turn right side up.

7. Prepare the glaze, if using: Combine the lemon juice and sugar in a small saucepan over medium heat and cook until the sugar has just dissolved. Drizzle the glaze evenly over the cake.

MOUNTAIN PASTURE FARM

Ray Ellsworth loves blueberries. According to his wife and co-blueberry picker, Sherri, he's got a closet full of navy blue shirts. That is, shirts stained from blueberry picking. (Stains aren't the only misadventure from owning and operating a certified organic blueberry farm, Mountain Pasture, in Becket, MA. When we visited, Ray told us that he was weeding in early May, only to look up and see a mama bear—and two cubs—100 feet away. She left, Ray says. "It was too early for blueberries.")

While Kentucky-born Sherri admits "I didn't know what a blueberry was" until her first date with her now-husband—they picked blueberries, of course—Ray says his proclivity for harvesting the fruit comes from both sides of the family. Mountain Pasture is on land the Ellsworth family has owned and farmed since the mid-1800s. It was a dairy farm until the 1960s when "homogenization and pasteurization laws put the dairies out of business," says Ray. That's when he and his family moved away, selling 600 acres, retaining only the small part he and Sherri now farm.

To be fair, he also attributes learning his blueberry picking techniques from his mother, who grew up in Washington, MA. "When you pick a bush, you pick the blue," Ray counsels. "And when you're done, you shouldn't have any blue left. Either you keep the blueberries or recycle." By recycle, Ray means composting them. "You never leave berries on the ground because it's just a breeding ground for bugs." The regulars who come to pick their own berries at Mountain Pasture know what to do, Ray says. "They grab two buckets and go. The newer folks, I have to tell them to pick berries with no breaks in the skin. Berries that are firm, not soft. And tell them the second bucket is the throwaway bucket."

The farm has become more sophisticated since Ray and Sherri's dating days. Ray, an accountant who is still working, cleared forested land and in 2007, started cultivating the 1-acre, 1200-bush berry farm. Despite being a more reluctant farmer—she calls herself "a farmer's helper"—Sherri loves baking with the fruit, and favors a lemon-blueberry quick bread. See the Glazed Blueberry Lemon Bread on page 232.

When Ray began Mountain Pasture, he was astonished at how many different bugs existed. Their first year in Becket, tent caterpillars stripped every leaf off the existing wild bushes. When he started planting blueberries, they were still there. He uses a special netting purchased from Canada to protect his patch from birds and bugs, especially the spotted-wing drosophila, a relatively new invasive fruit fly originally from East Asia that turns berries soft. Because of this pest, Ray says, "the commercial farmers have to spray a lot more than they used to. But the trouble with insects is that they build up a resistance to pesticides." A sustainable practice like his means using mechanical means or natural predators—frogs, spiders, hummingbirds—to fend off the bad guys.

Ray sells whatever he produces, stacking up the berries in his car to drop off at Guido's Fresh Market-

place, the Berkshire Food Co-op, or in Cummington, MA. Prime season for blueberries is from July 15 to August 1, although Ray runs into mid-September. He offers pick-your-own while the supply lasts.

Ray himself works three days a week off the farm as the town accountant for Stockbridge, MA. "I'm enjoying it. It gives me something to do on the days it rains." And he knows he can't make a living selling blueberries. "My experience has been that it's very hard to run a profitable farm. The prices we sell food for, because that's what the market will bear, are not enough." Even as an accountant, he's perplexed how produce can be sold as cheaply as it is. Take blueberries (of course!), he says. At the start of the season here, one chain—he's reluctant to mention the name—will bring them in for $1.50 a pint. He says it has to be a loss leader. "There's no way you can produce and sell berries and make a living at that price or anything close. And I get a fairly decent price because mine are certified organic."

ACKNOWLEDGMENTS

With great appreciation:

— to the dedicated Berkshire farmers, chefs, and food producers—those we interviewed and those we did not. You inspire us with your passion for maintaining healthy soil, your humane treatment of animals, building community, and producing flavorful foods.

— to Chef Brian Alberg, our exquisitely talented collaborator who created most of the recipes. Thank you for your impeccable work ethic, but also your sense of humor, which kept us on track.

— to Barbara Zheutlin, friend and former executive director of Berkshire Grown, who offered expert guidance from the moment we broached the idea for this book.

— to our lead recipe tester, Sarah Strauss, and her colleagues, Karen Meirs and Suzanne Podhaizer. Thank you, Sarah, for your professional and friendly counsel, delivered with such cheeriness even during late-night calls.

— to Elizabeth Baer of culinursa.com, friend, recipe tester, editor, and adviser. We are indebted for your all-around willingness to do whatever necessary to produce a quality book.

— to our partners in so much of what we do, the team at SME, Neil Raynor, Patti Maddamma, Margaret Cocozziello, and Loren Umana, and to Rosmeri Salman.

— to Rob's photography mentors Stephen Donaldson, acclaimed photographer of the Berkshires, and Michael Marsland, former Yale University photographer, who helped him find new ways to capture the region's beauty and the distinctive character of those who farm and produce food.

— to our literary agent, sage adviser, and friend, Karen Gantz Zahler, who made this book possible.

— to The Countryman Press team, including editorial director Ann Treistman, editorial assistant Isabel McCarthy, and former associate editor Aurora Bell, for your combined efforts and wisdom in bringing this book to fruition.

— to Carrie Bachman, president of Carrie Bachman Public Relations, and Lisa Ekus and Sally Ekus of the Lisa Ekus Group, LLC, for sharing your exceptional expertise in cookbook marketing.

— to our friends and extended family who innocently showed up at our house for dinner and discovered they were participants in "cookbook suppers," asked to try yet one more recipe version, and offer—mandatory—criticism.

— and finally, to our beloved children and their significant others, accomplished chefs and major foodies themselves: Elana, Ari, Eli, and Rafi, Ben Goldman-Israelow, Deborah Block, and Astrid Schanz-Garbassi. We are grateful for your love, sustenance, recipe testing and editing, as well as your willingness to sample endless recipe versions.

Elisa Spungen Bildner and Rob Bildner,
Becket, Massachusetts, June 2019

INDEX

ABOUT THE AUTHORS

Elisa Spungen Bildner is a former lawyer, CEO of a food manufacturing company, newspaper reporter/editor (*Star Ledger*, Newark, NJ) and journalism professor (Rutgers University and New York University). She has written numerous articles for consumer, trade, and scholarly publications.

She is also a professionally trained chef (School of Natural Cookery, Boulder, CO) and practicing yoga instructor. Spungen Bildner has chaired the boards of several national/international nonprofit organizations and currently sits on a number of boards. Spungen Bildner has a BA from Yale College, a JD from Columbia University, and an MS in Nutrition from the University of Bridgeport.

Robert "Rob" Bildner is a former attorney who left the practice of law to create, run, and eventually sell several food distribution and manufacturing companies. He currently owns a fine wine and spirits shop.

In addition to his background in the food business, he is active in the philanthropic world. Bildner and his wife, Elisa Spungen Bildner, established the Foundation for Jewish Camp, and he continues to serve on a number of nonprofit boards.

Bildner, who photographed the farms and restaurants in this book, studied photography in workshops around the world. He is a graduate of Yale University, University of Pennsylvania Law School, and the Jewish Theological Seminary (MA in Jewish Studies).

Chef Brian Alberg is the vice president of culinary development for Main Street Hospitality Group. He is responsible for kitchen culture and food for their ventures, from The Red Lion Inn to their newest establishment: The Break Room at Greylock Works.

A graduate of the Culinary Institute of America in Hyde Park, NY, he is an active member of the James Beard Foundation and serves on the Norman Rockwell Museum and Railroad Street Youth Project boards. He is a past president of Berkshire Grown and the founding chair of Berkshire Farm & Table.